KB058113

ENCOUNTERS
WITH
GREAT MINDS

HWANG CHANG-GYU

ENCOUNTERS WITH GREAT MINDS

A story of the global No. 1 in semiconductors & 5G

SIGONGSA

This book describes the unprecedented career of Dr. Chang–Gyu Hwang, Chief Executive Officer (CEO) of Samsung, Chief Technology Officer of the Republic of Korea (South Korea) and finally CEO of KT Telecom. But the book is much more than an autobiography. It is full of philosophical thoughts. The content bridges time and space. It combines Eastern and Western wisdom. And it is more emotional than similar works of Western authors.

This alone is of great value, because it helps the reader to better understand Eastern management. There are few people who have worked with as many significant innovators of our time as Dr. Hwang. These include Steve Jobs, Klaus Schwab, Marc Benioff, and Jensen Huang, as well as Intel founders William Shockley and Andrew Grove from his time at Stanford University. I highly recommend the book to entrepreneurs, managers, and especially ambitious young people. It is rare to find such an enriching insight into the world of big global high tech business.

– Hermann Simon I Businessperson and author of global bestsellers *Hidden Champions Confessions of the Pricing Man: How Price Affects Everything*

Dr. Hwang embodies the essence of the nomad spirit. Throughout his life he has tilled the soil of new digital lands, creating the future. Everyone can benefit from the wisdom and insights shared from his remarkable career expanding the boundaries of technology.

— Marc Benioff, Chair and CEO, Salesforce

On the Meaningful Experience of Encounters

I have no religion. Instead, I prefer the word "meditation."

Slowly, I contemplate the faces in my memory one after another. There are countless people, ranging from household names such as Lee Kun-hee, Steve Jobs and Klaus Schwab, to important figures from history books like Admiral Yi Sun-sin, and the dozens of team members with whom I have shared many joys and sorrows. They are all my teachers.

I'm a very lucky person. While still in my early 20s, I could determine the course of study that I would pursue for the rest of my life, and thanks to my excellent colleagues, I was able to achieve numerous things that would have been impossible to accomplish alone. I succeeded as a leader of a company that pioneers change and innovation after transforming myself from an engineer into a manager.

But there were greater blessings still to come, as I was fortunate enough to meet numerous "good teachers." I met them both inside and outside of school. They have been with me throughout my life, sharing their wisdom in ways that are sometimes small and sometimes great.

How can I achieve technological innovation to develop the economy and change society? This was a question that has penetrated my existence.

It began simply with the idea, "let's get ahead of Japan." In the 1980s, when I returned to Korea after a demanding period of study at the University of Massachusetts (UMass) and Stanford University and work in the United States, I vowed to never go abroad again. I declined a talent scout's offer from a renowned global company and turned down their proposal for an executive position. Instead, I decided to start working for a Korean company, all because of my firm resolve that "Koreans too could beat Japan." At that time, while Japan was showing off as a semiconductor powerhouse after surpassing the United States, Korea was lacking.

Fortunately, however, that was only temporary. When Korea developed the world's first 256M DRAM and announced the "New Memory Growth Theory," also referred to as "Hwang's Law," we were no longer a nation that had to copy technology after spending massively on royalties. As my colleagues and I ushered in the era of mobile devices along with Apple, the world took notice, shining a spotlight on my own country and asking: How Korea could achieve that much in only a decade? Now, Korea is always a part of the discussion when talking about the future of the world's semiconductors.

When I was young, I didn't think I would make a good manager. I thought I would spend my life as an engineer. Many people helped me become a leader, and I achieved many things that I couldn't have done without the support of others.

I had undeservedly gained recognition as a model "leader of innovation" because of my unique background as a manager. I had to overcome my limitations as an engineer when I was tasked with creating a driver for national economic growth as the first leader of the R&D Strategy and Planning Team (National CTO) under Korea's Ministry of Knowledge and Economy.

To foster growth in Korea, I had to grow myself. Thus, I broadened my knowledge by listening to the voices in the field. This allowed me to lead the development of various technologies that have become widely commercialized.

Becoming the head of a company was another challenge. Innovation in management was as difficult and challenging as innovation in technology. I made a proposal to the employees that we should build an organization that changes society, going beyond economic development. I raised my voice urging them to work together and find a way to turn possibility into reality. I felt that the management workplace was one in which sincerity held currency. When hearts were moved in the organization, the organization itself was entirely transformed anew, and organizational innovation then walked hand in hand with technological innovation.

While seeking solutions to questions that have gripped my life, my hair greyed, and I became a seasoned veteran in the halls of management.

I, on the other hand, have held on fast to "technology" and "people" for three decades through thick and thin. Flash memory, mobile DRAMs, solid-state drives, "GiGAtopia," and 5G have become common nouns today. When I first laid these technologies out, I sought to predict the answer to the question: How will these technologies change the world? "Hwang's Law" has remained steadfast and held its ground while Korea has undergone two major upheavals. In the meantime, nicknames like

"Mr. Flash" and "Mr. Semiconductor" followed me around.

Steve Jobs would fondly address me, saying "Hey, Mr. Flash" whenever I sent him a new product or after we'd reached another business deal. His friendly voice still rings in my ears.

Meanwhile, Korea released the world's first 5G system a full two years ahead of the global timeline, and it boasts not only high speed but high-capacity connectivity without buffering. This technology will serve as infrastructure for the Fourth Industrial Revolution. Going forward, the connectivity provided by 5G will better civilization.

The above-mentioned technologies did not result from my efforts alone, and I do not say this just to be humble. Since the days of my prime, I have deeply felt that I couldn't accomplish anything by myself. Getting anything done requires open communication with others. So, I did just that. I've always liked people by nature. I was never tired of meeting countless times with people who are always agonizing over technological development. Rather, I was fascinated with their carefree and progressive spirit. The inspiration I received from them enabled me to fulfill greater goals that exceeded my own capacity. The results came from the learning I experienced through every encounter.

This book contains "encounters" that I have had over the past thirty years. Some of these individuals are still around to learn of its publication, while others have departed, leaving only traces of their lives behind. Writing this manuscript led me to meditate on each and every one of them while poring over documents from decades ago. In some parts, I could only rely on old memories. If there are any mistakes or errors, I ask the reader to blame these "old bones" for showing that even the very best of teachers can sometimes end up with an unworthy student. They have always been good teachers.

I would like to use this opportunity to extend my gratitude to my predecessors who laid the cornerstones for the semiconductor business, as well as to my colleagues and juniors who have quietly exerted their expertise in their respective areas of specialization, during good times and bad, with the wholehearted determination to "make the best semiconductors in the world."

In my days as National CTO as well, I was helped by experts both in Korea and abroad. Without their commitment, I wouldn't have been able to accomplish the task of growing Korea's national technology. Last, I want to express my appreciation to the Korea Telecom (KT) employees and executives with whom I spent six years. All of them readily participated in the task of changing the world.

These days, everyone is busy and cannot spare a moment. When I was in office, I also was too occupied to read a single book to the end in one sitting. I tend to fret when I am unable to grasp what a book is about right away. I imagine many readers may also wonder what the message of this book is as soon as they open it.

The message is simple. I recommend that you set aside the pessimistic view of the "hopeless generation" and take just one step forward. I can tell you one thing for sure—not a single person I mention in this book earned his or her position without facing challenges or obstacles. Those who shared their wisdom with me followed rational optimism, did their best in what they did, and kept a respectful and considerate attitude. They had sufficient abilities and qualifications, and success was like a tail that tagged along.

No one is perfect, and no one can survive alone. One should think beyond the self to the group. Then, the experiences from every encounter will become even more meaningful. Finally, I hope my personal stories will serve to inspire readers who wish to widen the boundaries of their knowledge and wisdom.

Table of Contents

Notes
- The titles used for people mentioned in the book are based on the time when the author met them. In some cases, titles were omitted, depending on the person and flow of the book.
- There is a Device Solution (formally known as Semiconductor Business Division) in Samsung Electronics. When mentioning Samsung Electronics, the company may be referred to as "Samsung" or "Samsung Semiconductor," depending on the flow of the book.
- The "b" (bit) unit for semiconductor products was omitted. E.g., 64Gb NAND Flash is expressed as "64G NAND Flash."

Insight

Have
Your Own Vision
for the Future

01   Make bold decisions for the future

| Lee Kun-hee |

People often say that the future is for those who are prepared. To that statement I would add "the future is for those who decide with insight." No matter how prepared people are, if they don't foresee the future and make their decisions accordingly, their efforts will be good for nothing. Also, opportunities in life always come without warning.

The future is for those who make decisions with insight

In October 1988, the director of the Planning Office of Samsung Semiconductor came to my office at Stanford University. He wanted to offer me a job me since Samsung was now testing its fate in the semiconductor business.

At that time, Samsung Electronics was devoting all its might to recruiting the brightest minds from overseas, following Chairman Lee

Chapter 1 Insight: Have Your Own Vision for the Future / **19**

Kun-hee's decree that technological development was the only way for Samsung to survive.

I was working as a researcher at Stanford University after receiving my doctorate in Electrical Engineering (related to semiconductors) from the University of Massachusetts and refusing scouting offers from global corporations like IBM and Texas Instruments. Several prominent American universities had even invited me to teach at their schools.

While I was putting off any decisions after telling them I would think about their offers, I was invited to a seminar organized by a major Japanese semiconductor company. I spent ten days in Japan giving brief consultations to six semiconductor companies. Following a lecture at Osaka University, my impression of the semiconductor industry in Japan was one of "amazement." I easily recognized the excellence of Japan's semiconductor industry as I had also consulted with Intel, the world's top semiconductor company.

On the last day of the schedule, I had dinner with the assistant head of the Hitachi Research Laboratory. He questioned me about the level of semiconductor technology in Korea. I couldn't immediately answer as I had lived in the United States for quite a while. Instead, I asked for his thoughts on the matter.

"Frankly, Samsung Electronics is making semiconductor products, but they are not up to standard. There is a huge gap between the basic and applied technologies of Korea and Japan, and it will take quite a while to narrow that gap." Staring at the nonchalant expression on his face while he answered my question, I felt rage and an indomitable spirit beginning to roil inside of me.

On the airplane leaving Japan, I decided to accept the scouting offer from Samsung Electronics. Moreover, I thought it would be meaningful if I could beat Japan using semiconductors, something to which I had already dedicated my entire life.

However, I had one major concern as I was about to join the company. Samsung had offered me an executive position.

I would be provided with a big salary, car and secretary, and a private office. The offer sounded great but was not easy to accept. It would require me to completely put down my roots at Samsung Electronics and engage long term in research projects as a "contract" executive, which did not seem appropriate to me. Besides, I would be working on "technology management" and not the "development of future technologies." When it came to R&D, there was a belief that it was important not to step outside the laboratory. So, I declined the executive position and set my sights on becoming a director.

Despite having the clear goal to "develop future technologies," I didn't have just smooth sailing from then on. I worked hard to be seen as a leader who takes the initiative and sets an example, while having to solve problems such as Korea's closed organizational culture, developers with low morale, and the wide gap between vision and reality.

As a result, it became clear that all my decisions were correct. I took three full years to become an executive. Although it wasn't a short period, considering that I could've been an executive from the start, those three years were more than meaningful. Most of those who had accepted jobs as contract executives quit in the middle of their contracts and left. Meanwhile, the trust and support I had earned while putting in time and effort working hard with the other employees became the solid foundation that led to my achievements as an organizational leader.

More than anything else, my encounter with Chairman Lee Kun-hee assured me that my choosing Samsung had been a good decision, and now I was certain beyond any shadow of doubt that there was a bright future for Samsung.

Chairman Lee Kun-Hee's "great decision" in making a top-notch corporation

On August 29, 1994 (coincidentally the 84th anniversary of National Humiliation Day, marking the start of Korea's occupation by Japan in 1910), Samsung announced that it had developed a 256M DRAM for the first time in the world. A few days later, led by Chairman Lee, there was a briefing on new product development and a meeting of Samsung Group presidents.

The briefing had been prepared to showcase Samsung Electronics' development of a brand-new, top-quality TV and the 256M DRAM as examples representing the company's success. Samsung founder Lee Byung-chull's living room at his house in Hannam-dong was turned into an exhibition hall for the new TV and 256M DRAM. As the director responsible for development, I oversaw the proceedings and explanation of the 256M DRAM.

Displayed at the front of the living room were the Samsung TV along with the TV from a different company touting its own brand. The competing products of Korea and Japan had been placed side by side so that people could visually compare their design, color, and quality. This alone made for quite a sight to see. On the other side of the room had been set up the blueprints for the 256M DRAM and an electron microscope. The actual size of a 256M DRAM is smaller than a thumbnail. Since it is difficult to imagine the technology in the 256M DRAM by looking at it with the naked eye, we decided to provide an electron microscope so that it could be viewed up close.

Actually, the amount of exhibition space given to the 256M DRAM was small in comparison to the area dedicated to the large household appliances. Nevertheless, I had confidence that "our technological capabilities were second to none."

When Chairman Lee entered the living room trailed by dozens of Samsung Group presidents, the briefing on Samsung's new TV started. It only lasted 30-40 minutes. Chairman Lee asked some questions regarding various aspects of the product such as the design, color, and user interface (UI), and offered a few words of advice and encouragement, saying, "We still have a long way to go."

Then, it was time for the presentation of the 256M DRAM. I introduced myself as the person in charge of its development, and delivered an overview and explanation regarding semiconductors and their development process. More than five minutes into my explanation, however, Chairman Lee still had not uttered a single word. It was because the explanation about semiconductors differed greatly from that given for the new TV. My presentation was rife with technical terms and jargon exclusively used by engineers, and the only thing visible was the thumbnail-sized chip and its blueprints. It wouldn't have been easy to understand even if one had paid their fullest attention. I thought to myself, this isn't going anywhere, and gathered my wits.

"Chairman Lee, the population of the United States is 270 million."

The author explaining the newly developed semiconductor chip to Chairman Lee Kun-hee.

This was totally out of the blue. Chairman Lee raised his head and looked at me with a confused expression, wondering why I was suddenly talking about the US population. I had succeeded in changing the subject and grabbing his attention, so I hurriedly continued my explanation.

"Even though the US has the world's largest economy, and it leads in technology and culture, its population isn't only made up of brilliant and talented people. There are also many people who are a burden on its society. But it's still the strongest country in the world.

Within this 256M DRAM that we made, there are the same number of cells as there are people in the US population. But if just one of these 270 million cells is defective, we won't be able to sell the 256M DRAM."

Chairman Lee then smiled at me brightly, glanced over at the group of presidents, and broke into laughter saying, "That's a great analogy."

I was able to deliver the rest of my presentation in a much brighter atmosphere after this change of mood. I helped Chairman Lee Kun-hee observe the internal structure of the 256M DRAM using the electron microscope and gave additional technical explanation on the blueprints.

Wearing a beaming smile, Chairman Lee listened to me intently for over thirty minutes. Then the briefing ended.

My scheduled task was also finished. Next on the agenda was the meeting with the president of Samsung Electronics as well as the other group presidents. I was gathering up my things and getting ready to go back to the office. Chairman Lee, who was now on his way to the meeting, turned to one of his secretaries and said, "Tell Director Hwang to come in, too."

This is how I was unexpectedly invited to the meeting with the Samsung Group presidents, including the Samsung Electronics president. At the meeting as well, Chairman Lee mentioned semiconductor development several times, even commenting, "I really enjoyed that event."

A month later on September the 26th, Chairman Lee threw a "party to celebrate Samsung's development of the 256M DRAM." He talked about its significance and importance both at home and abroad and encouraged the engineers who worked on the project.

In addition to Chairman Lee Kun-hee and Samsung President Kang Jin-ku, the reception, which took place at the Shilla Seoul Hotel in Jangchung-dong, was attended by Deputy Prime Minister Jeong Jae-seok of the Economic Planning Board, former Minister Kwon Ih-hyeok of the Ministry of Education, and Director Kim Sang-ha of the Chamber of Commerce & Industry. After toasting with over 550 dignitaries from various circles, I took the rostrum and introduced myself as the person in charge of developing the 256M DRAM. The whole process was like a sort of "hazing," not only as an engineer, but also as the person responsible for leading the development team. After this event, I frequently had the opportunity for one-on-one meetings with Chairman Lee.

Of all those encounters, the often-mentioned "Zakuro Meeting" left the deepest impression on me. Zakuro is a shabu-shabu(Japanese-style hot pot) restaurant located beside the Hotel Okura Tokyo in Japan, and the meeting was held in the restaurant instead of the hotel for security reasons.

The decision made in that restaurant came to be regarded as the most important event in the history of semiconductors; it affirmed Samsung Semiconductor's status and advanced the growth of the global mobile market. In addition, it led to the development of the innovative technology charge trap flash (CTF, refer to the page 137), the basis for the continuing growth of the global semiconductor industry.

In early August 2001, Chairman Lee called me to visit him in Tokyo when I was the President of Memory Business Division. He wanted to decide on a partnership with Toshiba. At that time, Toshiba was the biggest player in NAND flash memory (hereafter "NAND flash"). In the overall flash memory(refer to the page 132) market, Intel held the dominant position with a 25% market share, while Samsung's market share was only 4.6%. In the NAND flash market, Toshiba possessed advanced technology and held 45% of the market. By comparison, Samsung was in second place with 25%. Toshiba proposed a partnership under these circumstances. Samsung was now faced with the difficult choice between joining hands with the industry's top company and stably sharing a piece of the pie, or risking it all by betting on independent development.

About one year earlier, Toshiba had suggested a technology exchange with Samsung Electronics. They proposed a transfer of their NAND flash technology to Samsung Electronics in return for our transferring DRAM technology to them. After one or two meetings, Samsung declined the proposal. Later, another proposal for a joint venture came from Toshiba.

I first heard about Toshiba's proposal from a Samsung executive at the headquarters. I was on my way back to Giheung after a meeting with the Group presidents. An executive who had worked in the Office of the Secretariat at the Semiconductor Division asked me, "Did you hear about the joint venture proposal from Toshiba?"

I checked once I arrived in Giheung. There really was a proposal—it had been positively reviewed—and it was now in the hands of Chairman Lee. I quickly requested a meeting with Lee Hak-soo, the chief secretary of chairman Lee, and spent three hours reasoning why we needed to remain an independent business. Samsung Semiconductor had been preparing to develop the flash memory and was thoroughly analyzing Japan's technology ever since I started working as the R&D Head in 1998. Samsung had already made the necessary preparations to produce and manufacture flash memory without the need for additional investment.

"Flash is an important product that will determine Samsung's future and lead the mobile market. Although we are one to two years behind Toshiba in terms of technological development, we recently developed the 512M NAND flash memory chip and we're going to develop the 1G NAND flash memory device before Japan does. In the same way that Intel dominated the PC market with the CPU, we can lead the future market with flash."

I implored Lee Hak-soo to support our continuing as an independent business. Having listened to everything I said, the chief secretary Lee grasped the situation and placed an urgent call to Chairman Lee in Japan, asking him to meet "for a report." He said that since there was a differing opinion from those who had viewed Toshiba's proposal favorably up until now, he would need to go to Japan directly and report it. I followed him to Japan one day later.

Two days after chief secretary Lee's departure for Japan, members of the company who had come for the urgent meeting gathered at Hotel Okura Tokyo. Vice Chairman Yun Jong-yong, who had been on a business trip to Russia, was also there. I went from Korea to Japan with Lee Yoon-woo, the president of the Semiconductor Division. Before the start of the "report meeting," chief secretary Lee Hak-soo gathered all the members together, including me. He then announced, "For this meeting, I will let President Hwang deliver the report."

He had laid the groundwork so that I could take the lead in presenting my opinion about the joint venture proposal from Toshiba. The meeting was to be held over lunch in a restaurant called Zakuro. It was right next to Hotel Okura Tokyo, where we were staying.

With Samsung's top executives in attendance, Chairman Lee asked, "Do you think we can do it?" This was a question about our true capability to lead the flash memory industry as an independent company. I answered without hesitation. "Flash memory will be key to the future of the semiconductor industry. We can win if we strengthen just some of our current technology."

He threw out another question.

"Some say there is no future in DRAM?"

Again, without hesitation, I answered him. "In the age of PCs, DRAM was only a subcomponent of a CPU. This will change in the future. DRAM will be the main component essential for mobile devices, including mobile phones. We are already developing the low-power DRAM chip for mobile devices and even decided to call it 'mobile DRAM.' The demand for this will inevitably grow."

Chairman Lee's final question was whether I had confidence in this, and I answered with conviction that I would create a new mobile market.

I saw a smile on his face as he listened to my answer. Following that, with no hint of objection, he commanded, "Respectfully decline the proposal. We can keep going at our own pace."

Only later I found out that Chairman Lee Kun-hee had been aware of Toshiba's proposal in detail through various channels. He had only called to hear my opinion since I was the one leading the memory business.

Toshiba's plan to monopolize the NAND flash market by dragging in Samsung fell apart. Samsung Electronics had placed a bet on a winning move rather than opting for the path of safety and sharing the market with the top player.

It was only a few months later, in autumn of 2001, that Samsung successfully completed the 1G NAND flash chip, boasting the world's highest level of integration. The tables had now turned. Within a year of declining the proposal from the market leader to go its own way, Samsung Electronics closed the wide gap between Toshiba and reversed the rankings.

In October 2002, Samsung Electronics held an investor relations (IR) session. The company announced that sales from NAND flash memory were predicted to reach $1.1 billion. After the announcement, an analyst raised his hand, and with a puzzled expression asked, "Market research institute 'D' predicted the scale of this year's global market for NAND flash to be $700 million. Are you saying Samsung's sales will be bigger than the market?"

However, sales turned out to be just as Samsung had predicted, hitting $1.1 billion, which was $400 million more than the $700 million predicted by a market research institution. How was this possible?

In the past, most of the components that go into electronic devices

< Share of overall flash market compared with Intel >

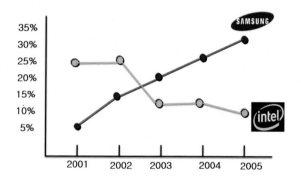

< Share of NAND flash market compared with Toshiba >

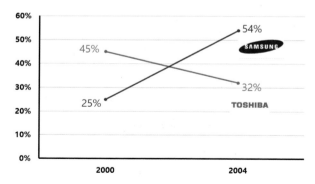

were sold according to orders placed by electronic device manufacturers. Component specifications were decided solely by the manufacturers, who then placed their orders with semiconductor suppliers.

That was not the case with flash memory. Samsung Electronics participated in the design process jointly with renowned digital companies. They decided on the specifications and product launch together. As flash memory became the key component driving the whole IT industry, it then became possible to actively make determinations of estimated sales.

By comparison, market research institutions have difficulty predicting sales because they cannot determine in real time which products and how much of them will be sold. One example showing just how wrong a market research institution's prediction can be was the digital camera market, which at the time had the highest demand for NAND flash memory.

In late 2002, it announced that the digital camera market for 2003 would amount to 23 million units. It turns out however that the market grew by 95% over the previous year and 45 million units were sold. The supply of NAND flash memory was only half of market demand, resulting in an extreme shortage. Because of this, the theory of memory market decline was totally dismissed.

As time passed, Samsung Electronics' come-from-behind victory was confirmed. Its market share of NAND flash surged from 25% in 2000 to 45% in 2002, and to 54% in 2004. On the contrary, Toshiba's market share plummeted from 45% in 2000 to 32% in 2004. The situation had been totally reversed in only two years. Samsung started with a 3% share of the overall flash market in 2000, growing to 14% in 2002 and to 35% in 2005, which it has maintained until today.

I kept my promise with Chairman Lee at the Zakuro Meeting. Samsung had overtaken Toshiba. During a case study by Harvard Business School (hereafter HBS case study), I heard an objective evaluation from professors and students that "it is almost unheard of in the history of business that a top market player has been surpassed in such a short period."

"How will your subordinates get the chance to be winners?"

Chairman Lee Kun-hee's precise judgment and full support laid the foundation for all our achievements. Although I would still give him the same answer if I could go back to that day, there were times when I have been immersed in the thought, how could I have had such confidence? What made me so self-assured in my youth of my conviction about the flash memory market was the thorough preparation I made based on my analysis of future trends and strategies through research. That said, there is something more to Chairman Lee's leadership that cannot be explained simply by his having an abundance of insight to the future.

The year 2001 was one of crisis. As well as being full of uncertainty it was the worst year in the IT industry's 50-year history. Many were concerned as to whether semiconductor companies would run deficits. Meanwhile, another concern weighing heavily on me was the investment in the mass production of the 12-inch (300 mm) wafer, which was already developed.

A wafer is a thin round disk used as a substrate material for semiconductors, and the 8-inch (200 mm) wafer has been commercialized for memory products. Due to the characteristics of memory semiconductors, in which unit price has to be lowered through mass production, the 12-inch wafer was more competitive than the 8-inch wafer was.

However, during an IT recession period it would have been unreasonable to boost the development and mass production of wafers, since it requires an investment running into billions of dollars. Then one day, I received a call from Chairman Lee.

"President Hwang, things are pretty tough for you these days, eh? How's the R&D going?"

After some brief pleasantries he got right to the point.

"How are other countries doing with development of the 12-inch?"

At the time, the German corporation Siemens had invested in the 12-inch wafer after receiving government support and was about to start mass production. Listening to this, Chairman Lee didn't beat around the bush but jumped right to the next question.

"And what about our development?"

He knew that we had already developed the prototype one or two years ago and that I had received an internal award for technology development. I explained that although we were almost ready for mass production, there was some hesitation over investment due to the horrible IT recession. But Chairman Lee showered me with reproof.

"President Hwang, you've been chasing big goals. You've already made it to No. 1 and come this far. If you don't invest now, how will your subordinates get to become No. 1, and how are we going to maintain the top position globally?"

He promised to provide us with full and active support and urged me to begin mass production of the 12-inch wafer. Because of his support and encouragement, mass production of the now-commercialized 12-inch wafer was launched without any problems.

The media described the investment decision as a "risky and daring investment." Samsung Electronics jumped into the market with its 12-inch wafer, or what was alternatively referred to as the "cartwheel of determination and success."

Over the next two decades, the number of 12-inch wafer production lines increased from nine in Hwaseong to 17, including those in Giheung and Pyeongtaek in Korea, Austin in the US, and Xi'an in China. Equipped with world-class technology and production capability, these facilities now serve as a dependable mainstay of the Korean economy.

Decide the future you want today

I had another encounter. In 2003, there was a meeting of economic leaders presided over by the Korean President that took place at COEX (one of Korea's main convention/business centers). I went to the meeting with Chairman Lee and gave a presentation as a representative of the Samsung Group. On the way out, Chairman Lee said to me, "Let's have a cup of tea."

Our conversation covered the current state of the semiconductor industry and the development roadmap for the future, and we continued as we arrived at the reception room of his home.

The Chairman asked whether software wasn't becoming more important in the IT industry, and in that regard, whether it would be necessary to expand relevant human resources. I answered that software is essential for semiconductors as well. Moreover, after listening to an explanation that typically only doctoral-level experts can understand, Chairman Lee asked, "What if we set up creative research teams to develop future insight for the next decade?" I felt the significance of his suggestion despite the light mood of the conversation.

As soon as I got to work the next day, I made a proposal to the research center staff and design team. "Let's make some technology teams that can overcome our current limits," I suggested. We formed seven to eight future research teams centered on core personnel specializing in processes, devices, and design. Along with the device project related to an advanced concept flash memory technology, they would also handle projects related to design and processes. These project (working groups), made up of as few as three to four members, or as many as ten, conducted creative and challenging tasks. Indeed, following my appointment as head of the R&D center a few years earlier, I established a research team that had been gathering various ideas.

When it comes to semiconductor technology, CTF can be seen as its most innovative and representative form. In 2001, at a seminar of invited space scientists held at the Samsung Advanced Institute of Technology, former CTF team leader and current vice president of SK hynix Choi Jung-dal stated, "The technological possibilities of using nonconductors were the creative impetus for the innovative technology known as CTF." NAND flash, which uses existing conductors as "floating gates," is prone to performance degradation because of serious inter-cell interference resulting from scaling. CTF technology brought about an innovative paradigm shift by enabling the stacking of thin-layered (almost atomic level) cells, as if constructing a skyscraper, which led to a simplified structure and increased capacitance. Choi later talked about the difficulty in developing this new technology. He was the person in charge of development, and he found it difficult to obtain the characteristics he

The author presenting a 4G NAND flash wafer with 70nm circuitry to Chairman Lee Kun-hee at a dinner held to encourage flash memory developers in October 2003.

wanted. At the time, because it was not easy to get systematic help from other departments, it was impossible to solve the backlog of problems. He is said to have been so troubled at times that he wanted to just give up.

Around that time, future research teams started to be formed due to Chairman Lee's interest in future planning, and this was carried out with lightning speed. The Chairman also required that the research teams basically be subject to evaluations. The teams conducted various research projects that could not have been previously attempted due to low potential for success and organizational realities. After the CTF technology was developed, but prior to the completion of any products, a meeting was arranged to provide Chairman Lee with a report. We heard from the Office of the Secretariat that there would be a dinner, an occasion organized to encourage the leaders of the design, process, and device teams. With several other executives in attendance, I introduced each one of the team heads.

"We no longer have to pay royalties to Toshiba and SanDisk. From now on, it'll be the other way around. We will be the one receiving royalties."

I talked about the development of the source technology for flash memory as I showed them a research paper on CTF technology that would be announced for the first time in the world at the 2003 International Electronic Devices Meeting (IEDM), the world's most authoritative conference on device technology.

I could see the heartfelt emotion in Chairman Lee's eyes. Nodding his head and smiling at me, he said, "We now have world-class technology in the semiconductor sector." Even at that time, a lot of companies, including Samsung Electronics, had to pay royalties to foreign companies to manufacture products.

They were paying huge royalties to Japan, which had taken over supremacy in semiconductors from the United States. But Samsung, being first to develop this new technology, had turned the tables, and Chairman Lee recognized the significance of this better than anyone. He knew that source technology represented both power and the future!

CTF is innovative technology that completely overcame the technical limitations of the floating-gate NAND flash, and my report on it, which was also announced at the IEDM conference in 2005 and 2006, was selected the "most innovative paper." It resulted in securing several patents for source technology, hundreds for application technology, and became the standard for flash technology.

This was of course possible because of the great support from other

CTF-based 64G NAND flash with 30nm circuitry, developed for the first time in the world.

departments. Following Chairman Lee's direction, I added six or seven members to the research teams and worked with them to solve problems that had accumulated. But most of all, I made sure that the design team got all the support it needed.

With any technology, to finish a product the developers and designers must communicate and sound each other out about what can be realized. Development accelerated after boosting support for the design team.

Finally, about two years later, the hard work and fighting spirit of the teams culminated in a major event, the completion of CTF technology.

In 2006, we developed a 32G CTF NAND flash memory with a 45-nanometer (nm) design rule for the first time in the world. And in 2007, we succeeded in developing the technology to stack layers, enabling a switch from the existing flat structure to a 3D structure.

We then developed 24-layer 30nm 64G CTF NAND flash with the world's first 3D structure. Today, a 128-layer version has been commercialized. The cost competitiveness, degree of integration, and performance are far superior to Intel or Toshiba's floating-gate flash. Our competitors are now using CTF technology as well. It seems that Samsung's CTF flash memory technology will be in use far into the future.

Later in 2014, when I was the chairman of KT, I met Samsung Vice

Chairman Lee Jae-yong at the Blue House (Office of the President) along with various dignitaries from financial circles on the occasion of Xi Jinping's visit to Korea. As soon as he saw me, he greeted me by grabbing my hands and said, "Thank you so much for developing CTF with Samsung."

"Well, we developed it, but it was everyone on our staff working so hard that made Samsung what it is today," I responded.

On these foundations, Samsung Electronics maintains a firm hold on its current position as the world's No. 1 semiconductor company. In 2020, despite the blow from the COVID-19 pandemic, Samsung spectacularly recorded $201 billion in sales, with $29.7 billion in operating profit.

Chairman Lee Kun-hee not only had insight into the future—he was a CEO who provided leadership through empowerment. The Chairman was invited to countless events to which I was often sent in his stead. In October 2005, I delivered a keynote speech in his place at the Nikkei Forum. Many prominent figures, including Nissan Chairman Carlos Ghosn and Dell Chairman Michael Saul Dell, attended the venue. Chairman Lee pursued the cultivation of talent, delegation of authority, and trust-based management for the future of Samsung. His leadership has been a great inspiration to me.

Insight—The Power to Move Forward in an Age of Crisis

In February 2002, I announced my namesake "Hwang's Law" at the International Solid-State Circuits Conference (ISSCC, the largest semiconductor conference in the world) in front of more than 4,000 semiconductor experts. It predicted that the demand for the memory semiconductor would explode, and that memory density would increase exponentially, doubling every year. This was the "New Memory Growth Theory." Breaking away from Moore's Law, which was an acknowledged, established theory, it caused great repercussion not only in the academic world but also within the industry.

It was in 2001 that the ISSCC proposed that I be the keynote speaker. At that time, the CPU-led personal computer industry was the center of the digital world. New PCs hit the store shelves following the release of CPUs, with upgraded functions, and CPU speeds determined the price of PCs. DRAM was only one of the PC's components.

When the PC market enters a downturn, the DRAM has a hard time creating its own business niche. To make matters worse, we were going through the worst IT recession in 50 years. The price of 128M DRAMs, which was $10.00 in March 2001, plummeted to $0.80 in October.

Due to these circumstances, the optimistic view that the semiconductor would lead the mobile era in the following year of 2002 was beyond everyone's expectation. It was the beginning of a great reversal.

Many market watchers could not help but be surprised because the theory accurately points out the inflection points for the market and technology.

"Until now, CPUs were priced depending on their clock speed. In the future, the mobile era will emerge, and mobile phones will replace personal computers. By then, clock speed will no longer be important. Speed will be determined by the network environment. Text is the current unit of information. But in the future, it will be music and video.

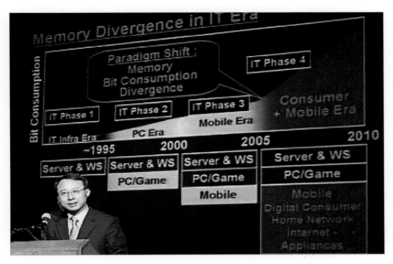

The author presents "Hwang's Law" at the ISSCC in February 2002.

Therefore, the price will be determined by flash memory capacity. This is the key to the "New Memory Growth Theory," or in other words, "Hwang's Law.'"

After receiving the request to give the keynote speech, I had no choice but to dedicate myself more to research despite the totally unpredictable and unfavorable conditions. I read innumerable studies and predicted trends, and I met more often with various experts to read customers and markets.

While everyone was talking about the IT recession, I moved in the opposite direction based on the New Memory Growth Theory. With more than 200 members on our product planning team, I monitored industry trends and customers, looking for technology investments. I participated in strategy meetings in which all the departments would

The author giving a special lecture at the MIT Gates Building in 2004.

gather to quickly and accurately "renew" information.

The next year, 2003, the global demand for flash memory doubled the supply. To this day, the prices of smartphones and pads are determined by their memory capacity.

In 2004, the UMass Distinguished Alumni Awards ceremony was held at the State House. A special lecture was given in the afternoon at the MIT Gates Building for the purpose of attracting talented youth from the eastern United States.

As it so happened, the lecture began with about 400 students filling the hall, while the doors on both sides of the building were kept open so that the 100 or so students standing outside could listen.

With bated breath, the students listened closely to my talk on the semiconductor market. After I finished the approximately one-hour lecture, I was hit with a flood of questions.

Because of this, the lecture ran an additional 10 minutes longer than expected. Then, I received one last question just as I was wrapping things up.

"I work for Toshiba as a semiconductor researcher, and I am currently studying for a PhD at MIT. As far as I know, Toshiba was the first company in the world to propose and develop NAND flash, and they hold an unrivaled position in the industry. But you said here today that Samsung Semiconductor has overtaken Toshiba and is even out ahead of them by a big margin. What is the exact reason for this?"

The lecture hall suddenly fell into a hush at such a provocative question. I took a moment to gather my thoughts before responding.

"Are you from Japan?" I asked.

A burst of laughter came from the audience, which also included dozens of Korean students. That bought me nearly half a minute, and then I calmly answered. As the student had pointed out, Japan did indeed occupy an unrivaled position in the semiconductor industry for a good while—until just recently—and I knew the reason why.

"Japan has the world's greatest "pillar" of technology in its unsurpassed collective of artisans."

And now, it gets to the part that I really wanted to pass on to the audience.

"By comparison, Korea does not have the same technological depth, but Koreans are highly motivated, and they are also good at integration."

I paused for a moment. Again, silence filled the room. As the silence started to break, I finished my answer.

"And there is one other difference that is more important than anything

The author giving a special lecture at Harvard University's Burden Hall in 2005.

else, and that is the leadership of Chairman Lee. Chairman Lee made everything possible."

While I was working for Samsung Electronics, I was an engineer with dreams. Chairman Lee believed in my dreams more than anybody else. No matter how sluggish or how much the semiconductor market fluctuated, he never wavered from making bold decisions and providing full support. This is what made Samsung Semiconductor into what it is today. It took barely two years for Samsung Electronics to surpass Toshiba and widen the gap between them in the NAND flash market.

For more than a decade, Intel had the entire flash market to itself while Toshiba was also playing solo in NAND flash. It also did not seem as if things would change any time soon. The world of industry has described Samsung Electronics' pursuit and takeover of the No. 1

position as unprecedented and unlikely to be repeated. That was a fact.

The audience gave me a big round of applause after I finished my explanation. Then the lecture ended.

In early 2005, the market exploded when flash memory was loaded onto the iPod Nano. The IT market went through a mobile big bang over the next decade, which led into the mobile era. Hwang's Law of flash memory being doubled every year was holding true.

In 2005, I gave a lecture to more than 1,000 professors and students gathered at Burden Hall, the largest lecture hall at Harvard University. The event was held to commemorate the first anniversary of the HBS semiconductor case study with the entire freshmen class of Harvard Business School. For Samsung, this was also an opportunity to secure human resources, which Chairman Lee had emphasized as his top priority. I addressed how I was able to foresee the mobile era. Our supplying of semiconductors to Apple became the genesis of our cooperation with them.

In 2016, I revisited Harvard University as the CEO of Korea Telecom. This time around, my lecture was on network innovation (GiGAtopia) in the business-to-consumer (B2C) domain. Through another round of major change I had gone from being a leader in business-to-business (B2B), to become a manager in B2C.

The influence of semiconductors was still powerful for a leader in the telecommunications market as well. I presented the 2TB solid-state drive (16 terabit, refer to page 134) in front of more than 800 students. In 2001, I had presented the 1G, and in 2002, the year I announced Hwang's Law, I presented the 2G.

Counting from 2001, flash memory with capacity double that from the previous year has been commercialized every year for the past 15 years. Moreover, as 5G becomes commercialized, the increase in demand for memory capacity will lead to continuous market growth. And the explosive increase in the use of video will only add to even further growth in the memory market.

Through learning and experience, I have come to realize that insight is a powerful tool in times of crisis. Everyone gets an equal amount of time. Those who wish to turn their dreams into reality should make daring decisions using their own vision for the future. If it is an investment for your future, you will never regret it.

02 Unwavering passion comes from having a clear vision in your heart

| **Steve Jobs** |

Everything seems possible in your 20s. The same was true for me. My interests settled in academia and studying, of course, but also in music and sports.

Mostly, I could be found in the library or research lab searching for and studying materials on semiconductors. At other times, I would go to the National Theater to take in a performance, or to the campus during a holiday to participate in a tennis tournament. I built up my social skills as the alumni president at SNU College of Engineering and Busan High School.

Naturally, I became accustomed to multitasking in those days, and every now and then I would coincidentally encounter "moments when I could see which way to go."

Finding Andy Grove's book in Gwanghwamun—
Encounters with two geniuses

In 1975, I came across Andy Grove's book, *Physics and Technology of Semiconductor Devices*, at a bookstore in Seoul's downtown area of Gwanghwamun.

The name Andy Grove may sound unfamiliar to someone outside the engineering field, but he is a highly regarded figure, together with Gordon Earle Moore, the man behind Moore's Law, and Robert Noyce, the founder and CEO of Intel.

After joining Intel upon its foundation in 1968, Andy served as its CEO from 1987 to 1997, turning Intel into the world's top semiconductor company. He was the prime mover who led the company to its No. 1 ranking in the world, and he is also responsible for building the PC-centered IT industry. The eponymous IEEE Andrew S. Grove Award exists to commemorate his achievements and is bestowed by the Institute of Electrical and Electronics Engineers (IEEE), the world's most prestigious organization in the field of electronics and based in the United States.

In his book, Andy Grove writes about the "properties and movement theory" of the integrated circuit (IC) and semiconductor devices. While I was still a university student, the IC, where several electronic circuits are arranged on a silicon substrate, was new technology. The more I learned, the more I became intrigued as the thumbnail-sized chip encompassed all the fields of science and engineering, including electronics, physics, and chemistry.

I became more and more fascinated by the allure of semiconductors as

I read the book. It occurred to me that semiconductors were at the center of the shift from analog to digital, and I planned for the future, thinking of Andy's book as a sort of signpost.

I decided to go to graduate school with a clear vision to study semiconductors. But in fact, it was not easy to major in this subject in graduate school in Korea. Even when I started studying, Korea's semiconductor industry was far behind the level of advanced countries. Korea Semiconductor Co., Ltd. was the only semiconductor maker in the country, and it had just been acquired by Samsung Group.

I needed to carry out experiments for my master's thesis, but since there was no laboratory, I built a small lab where I did experiments with a 2-inch wafer (silicon substrate) that I got from Korea Semiconductor. At the time, Korea Semiconductor produced chips for digital watches, but it was difficult to even get hold of a normal wafer, so I had to use a broken one for my experiments. Still, I gladly devoted myself to research, studying and giving presentations together with other students from Seoul National University (SNU) and Korea Advanced Institute of Science and Technology (KAIST).

Then in 1977, there was another important event. William Bradford Shockley, who won the Nobel Prize in Physics in 1956 for his work in developing the transistor, visited SNU to give a special lecture. Although I missed the lecture by a hair's breadth, I was able to hear about it later in a retelling by another seminar member. Shockley, in his own semiconductor world, pronounced the word "semiconductor" as *se-mai-conductor*, and "ion" as *ai-on*. Through direct and indirect encounters such as these with the giants of semiconductors, I felt my path in life becoming clearer.

I earned my PhD in electronic engineering at UMass, and continued to immerse myself in studies and experiments at Stanford University in Silicon Valley, the mecca of the semiconductor.

I was able to decline job offers from global companies such as IBM and Texas Instruments because I put my vision of doing semiconductor research ahead of monetary success. While at Stanford, I consulted with Intel and HP, had access to cutting-edge technologies, and engaged in active exchange with experts.

There, I had thrilling encounters with my idols. The office right across from my research lab at Stanford was the lab of an honorary professor in his late 70s. That professor was none other than William Shockley, the Nobelist who once gave a lecture at SNU. I still vividly remember how excited I was upon discovering him as he entered his lab with his wife's assistance.

A few days later, I knocked on the door of his lab with my doctoral thesis in hand. My paper, which was titled "Properties and Study of High-Speed Semiconductor Devices" applied Shockley's hot electron theory. When a strong electric field is applied to a semiconductor the electrons receive high amounts of energy, something which Shockley called the "hot electron." My thesis wouldn't exist without his theory.

Although he was usually characterized as being opinionated, he greeted me kindly and carefully perused my thesis. I told him how in my 20s I had heard indirectly about his special lecture and the moments that gave me the determination to study semiconductors. It was a very thrilling and nerve-wracking experience.

In yet another moving encounter, while visiting Intel for a consultation, I met Chairman Andy Grove in the company cafeteria. He was a true giant in the global semiconductor industry, and I do not exaggerate by saying he

William Shockley, who won the Nobel Prize in Physics in 1956 for developing the transistor for the first time in the world (left). Andrew Stephen Grove, who joined Intel in 1968 and served as its CEO for 25 years (right).
Source: Wikipedia

was the one figure who had the greatest influence on my life.

With his strong charisma, he turned Intel into the world's largest semiconductor company. I went without hesitation right up to him and exchanged greetings.

One day, during a period when I was doing twice-a-week consulting work at the Intel HQ, I greeted him again after having lunch. We chatted as we walked from the cafeteria to his office. Although it was the CEO's office, it had a desk only slightly larger than those of the other researchers, and there was just enough space for a meeting. I could feel the atmosphere at Intel, a place without walls where everyone communicated openly regardless of their position. Once again without hesitation I talked about the coincidence of finding his book in Gwanghwamun, my vision for the semiconductor, and my research projects.

He was dressed casually and listened earnestly to what I was saying. He asked questions like, "What is the 0.35μm transistor technology for the next-generation CPU like, and what are its properties?"

Again I felt fortunate to have set a vision for my life after discovering Andy's book and immersed myself in my studies, and to then encounter two geniuses who are legends in the history of semiconductors one after another. It was because of these encounters that I was able to have a clear vision of my goals and pursue them fiercely.

Looking back upon the years I spent in the lab, it was a time of "complete combustion." I wouldn't exist as I am today without my total immersion in those days. I would go on to meet a few more teachers who also experienced this complete combustion. One of them is Steve Jobs, a friend who is no longer of this world.

What we have to do is change the world

On December 6, 2004, I visited Cupertino, California. I was in that strangely named city for "important decisions" (read "negotiations") that would have an enormous influence on the world in which we live.

Steve Jobs, Tim Cook (then the COO of Apple), Jonathan J. Rubinstein (Development Head), Jeff Williams (Purchasing Head), and two or three other key decision makers from Apple were sitting across the table. What follows is the story of how we came to sit side by side with Apple's top management.

Three years earlier in 2001, the world began to become mesmerized with an odd little mobile audio device. The device came loaded with a small hard disk drive (HDD) and utilized MP3 technology developed in Korea in the late 1990s. It was highly portable and stored over 1,000 songs, and people were crazy about it. It was the "iPod," the device that introduced Apple's smart ecosystem to the whole world.

The reason consumers were infatuated with the newly released iPod was not simply because it was a single device that could store a lot of songs. The intuitive design and unprecedented music ecosystem (iTunes) that it provided were something original that only Steve Jobs could create. Through the iPod, Apple succeeded in transforming itself from a PC manufacturer to a leading player in the mobile sector, and opened a winning path that would lead quickly to the top of the US market.

However, the experts were not so smitten with the Apple iPod. It had distinct technical defects. Although it was a mobile device, it was vulnerable to shock and didn't operate well in sub-freezing temperatures. Also, the battery would run down quickly, meaning users had to carry a charger if they wanted to use it for more than two hours.

Another characteristic of the iPod was that it was inconvenient to carry despite being a mobile device. Its numerous "inconveniences" stemmed from the chronic problem of having been loaded with the hard drive. I believed that these problems could easily be solved by replacing the hard disk with flash memory developed by Samsung, but this was easier said than done.

Not long after the release of the iPod, Samsung proposed to Apple that it load the iPod with flash memory instead of a disk drive. However, Apple would not even give Samsung the time of day as it already held a monopoly over the market. Apple's market share in the US was as high as

70%, so the company didn't feel the need to start an all-out war over the use of an expensive flash component. Steve Jobs in particular stubbornly clung to his idea that the iPod should contain 1,000 songs and stuck to using the hard drive, as long as the price of flash memory didn't plummet.

Still, Samsung Electronics could not let Apple slip away because their potential as a client was too huge. Moreover, Samsung had been struggling to secure a large market after finally succeeding in developing flash memory, which had better shock resistance and longer playback time because it consumed less electricity than an HDD. Samsung needed to reel in Apple if only to expand the influence of flash memory in a world growing more mobile-centered by the day.

Flash memory was more competitive than the HDD in every aspect, including functions and convenience, and the speed of its technological development increased, which gradually enhanced the price competitiveness as well. In June 2004, with full confidence in our product, I sent Apple an MP3 equipped with flash memory. I hoped that Apple would

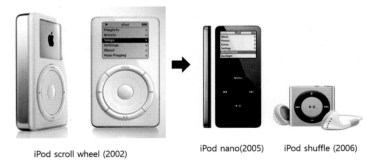

iPod scroll wheel (2002)   iPod nano(2005)   iPod shuffle (2006)

The iPod, released in 2002, the iPod Nano, equipped with the flash memory (2005), and the iPod shuffle (2006).

compare the products and see the striking differences between its hard drive-based product and the MP3 designed with flash memory.

From that point on, it became a boring waiting game. After about three months, Steve Job called us in person.

He invited us to a place he called the Reception Hall in Palo Alto, California, a city that was home to quite a few IT tycoons. At that moment, I knew that our head-on strategy to prove the competitiveness of flash memory had worked. Once my excitement died down, I arranged to fly to Palo Alto in late November after attending a meeting at IBM. Unfortunately, my meeting with Apple was not without obstacles. I was stranded at the airport in North Carolina, from where I was supposed to fly to Palo Alto. On the way to board the flight, which had already been placed on standby, they announced that the airplane couldn't take off due to a discharged battery in an important piece of equipment. It was impossible to fly to Palo Alto because it would take one to two days to repair. I felt my heart hit the floor..

I took a few deep breaths and called Steve Jobs. I explained the situation and made sure to apologize. I didn't expect his reaction. I thought he would hang up saying, "Well, let's take a rain check." Instead, in a tone dripping with disappointment, but also showing he was anxious to set up the meeting, he asked, "Can you come in early December?" I was now strongly convinced that Apple would adopt Samsung's flash memory, and I promised to return to Palo Alto after attending a 30th anniversary event for Samsung Semiconductor.

After that phone call, I knew that Samsung flash memory loaded into the Apple iPod would become a reality but that there also remained a challenging process to undergo before signing the formal contract.

Furthermore, I could now envision the "age of the mobile-smart device" that would unfold across the whole world. My intuition told me that a new future was just around the corner, where internet connectivity would be possible regardless of space and time, and people would be able to download any information they needed.

Opening of the "mobile-smart era" by Samsung and Apple

On the day I was supposed to go to Apple in Cupertino, Samsung held an event to celebrate its 30th anniversary in the semiconductor business. Chairman Lee Kun-hee came in person to Samsung Semiconductor's Hwaseong Complex to deliver a congratulatory address.

The manufacturing line for the 12-inch wafer was completed by then, and additional construction was being carried out nonstop. I had to report various issues as the person in charge of semiconductors. Among the pending issues was the securing of semiconductor-related human resources, and the following year, Sungkyunkwan University opened a Department of Semiconductor Systems Engineering.

The flash memory contract with Apple was a significant issue. After hearing about my business trip to Cupertino, Chairman Lee instructed me to make a good impression on Apple. I thought he had told me that because of his previous experience with Nokia being a great asset for Samsung (I will explain the collaboration with Nokia later). Everyone expressed their expectation that the collaboration with Apple would be another great opportunity for Samsung.

A few days before my departure, Vice President Lee Jae-yong called me

The author and Lee Jae-yong meet with Steve Jobs at Apple HQ.

to say that he wanted to accompany me on the business trip. I willingly agreed because he was also in charge of the semiconductor business.

On December the 6th, the meeting room at the Apple HQ was filled with tension. As Apple management later revealed, Samsung had already been decided on as the flash memory supplier. Still, the negotiation process prior to signing to the contract was arduous. The problem was the price.

I made an offer that Apple couldn't easily accept. Steve Jobs jumped into the price negotiations by naming an unimaginable order quantity. The tough negotiating continued in a tense atmosphere for over three hours. Earlier, before entering the meeting room, Lee Jae-yong had said to me, "President Hwang, I'm an observer today," a statement that had given me extra confidence.

What impressed me the most that day was Steve Jobs laying out his plan for a "smart kingdom to be opened by Apple." In his turtleneck and jeans, he started to write out his plan on the whiteboard. Using straightforward language and gestures, he described the products and launch roadmap he was envisioning in an overwhelming tone. Soon, the whiteboard was packed with diagrams and letters. I can still vividly recall the words written in Steve's own hand, "iPhone," "iPad," "iTV," "MacBook Air," and others. In that room, into which Steve Jobs unleashed his built-up passion, I could easily imagine the power of these soon-to-be-released Apple products and how they would change the world as they began hitting the global market.

Finishing his presentation, Steve Jobs said he would use Samsung Electronics' flash memory for the soon-to-be released iPod. He stressed the tremendous quantity ordered, saying that Apple would build its ambitious "smart kingdom" with Samsung's flash memory. But this was a ploy followed by a demand for us to lower the price. However, I calmly answered, "Samsung Electronics has other clients just as important as Apple. Considering their trust in us, we can't do that." Indeed, any relationship with a client is not something that can always be measured in dollars and cents.

Nevertheless, Steve continued with his tough demands. Quantity and price are important in a negotiation. Perhaps Steve Jobs thought he had the advantage here, considering Apple's position and its future lineup. I, on the other hand, concentrated on the fact that as much as Samsung needed Apple as a client, Apple also needed Samsung as a partner. By that time, Steve couldn't imagine Apple's products without Samsung's flash

The author giving Steve Jobs the 60nm 8G NAND flash wafer after their meeting.

memory.

Having spoken fervently for quite some time, Steve Jobs came around the table in his turtleneck and ripped jeans where he squeezed himself in to sit between me and Lee Jae-yong, and continued to talk. He was trying to convince Lee, who had only been listening without saying a word for three and a half hours. Seeing that we were still sticking to our position, he went back to his seat.

As soon as he did so, Lee leaned toward me slightly and said, "What if we invite Steve to Korea?" His point was, since it was difficult to decide right away, we should set up another meeting to get home advantage. The meeting ended with, "Let's discuss the details again later."

As we wrapped up the first meeting by shaking hands with Steve Jobs,

I gave him the 60nm 8G NAND flash wafer, which Samsung Electronics had developed for the first time in the world. The wafer was the second among five from the first run after successful development ("run" refers to a set of 10-20 wafers processed together during the semiconductor fabrication process). I presented it to Steve as a symbol of Apple's membership in the flash world.

Once I had gotten back to the hotel, Lee Jae-yong called to suggest we have a glass of wine. We reviewed what we'd done during the day and discussed our remaining schedule. Lee carefully suggested, "President Hwang, what if we accept their conditions for supplying the flash on condition that they buy our System LSI?"

Samsung had put immense effort into improving the competitiveness of the System LSI (large-scale integration), a semiconductor with various applications in industrial devices. However, it would not be easy to break into the stronghold of Intel, the dominant player in the global market. Intel's power in the CPU sector was that enormous. Using the leverage of flash to supply the application processor (AP) to Apple would greatly facilitate the entry of Samsung Electronics' system LSI into the global market. For reference, the AP is a CPU for mobile devices, a core semiconductor that processes the operation of applications and graphics. With the advent of new services and multimedia content, mobile devices like smartphones and PDAs required a CPU—and that was the AP.

I calmly listened to Lee and nodded since we usually share the same ideas. I didn't say it out loud, but I could easily recognize Lee's insight as a manager.

Returning to Korea, I sent a suggestion to Apple that they couldn't refuse.

"It is difficult for us to completely agree with your bid, but we will partially accept your request regarding the price of the NAND flash. Instead, please examine our suggestion about using Samsung's AP."

Only then did Steve Jobs accept my proposal. Apple signed a contract to receive not only the NAND flash, but also Samsung's AP and mobile DRAM. This made Apple the biggest client for Samsung's Semiconductor Division.

It might have been a coincidence that two Samsung leaders had the same idea, but thanks to that, Samsung's development of the AP went into full swing. It significantly strengthened the business and enabled its AP to be installed on Apple's products in a relatively short time.

In 2007, following preparation and testing period lasting a year and a half, Samsung was able to begin exclusively supplying the AP for the iPhone in 2007. Earlier in 2006, it also supplied the MPU (a product with simpler functions than the AP) for the MP3 player.

The System LSI Division, which had faced some earlier difficulties in management, transformed into a division that made billions of dollars in profits just by supplying Apple with the AP as its sole product. Samsung's AP capability strengthened during this exclusive supplier relationship that lasted six years. It became clear that flash memory was the core component in Apple's ambitious smart kingdom. If Steve Jobs had his clear vision, Samsung had the cutting-edge technology that Apple needed. Samsung was the ultimate partner for Apple in turning its vision into reality.

The beginning and completion of the global mobile revolution

In 2005, the iPod Nano, loaded with flash memory, was released. As expected, it was a phenomenal success. This was no surprise. The iPod Nano was thinner, lighter, and had a playback time that was five times longer than the existing product. With the success of the iPod Nano, the sales of flash memory and the market share of Samsung Electronics increased exponentially. Sales surged by 47% in one year, and its share of the flash memory market soared to 35%.

For the next few years, the growth of Samsung Electronics was on a par with Apple. After the MP3 player, Apple solidified its position as the leader in the portable multimedia player (PMP) and smartphone markets, as it released the iPod Touch in 2006, the iPhone in 2007, the iPhone 2G in 2008, and the iPhone 3G and 3GS in 2009.

Apple's share price, which had hovered between $7.00 and $20.00, shot up to over $200.00 after Apple's launch of the iPhone. This share price doubled to $400.00 in 2011, after the flash-based solid-state drive (SSD) was installed in the iPad.

In 2006, while I was still president of the Semiconductor Division, Samsung Electronics announced its development for the first time in the world of the 64GB solid-state drive. The SSD is a semiconductor memory storage device that replaces high-capacity hard disks and overcomes limitations in microfabrication by improving density with vertically stacked layers, like in an apartment building.

The SSD is very small, has low power consumption, and makes little noise. It also provides much higher speed, which differentiates it from existing products equipped with the HDD.

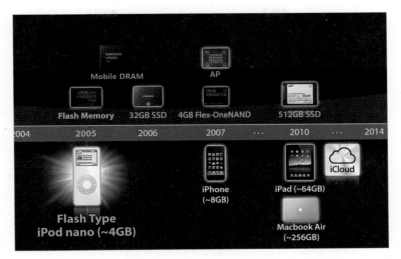

Mobile DRAM

AP

Flash Memory   32GB SSD   4GB Flex-OneNAND   512GB SSD

004   2005   2006   2007   ...   2010   ...   2014

iPhone
(~8GB)

iPad (~64GB)

iCloud

Flash Type
iPod nano (~4GB)

Macbook Air
(~256GB)

Apple products loaded with various Samsung Electronics memory semiconductors and AP.

There is one other hidden anecdote behind the birth of the solid-state drive. On my flight back to Korea after the meeting with Steve Jobs, I anticipated the market need regarding storage in laptops and the memory systems of businesses, and predicted the fast growth of high-capacity flash memory. The moment I was back in the office, I immediately put together a team composed of 200 members from the HDD Team under my department, the System-on-a-Chip (SOC, the technology that embeds several semiconductors with different functions on a single chip) Team under the Department of System LSI, the Software Team, and the Product Planning Team.

It was the so-called SSD Team. I was able to secure 40-50 talented members of the Software Team from the Samsung Electronics headquarters thanks to Vice Chairman Yun Jong-yong's support.

Our first target was the laptop. Until then, every PC and laptop was equipped with the HDD. Flash memory was not considered as competitive due to its high price and small storage capacity. I thought if we could enlarge the memory capacity and lower the price through technological development, the SSD would be able to compete.

First, we produced a 16GB SSD and a 32GB solid-state drive that would be used for camcorders or in industrial applications. This allowed Samsung Electronics to enter the flash-based storage market in 2005 and develop a laptop equipped with a 32GB Solid-state drive in 2006. In 2007, Apple launched the MacBook Air equipped with a 64GB SSD.

If Steve Jobs was responsible for predicting the mobile era and initiating the global mobile revolution with Apple's products, then Samsung made this revolution possible and added the final touch with its independently-developed semiconductor memory.

The MacBook Air and iPad, released in 2010, created a new market that eliminated the boundary between laptops and smartphones by adopting Samsung's solid-state drive to replace the existing HDD. This was possible because Samsung's solid-state drive was thin, and had high capacity with high-speed data reading and writing capability. Despite its high price, the MacBook Air created a sensation in the market with its light, thin, and stylish design. Its weight and speed were overwhelmingly competitive compared with other laptops.

The next big target I went after was the server market. High-speed random access memory is the most important aspect of an internet server.

It is not victory, but change and innovation that make us happy

The data-processing speed of the flash memory on an internet and cloud server was much higher than that of the HDD. It also had satisfactory reliability and durability, and low power consumption. I predicted that the market would significantly grow as the flash-based solid-state drive became essential for servers. And the SSD market for servers did grow exponentially.

I was able to create a global success story in my own way by observing the market flow and development speed of technologies. Just as we pushed for introducing flash memory to Apple, another of our important strategies was to create a market that did not yet exist by arousing our clients' hidden needs. The meeting between Apple and Samsung brought about the start of the global smart revolution, while Samsung's development of flash memory gradually led the completion of the revolution. It was natural for both Apple and Samsung to become the top global player in their respective fields.

One year after striking the deal with Apple, I met Steve Jobs again at the first Apple store in Tokyo. He greeted me with a bright and energetic expression, "Hey, Mr. Flash!" Unlike the person I saw at the negotiation table, he seemed to be a person who was treating Samsung Electronics as a true partner that would share the future with Apple.

After several meetings with him, I heard about his relationship with Lee Byung-chull, the founder of Samsung.

Apple, while it was still in early stages, found a defect in a component it had ordered from Samsung. Steve Jobs himself complained and Lee urgently dispatched engineers to smoothly solve the problem. This was

A 2G iPhone sent to the author from Steve Jobs

the first occasion on which Steve Jobs had a good impression of Samsung Electronics. It was as if Founder Lee's words about looking towards the future and doing everything with sincerity were echoing in my ears.

"Instead of satisfying the current demand, you should create a future demand based on imagination," said Steve Jobs. He was still firm on his ideas during our meetings.

He wanted to prepare for the future by being a step ahead instead of settling in the existing market. Steve's words left a deep impression on me, as I also had the idea that a company's mission is to prepare for the future with insight.

"Dr. Hwang, what is the limit of a technology?"

This is the most impressive question he ever asked me. He kept asking this question over and over again. It was because he had to figure out how far the semiconductor could be developed so that Apple could create innovative products five or ten years into the future.

If we couldn't get together, we would talk on the phone. I explained various new technologies, including the innovative technology CTF, and reported on the expanding boundaries of technology. I was deeply moved by his passion and ability to anticipate products and technologies one or two decades ahead of our time. Still to this day, I often pose the question, "Why isn't there another innovative leader like Steve Jobs?"

The uncommon insight that led the global mobile revolution wasn't generated overnight. The potential to make dreams come true began with a "thorough analysis" of market trends and the "willingness" to create a future market with one's own hands.

Steve Jobs is well known for his brilliant inspiration and perfectionism. He was also a leader with unparalleled sense in utilizing technologies and sharing his visions to realize his inspiration and perfectionism. His unique vision and passion turned his dreams into reality.

When I was leading one innovation after another after declaring Hwang's Law, many journalists would say to me, "You and other researchers must be under extreme stress to double memory capacity every year."

I was always ready for that kind of comment.

"Of course. We are physically worn out. But try to imagine Samsung's semiconductor technology used on products that the young generation is crazy about, and the creation of new markets one after another. Imagining these things makes us welcome such challenges. That's enough to get rid of any fatigue."

Along with our researchers, I had a clear vision that the "future is something that we create." And though our achievements felt rewarding and made us happy, failure gave us an opportunity to grow.

I'd like to give a small bit of advice to those who want to become another Steve Jobs. If you strive for changes and innovation, you will also have an insight into the future. It is your heart's unwavering vision that will give you burning passion.

03

Don't hesitate
to grab the opportunity

| Yi Sun-sin |

I had this one habit while I was still a student. I would write Chinese characters in the margins of my textbooks or notebooks when I started to lose focus or had a break from schoolwork. Thanks to my grandfather, I was familiar with Chinese characters.

I usually wrote down characters that came to mind. One day, I wrote 必死卽生 必生卽死. It was after I had read *Nanjung Ilgi* (亂中日記), a war diary that Admiral Yi Sun-sin wrote during the Imjin War with Japan (1592-98). As I wrote the eight characters over and over again, I became fascinated by the power that these words carried:

"Those who seek death shall live. Those who seek life shall die."

I read several books about Admiral Yi. He established great aspirations and proceeded to realize them. I felt great reverence for the admiral, who led his fleet to victory in the Imjin War. The fervor I had felt during my teens didn't subside. The lessons from Admiral Yi Sun-sin encouraged me at times when I needed to be courageous to face the future without any hesitation.

"Twelve battleships still remain in Your Subject's hands."

Every Korean knows about Admiral Yi Sun-sin. However, not many know the stories about the various facets of the man and his life. I, too, only could only put together an annotation on those facets after I repeatedly read the book, *Yi Sun-sin, I'm Already Prepared*, by Kim Jong-dae. (Kim graduated from Busan High School, my alma mater; studied at Seoul National University School of Law; and retired as a judge of the Constitutional Court of Korea.)

"Admiral Yi had an imposing air as he was rigorous and prudent. He loved others and was humble in front of scholars. He was trustworthy, deeply learned, and broad-minded, and he did not easily show joy or anger on his countenance."

This passage comes from a necrology, a record about the kind of person he was, written after his death.

The life of Admiral Yi was truly filled with bitterness and suffering. He had no supporter who would cover his flaws or encourage him to fight with all his might. He received a royal edit ordering him to fight to the death, so he had no choice but to go out and face the enemy once more. However there were no resources remaining for him. Won Gyun, a naval commander who had slandered Yi Sun-shin, had been routed and even lost his life at the Battle of Chilcheollyang (north of Geoje City) in the seventh lunar month of 1597. Nearly all the *panokseon* ("board-roofed" battleships) and naval forces that he had trained had been wiped out. The Koreans lost more than 20,000 seamen, including the commander, and over 100 battleships, including three iron-clad *geobukseon* ("turtle ships") had been sunk.

The majestic fleet he had built up during four years of hard work was

70

reduced to ashes in a day. Only three months earlier, Admiral Yi was about to be executed in the capital. He was released from prison with the punishment of having to fight in the war as a commoner. That was on the first day of the fourth lunar month, 28 days after he had been imprisoned. He lost his position as the Commander-in-Chief of Samdo Naval Forces and was placed under the command of Kwon Yul in Chogye, Hapcheon.

However, Admiral Yi's mother passed away ten days later. She was going to move closer to her son and was traveling by ship from the capital (Hanyang) to Asan. Her vessel was hit by strong winds and waves, and she passed away at the age of 83. After holding the funeral with help from others, Admiral Yi resumed his race south on the 19th day of that month.

Admiral Yi collected himself together and arrived at Kwon Yul's camp in Hapcheon on the eighth day of the sixth month, two months after he had left the capital. The Samdo Naval Forces had been destroyed during the Battle of Chilcheollyang, where Won Gyun had suffered successive defeats.

Admiral Yi received permission from Kwon Yul and promptly went to the place where the Koreans had met defeat. He did so because he had to observe the area, regroup the scattered surviving seamen, set a new plan of attack, and establish strategies for saving the country. Risking great danger, he arrived at the seashore overlooking where Won Gyun had lost. When he reached the coast of Jinju and Noryang, sailors and commoners alike ran to him and wailed. On the third day of the eighth month, Admiral Yi received an edict from King Seonjo reappointing him as Commander-in-Chief of Samdo Naval Forces. However, no support was forthcoming from the court.

Admiral Yi set off again on the day he received his commission. He went up to Hoengcheon, followed the river Seomjin-gang upstream, and passed Hwagae Market in Hadong. It was crowded with commoner refugees. He dismounted his horse to grasp their hands and urge them to stay strong during the rest of the war. The young men among them followed him. In this way he toured the inland regions of the southern provinces for a month, covering as far as 300 km and facing constant risk of being spotted by the enemy.

It was at Byeokpa-jin, on the island of Jindo, where Admiral Yi reorganized his forces and prepared for battle. The Japanese navy noticed this move and thought, "Admiral Yi is about to take action again. If we don't wipe them out this time, our marine transport will not be safe." They mobilized their forces, prompting Admiral Yi's sailors to desert and leaving him at a dead end. Moreover, he received the order from the court that he should abandon his ships and return to shore to fend off the enemy. They thought he stood no chance with his depleted fleet and only the remnants of a defeated force. After much consideration, Admiral Yi defied the court that had attempted to abolish the naval forces with these words:

"Your Highness, twelve battleships still remain in Your Subject's hands. If we fight with all our might, we can still win this battle."

The famous Battle of Myeongnyang took place on the 16th day of the ninth month. It was the catalyst for Joseon to snatch away Japan's chances for victory in the war. It took four more battles before the seven-year war that had created a hell for so many people came to an end.

"Those who seek death shall live. Those who seek life shall die."

I felt closer to Admiral Yi when I was serving for the ROK Navy. After graduating from Seoul National University, and before I studied abroad, I applied to be an instructor at the Republic of Korea Naval Academy. After I completed my master's course, I was commissioned as a first lieutenant.

One of the Naval Academy's outstanding monuments in Jin hae is the "museum." It was built to educate people about Admiral Yi Sun-sin's patriotism and his activities during naval battles. As far as I remember, this place had the largest number of documents related to Admiral Yi at the time. I spent

The author as an instructor of the Republic of Korea Naval Academy in 1978

time there whenever I could. The original copy of the *Nanjung Ilgi* is displayed at the museum, and I liked reading it using a magnifier. I was deeply moved seeing the characters 必死則生 必生則死 written in Admiral Yi Sun-sin's own hand. During those days, I turned the vigor of my 20s into the chivalrous spirit I learned from Admiral Yi, who taught me to "always prepare and face the future without any hesitation."

I was determined that when the time came, I would embody Admiral Yi's risk-taking mentality and accept any challenge that came my way. I thought taking risks would be the only way to win and realize the historical changes I aspired to achieve.

Later, there were several moments in my life when I was reminded of Admiral Yi's mindset. I had the opportunity of a lifetime in 2001.

People often say you encounter a heaven-sent opportunity at least once in your life. But you might not recognize it at that very moment. You may realize it was good fortune only after you or others take that opportunity and make something out of it. However, it did not take me even a day to know that it was luck. The words "those who seek death shall live" and "those who seek life shall die" was embedded in my heart.

It was November when Samsung's Memory Business Division was busily preparing the NOR Flash Workshop. The existing SRAM-centered business had limitations when it came to expanding sales. Demand plummeted as Intel, the major client, embedded SRAMs in its Pentium chipset. The NOR flash was mainstream in the flash memory market, and Samsung's market share was less than 1%. The NAND flash, which I wanted to build up, represented barely 20% of the entire flash market.

We decided to step up our design work on NOR flash so we could enter the market mainstream, and then we planned the workshop. One of the important reasons for this was the modest share of NAND flash chips in the flash memory market. NOR occupied 96.5% of the entire flash market in 2000, and 88.4% in 2001. NAND took up the rest. We needed to contain Intel in the NOR flash market to at least expand the NAND flash market. We formulated a "double strategy," in which we would prevail over Intel on the one hand and grow ourselves on the other.

Of course, coming out on top in the NOR flash market was easier said than done. In late 1990s, Samsung Electronics went into both the NOR and NAND segments while setting up its flash memory business.

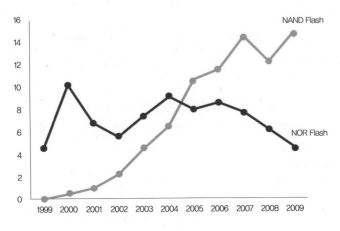

< Changes in Market Shares of NOR Flash and NAND Flash (1999-2009) >

NAND Flash

NOR Flash

• Unit: billion

Samsung was ready to take the second place in the world in the newly-formed NAND flash market.

However, Samsung Electronics' position in the NOR flash market, was negligible. The same went for its technologies. Although the company had NAND flash technology, it had little experience in developing devices in the NOR flash domain. Even some participants of the NOR flash workshop were skeptical. But I didn't have any room for doubt.

The day we were to hold the workshop in the afternoon, an employee ran up to me with an urgent message. A representative of the Nokia chairman had come to visit. I personally greeted the guest in my office. He said he came to deliver a message from the Chairman, and I was astonished by the message he brought:

"If you make a 64M and 128M high-density NOR flash by this

specific deadline, we will guarantee the market share you want."

At the time, 32M was the highest capacity for NOR flash devices. Nokia demanded a memory chip with 2x and 4x the current capacity. In addition, they wanted the 0.18 micron design rule, whereas the latest technology in the industry was 0.21 microns. Basically, they demanded the most advanced, next-generation technology. At first, I was very confused, even after listening to what he told me to my face. Besides, Samsung Electronics Semiconductor was ranked below tenth place in the NOR flash market.

"How could they make this kind of proposal?"

As I listened to their story, it was understandable. Intel was Nokia's sole NOR flash supplier, and Intel leveraged its monopoly to announce a price increase. Not wanting to be pushed around by Intel, Nokia had come up with an alternative approach by reaching out to Samsung Electronics. Fortunately, the representative sent by Nokia Chairman Jorma Ollila visited us on the day of our NOR flash workshop.

After having lunch, I put my brain to work, thinking over and over again. We would be working ourselves to the bone just to meet the deadline set by Nokia. We needed to spend a good year for the development and nine months for the approval. Normally, it took 60 days to complete a 300-step process, but we would have to cut this by two-thirds. However, if we did make the deadline, it would be proof of the saying, "Heaven helps those who help themselves." After the workshop, I concluded that "we must succeed by all means," and embarked on the tough schedule. As promised, the Memory Business Division succeeded in developing the product with the specifications required by Nokia in just nine months. Our employees took the prototype with them to

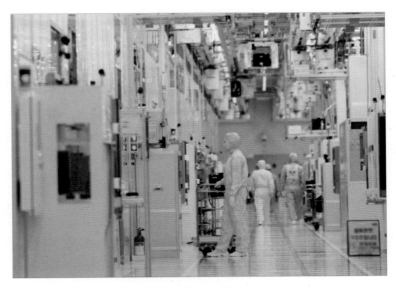

The production line for 12-inch semiconductor wafers

Helsinki, Finland.

A few days later, while on my way to Europe in early 2002, I received the test results for our NOR flash prototype designed for Nokia cellphones. I was dumbfounded. The results showed a 99.9% failure rate. It was embarrassing. But I thought even for a totally unqualified product, the failure rate couldn't be 99.9%. I was sure that there must have been something wrong during the testing process, and ordered a re-test. The test result that came out the next day was 100% successful.

Today, it's easy for me to say that it was just a minor mishap. But at that time, I felt like I had gone from hell to heaven overnight.

After that, we built a firm relationship with Nokia. First, they consulted about sourcing with Samsung Electronics. The Nokia chairman met with

Samsung's Chairman Lee Kun-hee who paid a visit to the Nokia headquarters in Finland to meet Chairman Jorma Ollila.

me, the president of their supplier, twice a year. He was known not to meet any supplier presidents, but I was an exception. This shows how important Samsung Electronics Semiconductor was for Nokia.

In June 2003, I went to Finland with Chairman Lee and Vice Chairman Yun Jong-yong to meet Chairman Ollila. Nokia's share of the global mobile phone market was 45% at the time. The meeting was prepared as Samsung Electronics became the major supplier of the NOR flash for most Nokia cellphones. Chairman Lee said to Chairman Ollila, "Nokia is the most important partner for Samsung Semiconductor."

We went back to the hotel that evening to have a conversation. To answer Chairman Lee's question, I was recommending several Samsung Group affiliates to Nokia.

That meeting between the chairmen of Nokia and Samsung was significant in many ways. First, it supported our main business, which is semiconductors. Second, we were able to promote business deals between other Samsung Group affiliates and Nokia, using the semiconductor as leverage. I could read the insightful strategy of Chairman Lee.

Losing Nokia, Intel's sales plummeted from $800 million to zero, and it was forced sell off that business division in 2007. By contrast, Samsung Electronics' sales in relation to Nokia's semiconductor memory reached some $2 billion in 2004, and Samsung Group's total sales grew steadily.

Every opportunity comes with risks from the outset

It was not just the surge in sales that made me realize our partnership with Nokia was a "heaven-sent opportunity" for Samsung Semiconductor. From the beginning, I anticipated that the trade with Nokia would not just end in a "rise of Samsung Electronics' market share in the NOR flash market."

My bigger picture was to have the company's position rooted firmly in the NOR flash market, and then expand the NAND flash market.

Nokia was somewhat oblivious, but I had plans to leverage the NAND flash with Nokia's NOR flash. Based on the trust we had built with each other, my plan worked out swiftly.

I stationed dozens of engineers at Nokia to swap out the NOR flash with the NAND flash. Then, I repeated the explanation over and over to the person in charge at Nokia.

"In the upcoming multimedia-centered 3G mobile market, we need to satisfy demand not only in terms of speed but also in memory capacity."

I was very persistent, and the person in charge said, "We are already familiar with the NOR flash. We will take it into consideration if it isn't inconvenient."

I changed our product's interface (program) to further their understanding. Samsung's strategy in predicting the market and creating the prototype was effective. The person in charge for purchasing from Nokia marveled at Samsung's demo.

None of our efforts was wasted, and it was like hitting a jackpot. In the process of replacing the NOR flash with the NAND flash, we created a "fusion memory" that combined the strengths of both. It was the OneNAND, which became Samsung's bestseller for the next two to three years. "OneNAND," which combines the capacity of the NAND flash and the speed of the NOR flash, is a NAND-based fusion memory with a dramatically improved operating speed.

It was significant as it replaced the NOR flash used in mobile phones, but it had a greater advantage since it enabled the NAND flash, with its higher density, to be used on the foundation for the NOR flash. At first, our strategy was to make a product for the NAND flash era where mobile devices would require high density, and then we would approach our client with the product. And because it simultaneously satisfied the qualifications in terms of both speed and density, Nokia's enthusiastic reaction to our prototype was as expected.

Still, several obstacles remained to the full-blown commercialization of OneNAND. First, there was an Israeli company that released a similar product. Samsung Electronics had to develop its version quicker than the competitor did, and meet Nokia's increasingly complicated demands.

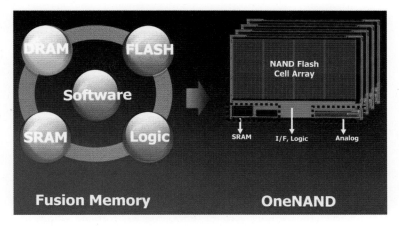

OneNAND, the world's first fusion semiconductor developed in 2003

Fortunately, the product made by the Israeli company consisted of two chips, which meant it was behind our OneNAND fusion technology in terms of functions and cost competitiveness.

We supplied the software one month ahead of schedule. In 2004, two years after Samsung first knocked on Nokia's door, the Nokia phone equipped with Samsung Electronics' OneNAND was released.

OneNAND, born in the process of searching for ways to promote the NAND flash in the NOR flash-dominated mobile phone market, created another revolution in the mobile phone market. OneNAND quickly made inroads into the NOR flash market, which had been the mainstream, and reorganized the flash market with NAND flash as the mainstream. Accordingly, the market share of Samsung Electronics' NAND flash, which was only 25% in 2000, surged to 54% in 2004. In 2006, Intel, which had been the top player in the NOR flash domain, abandoned it and made its way into the NAND flash market.

The trade with Nokia gave me the opportunity to change our "organizational culture" while at the same time generating profits and developing new devices. In the early 2000s, the semiconductor market was stuck in a recession, and Samsung's presence in the market was insignificant. This circumstance made defeatism run rampant within the organization.

Our trade with Nokia changed that mentality. The fruit we harvested by working with excitement was not just a one-time experience. Employees expressed their delight in the company saying, "We can do it if we try!" The virtuous cycle of innovation was forming within our organization in no time.

Confidence, our strongest ally, became deeply embedded throughout the organization. The world market share of our NOR flash increased from less than 1% to 15% in the process.

"How did you make such a decision?"

I was asked this kind of question in the company every time I succeeded in something. In hindsight, I wasn't totally free from the "risk of failure." The conditions proposed by our top client Nokia was beyond our technology back then. Time was not on our side, either. They set a really tight deadline. Even though I was fully aware of their overwhelming demand, I still accepted it. I had to.

That is because I know that every opportunity comes with risks. And I know that grabbing that opportunity is also accepting the risks that might accompany it. When grabbing an opportunity, the only remaining task is to reduce risks one by one through every possible effort. I performed my duties without complaint, to include revamping the organization, removing inter-department barriers, conducting integrated trials at the beginning of development, and improving communication between engineers and traders.

There is a saying that you can only grab an opportunity while it's in front of you. Once it's gone, it's gone. You can try to snatch it again, but that won't be as easy. Even a heaven-sent opportunity will have no rewards unless you respond and utilize it properly. It is crucial to thoroughly prepare and confront every obstacle that comes along the way. At the end of the road awaits a visible success and valuable experience that nurtured our organization

Whether it's a wooden or stone bridge, be the first to cross it

Based on my experience, there is a type of organization that has difficulty in practicing "risk-taking." I am referring to a conservative organization that prioritizes safety. It may be good to be professional in one certain area, but you should not be stuck in that area. Still, it is common to see a company with a long history trapped in one area, only to eventually disappear from it.

When I started working for KT, changing the company culture was an extremely important task. It couldn't be done with just a slogan. We needed a clear vision and goals to take steps in that direction. The "5G Declaration" was the signpost that showed us direction. But an assertive leader was necessary for any changes to actually happen within the organization. I was the one who raised a hand to take the lead for KT. In 2015, the Global System for Mobile Communication Association (GSMA) convened in Barcelona, Spain. GSMA hosts the Mobile World

Congress (MWC), the world's largest event in mobile communications, and leaders of communications companies from around the world participate. The number of attendees was about 20, including board members.

They took turns to speak. After the CEO of NTT DOCOMO (DOCOMO), Japan's largest mobile phone operator, finished his presentation, I raised my hand. The GSMA chair passed the microphone to me. "The DOCOMO CEO just said that 5G should be actualized at the Tokyo 2020 Olympic Games. But KT is already preparing for a rollout of 5G at the PyeongChang 2018 Winter Olympics. We have started to prepare the infrastructure in PyeongChang, and we are rapidly working on this project."

The meeting room went silent.

In actuality, this was the situation. The DOCOMO CEO had begun the 5G commercialization process, an effort to be unveiled at the Tokyo 2020 Olympics, in 2013. DOCOMO remained on schedule after receiving enormous R&D support from the government. Japan would become the first region with commercial 5G service, according to the GSMA roadmap, which included plans for standardization in 2018 and commercialization in 2020. However, Korea unexpectedly declared that it would be the first to realize 5G!

Japan probably didn't expect that there would be competitors since other countries' telecom networks were no match for Japanese technologies. I could see the bewilderment on the CEO's face. I didn't mind the awkward atmosphere and continued speaking.

"I am well aware of the schedule that the CEO talked about. However, we have the PyeongChang 2018 Winter Olympics two years before the Tokyo 2020 Olympics take place. I'd like to propose a partnership between the two companies, since KT is also working on the actualization of 5G. KT will actively transfer the 5G technological know-how to DOCOMO for the Tokyo 2020 Olympics."

After a short while, the GSMA Chairman drew a conclusion. "Actualizing 5G for the first time at the PyeongChang Winter Olympics would be a huge challenge for KT. If Japan shares the technology, it will be a win-win situation."

The next day when the MWC started, I gave a keynote speech, and I declared the plan for "5G Actualization at the PyeongChang Winter Olympics."

Some may find it hard to understand why I took the risk that could appear insolent in some way. However, I was so desperate. Admiral Yi Sun-sin's words "Those who seek death shall live. Those who seek life shall die" drove me to burn my own ship.

KT was in stagnation when I became the CEO. It needed a great and clear vision to rebuild the organization. "GiGAtopia" and "KT No.1" resulted in the process of searching for such a vision.

For an organization to survive and be renewed, its members shouldn't simply become complacent after accomplishing one goal. So, the vision I found for KT was the "5G World."

If Admiral Yi had twelve battleships while preparing for the Battle of Myeongnyang, I had a great amount of technological knowledge from serving as the National CTO. Though KT may have had management issues, its technology was by far the best in Korea. The company had carefully accumulated wire-line technologies one by one, so achieving the "world's first 5G commercialization" was not an impractical goal.

"We don't have time to knock on a stone bridge. Whether that bridge is made of stone or wood, it is a bridge we must cross. If others are running to cross that same bridge, then we must fly to be the first across it."

I assembled the employees and executives, and made sure to reemphasize "risk-taking." At first, even the executives were doubtful. KT had suffered the bitter experience of being expelled from the winner's market position by a huge margin. It fell a step behind during the transition from 3G to 4G. Its competitor provided 4G communications service by importing Huawei's devices and investing one year ahead of KT.

KT's market share dropped from 35% to 27%. This bitter lesson of being a step ahead was engraved in the hearts of KT's employees. Thanks to this experience, it was easy to get their compliance. The harsh experience of the past became a remedy for the present.

I had to strike while the iron was still hot. I chose 5G as the topic after accepting the proposal to deliver a keynote speech at the MWC in 2015. I was aware that Japan was already preparing for 5G, but it wasn't the time to just go easy on them. The only way to survive was to pioneer both domestically and abroad.

After the GSMA meeting, I went to meet the DOCOMO CEO again and talked about cooperation. My suggestion was to share what we have developed and come up with a win-win plan. I said, "I heard that DO-COMO is doing a great job. KT is also working things out well," to convince him to accept technological exchanges. Not long after, I was on a flight to Japan with KT executives.

DOCOMO's technological field was outstanding. Normally, the telecommunications market is proportional to the number of users, which was typically dependent on population size. Japan's population was 120 million, which was more than double Korea's. Moreover, the Tokyo 2020 Olympics was a national event. The Japanese government began to thoroughly prepare for it seven years ahead of time, and the support it provided to DOCOMO was tremendous.

I rallied all KT employees and executives to prepare for this technological exchange. We had to advance our technological expertise by making up for shortcomings and learning as much as possible from them, while sharing our technologies. Not just executives, but all employees supported this plan. We proceeded with unstoppable acceleration.

In fact, the moment I saw the NTT DOCOMO R&D Center for 5G in Yokohama, my jaw dropped. I could feel the Japanese government's strong support.

To sum it all up, the PyeongChang 20218 Winter Olympics was the perfect 5G world. We made it without one false move. The CEO and the executives of NTT DOCOMO were all there. They marveled at the 5G world that Korea had realized two years ahead of them. They didn't forget to ask for KT's support. KT happily provided full support after its big success at the PyeongChang Winter Olympics.

Our lead in the commercialization of 5G technology resulted in improved competitiveness for other large Korean companies and SMEs in the global market. Moreover, Samsung's Network Business Division, which manufactures 5G equipment, was able to increase its market share to over 20%. The competitiveness of Korean SMEs also began to make its presence felt in the 5G market.

To all those young people who question whether the present is a crisis or an opportunity

Every day, I read the characters 必死卽生 必生卽死 framed on my wall during my six years at the Gwanghwamun office. They were an enlarged copy of Admiral Yi Sun-sin's original calligraphy, printed using a high-performance enlarger. This was a meaningful and special gift for me.

It was early 2005. I received a letter from the president of the Naval Academy. He asked me to give a lecture at the annual gathering of all cadets. I was so busy that I couldn't reply, but he wrote me a letter once again.

Fortunately, I had an occasion to inspect the Nokia factory in Masan, which is near Jinhae where the Naval Academy is situated, and I was able to plan for the lecture.

Once I arrived in Jinhae, I started to recall memories from twenty years before. Riding a bicycle to and from the Naval Academy on a road lined with cherry blossoms; teaching about semiconductors and electronics to engineers in the Electrical, Electronics, Mechanical, and Marine Engineering Departments; looking at Admiral Yi's handwriting at the museum over and over again... Almost two decades had passed but the Naval Academy's building never looked better. And the museum was still there.

The title of my lecture was "Chungmu-gong (the posthumous position of Admiral Yi) and the Semiconductor Business." I stood on the platform after saluting the colonel, who was responsible for 1,250 cadets. I talked about how Admiral Yi's mindset had inspired me in my teens and 20s, and how I applied it to the semiconductor business. Among Admiral

Yi's various facets, including his impeccable leadership, outstanding knowledge, excellent tactics and strategy, and creativity to build the *geobukseon*, I focused on the concept of "prevention is better than the cure." In other words, "crisis management capability." That is because "risk-taking" is the first and foremost quality a leader must have in the 21st century.

While having a friendly conversation after the lecture, I curiously asked about the scroll with the characters 必死卽生 必生卽死 that I saw in his office. He said they produced 16 enlarged copies with a German enlarger in the 1970s, and fortunately there was one left. A few weeks later, I received the scroll in the mail. And ever since then, the scroll has always been on one of my office walls.

When I had a moment, I would look at Admiral Yi's phrases. I could visualize him in mourning clothes visiting the southern province after losing his mother in the rainy season.

"Soldiers fight the battle, but people prosecute the war," he said while offering condolences to parents who lost their children in the Battle of Chilcheollyang. For Yi, who thought of suffering people first despite his own tragedy, victory was not a coincidence. It was a reward from heaven for taking risks and a comfort for taking care of the people.

What significance does Admiral Yi have for my friends these days? Some young people I sometimes meet said, "It's difficult for me to open up my feelings." I advised them to get to know Admiral Yi during times like that.

In 2020, I retired from KT and took a trip to Jindo. Although I had to be very thorough with preventative measures given the COVID-19 situation, I was glad that I took this trip the moment I saw Uldolmok

The scroll the author received as a gift from the president of the Republic of Korea Naval Academy

Strait.

The narrowing waterway amidst uplifted terrain generates enormous whirlpools, which could be used to one's advantage in a naval battle. It is said that after he had been reinstated as the Commander-in-Chief of Samdo Naval Forces in in seventh month, Admiral Yi visited that area with local residents several times in the ninth month of 1597 to prepare for the Battle of Myeongnyang.

His statue in Uldolmok, together with ten pictures, symbolizes his kindness to people even when he himself faced a tough and difficult situation. I gazed at Uldolmok for hours, feeling the wind from the sea, leaving an even deeper impression on me. It was as if I saw Admiral Yi's lonesome and solitary life unfolding in front of my very eyes. How he gathered his remaining troops together to save a country that was endangered like a candle in the wind. I longed to learn from his spirit and share what I learned with others.

If you can't tell whether the present is a crisis or an opportunity, I recommend learning about the agony and decisions of Admiral Yi. I myself gained power and energy by looking back at his footsteps when I was confronted by difficult situations. Admiral Yi is among the most venerable of figures because of his love for the people and his courage to keep the faith and maintain justice even in hard times. I believe that young people today will find their way forward by emulating Admiral Yi, just as I did in my youth.

04 Strive for disruptive innovation

| Elon Musk |

Historically, new technologies have rarely been welcomed by the public at the time they come out. Most people stuck with horses and carriages after gasoline-powered automobiles first appeared, complaining about the trouble of having to shift gears, endure toxic fumes, and look for filling stations all the time. When Steve Jobs released the first Macintosh, many criticized it, saying that moving the cursor with a mouse fatigued the eyes. Yet these technologies now dominate modern society. Our lives have changed for the better thanks to those who have taken on challenges and have never given up.

For centuries, optimism and a challenging spirit have remained the characteristics for people who are determined to overcome obstacles. This is true in any area, but being optimistic and resolved to face challenges is even more important in the field of science. Adopting an exceedingly analytical and careful attitude creates the situation where one notices the downsides first.

If you give up on a task solely because it is difficult to do, you will be unable to realize the future you seek. Thomas Edison described his numerous failures in the process of inventing the lightbulb as "discovering 10,000 ways in which the lightbulb will not work." Every success is a result of countless trial and error.

Every present is disrupted, while innovation shapes the future

"Chills run up my spine when I think about five to ten years from now."

Chairman Lee's awareness of crises twenty years ago was an accurate diagnosis of reality today. At least, that has been true for memory chips, which are now among Samsung Electronics' leading products. At the end of 1999, soon after I became the head of the Memory Business Division, a report came out that said Intel was the predominant player in the flash memory sector (with a 26% market share). In the report, AMD was ranked second (16%), followed by Fujitsu (15%), and then Sharp (13%), while Samsung Electronics was in tenth place, with a mere 3% market share. The competing companies continued to claw away fiercely at Intel's market share (75% in 1992, 42% in 1995, and 26% in 1999), but joining this competition was a pie in the sky for Samsung Electronics, who lacked technology and product competitiveness.

I was spending all my time in the laboratory when one day I got a call from the Office of the Secretariat. They told me the Chairman was planning a two-day and one-night confab among the presidents of Samsung Electronics and other electronics-related Samsung affiliates to discuss the Group's "bread and butter going forward." I was ordered to give an oral presentation without preparing any handouts.

I had analyzed numerous statistical materials and technologies and was strongly convinced the future would be defined as "the mobile era." I pondered over what "future bread and butter" would break us out of the looming crisis. I believed I should start by informing top management on the direction in which the paradigm shift would take semiconductor technology development.

On April 19, 2002, I arrived at the meeting venue, Creation Hall, armed solely with a paper by Professor Clayton M. Christensen entitled "The Future of the Microprocessor Business," which I had recently read in the journal IEEE Spectrum. I was called to be the first presenter in a meeting where a group of more than 20 presidents and over 30 officials from the Office of the Secretariat were present.

In his paper, Prof. Christensen pointed out that although Intel's CPU was an expensive, advanced technology, it could soon face limitations and a dilemma. I put his message in my own words and proceeded to introduce an innovative way for breaking through the crisis. When other executives were handing out materials and checking the Power Point screen, I was busily reorganizing my own presentation in my head. The moment everything was ready, they called my name.

"I have in my hand a three-page paper written by a renowned professor from Harvard Business School. Professor Christensen wrote this after working as a consultant for Intel for three years. In essence, he warned Intel, the current top global player, that microprocessor makers who continue to cling onto Moore's Law could lose their market share in a fast-changing marketplace."

The paper by Prof. Christensen of Harvard Business School.

The air grew heavy in the meeting room. At that time, the computer was the main IT device, and Intel's CPU, the main component for computers, was being sold throughout the world at a high price. His was saying the transition from the PC age to a mobile age would lead to the collapse of the CPU paradigm and the emergence of a new paradigm driven by new technologies. His very assertion could be perceived as a mirage.

"Microprocessor makers, including Intel, are staking their business on a 'CPU evolution' like the one proposed by Moore's Law. However, in reality, customers are using just 10-15% of the CPU's functions. Although the technology is advanced and expensive, its absolute necessity for customers is subject to debate."

Then, I introduced "flash memory" as an innovative new technology that could drive the future. At the time, memory chips were treated as secondary components in computers. If the CPU was the active element, memory chips would be purely passive elements that would stagnate without the release of a new operating system. However, the stature of memory is expected to change in the mobile era.

"Prof. Christensen didn't go this far in his paper, but I think 'next-generation technology' that costs less and has greater utility will drive the new paradigm in the upcoming mobile era. What our customers need is a low-cost, innovative technology such as flash memory."

In other words, a world is coming that revolves around memory chips, not the CPU. In the mobile era, securing sufficient "storage capacity" will be more valuable than "speed," which is determined by the network environment. Technology such as the flash memory will reveal its true value in satisfying the need to store high-volume contents like photographs and video clips. Although this isn't included in the paper, my conclusion was that we needed to stake our future on the development of flash memory.

"If we use this technology, we can dominate the future."

After my 10-minute presentation, I returned to my seat. Without saying a word, Chairman Lee Kun-hee gave me a sign that he understood my strategy for semiconductor development.

After some time had passed, the thought occurred to me: "Why would Chairman Lee have me present first at a meeting of presidents?" The logical deduction I reached to this question was that perhaps he wanted to subtly persuade the group of presidents to decline cooperation with Toshiba at the upcoming Zakuro Meeting and instead put our energy into flash memory chips.

Prof. Christensen also wrote that disruptive innovations rarely come from advanced technologies. Rather, disruptions results from technologies that despite their being considered as traditional–develop faster and have the potential to penetrate the low-end of market with their low cost. The market can't grow if it has to pay a high cost consistently.

This was the conclusion of his paper. I also didn't think that the mobile era would require semiconductors with extraordinary functions. I predicted that storage capacity, rather than the CPU speed, would be the main driver in the mobile era. Flash memory represented a less expensive technology than CPUs do, but the speed at which it could change in response to market demand and its development pace were much faster than was the case with CPUs. Thus, Hwang's Law, which represents flash memory, overtook Moore's Law, which focused on the development of the CPU, and quickly found its place in the market.

According to Prof. Christensen's theory of disruption, a traditional, low-cost technology can cause the market created by the latest high-cost technology to collapse. For instance, this theory anticipated the CPU business, a high-cost, cutting-edge technology at the time, would be disrupted by traditional, low-cost technologies. I applied his theory of disruption to Hwang's Law, presenting a theory whereby the flash-based mobile market would surpass the CPU-based PC market.

I was put fully in charge of semiconductor development after the meeting of the presidents, and I stepped up the pace of flash memory

Christensen's theory
The Innovator's Dilemma(1997)

Hwang's theory
ISSCC (2002)

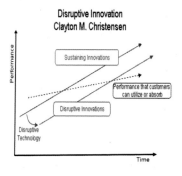

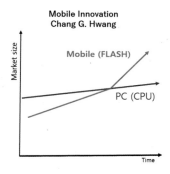

A comparison of Prof. Christensen's theory of disruptive innovation and the author's theory of mobile innovation, or Hwang's Law

development at Samsung. Then, Samsung's semiconductor operation was acknowledged as an independent business at the Zakuro Meeting, boosting in-house development and production. I announced my New Memory Growth Theory at the 2002 International Solid-State Circuits Conference (ISSCC), a prestigious global forum for presenting papers sometimes referred to as the Semiconductor Olympics. Soon thereafter I started to devise an omnidirectional strategy to expand the use of flash memory to mobile devices.

As a global marketing strategy, every department related to product planning and marketing endeavored to cultivate the global market. They prepared for the Samsung Mobile Solutions Forum in Taiwan, looked for opportunities in the USB market, and sought ways to expand the use of flash memory in the MP3 market.

The Samsung Mobile Solutions Forum was first held in Taiwan in 2004, and this event played a significant role in promoting Samsung Semiconductor's flash products over the next six years.

Taiwan was showing off their world-leading competitiveness in mobile devices, and their products became the first to be equipped with Samsung's flash-based mobile solution. In a way, Taiwanese companies played the role of a global strategic marketing with Samsung semiconductor solution. This strategy was inspired by the Intel Forum, which was run by the PC industry frontrunner for more than a decade. As expected, Intel also adopted Taiwan's PC components and chipsets since these were leading the market.

However, as I just mentioned above, the future doesn't come without a cost. Predicting trends in the future market is one thing and realizing those trends technologically is an entirely different matter. We had been moving full steam ahead on both DRAM and flash memory development at our laboratory from before the business strategy meeting, but because of technological limitations we could not avoid difficulties for an extended period. To overcome this, we continued to pursue innovations in design, processes, and materials. We managed to achieve the results we were looking for through a combination of desired outcomes in all three areas.

For instance, people at all organizational levels exerted tremendous effort with respect to design and process innovation. With flash memory, even though we developed certain products, they could not actively lead the market if they did not leave the factory in time. However,

< Changes in Flash Memory Market Share >

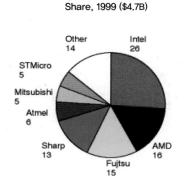

Samsung's Flash Memory Market
Share, 1999 ($4.7B)

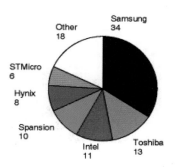

Samsung's Flash Memory Market
Share, 2005 ($20.5B)

•Note: Samsung Electronics' market share is included in the "Other" category in 1999, as it was below 5%

semiconductors are known as a facilities-driven business; building new production lines requires enormous amounts of money and takes much time. Intel had taken the production of their SRAM chips (used as computer cache, or temporary, memory and in telecommunication equipment) in-house, so our SRAM line output had plummeted. Therefore, I discussed with my engineers the possibility of switching SRAM production lines over to flash memory. Management and lower level employees came together to mobilize all our technologies to reset the production lines with minimum investment. Our flash memory boom would not have begun as fast as it did without their innovative efforts.

In less than five years, the numbers confirmed that my prediction and our challenge weren't wrong. Samsung Electronics' share in the flash memory market surged from 4.6% in 2001 to 34.4% in 2005, twenty-one percentage points higher than second-place Toshiba's share. Intel's market share fell to 11%. Toshiba's unchallenged technological lead was replaced by Samsung's technology. The birth of the charge-trap flash (CTF) became the turning point for Samsung's technological domination.

An innovative adventurer traveling a road without even a map

Current technology will eventually be disrupted. However, our challenges and innovation must race on without fail if we are to create the future we want.

I am recently reaffirming this truth through Elon Musk, an innovative adventurer. He is opening up a "new future" to humankind with his autonomous electric vehicles, private space shuttles, solar energy and more. He continues to take on challenges, promising to build fast-charging EV stations in the US and establish an underground hyperloop that runs at a speed of 1,200 kmh.

As far as I can remember, I first looked up his name on the Internet in the spring of 2013. I had read several articles about him before, but it was his Technology Entertainment Design (TED) talk that fascinated me.

When he did his TED talk in 2013, he was only 42 years old and had already achieved fruitful results after overcoming many challenges. He started a business (Zip.2) at the tender age of 24 after quitting the PhD program (Materials Science in the Applied Physics) at Stanford University. He sold PayPal, the Internet payment platform he cofounded as his second business, when he was 31 years old. By then, his fortune amounted to $200 billion.

Actually, he really started to get going from this time. He had begun penniless and made an immense fortune by establishing and then selling off two businesses. His next move was to take on the challenge of traveling "a path no one in this world has ever been on." The three companies he runs reveal the challenges he has overcome and the accomplishments he has made.

Founded in 2002, SpaceX accomplished a brilliant feat by becoming the first private rocket company to successfully launch, orbit, and recover a manned spacecraft. Tesla Motors (renamed Tesla subsequently), in which Musk invested in 2004 and became Chairman of the Board, produces and sells luxury sports cars, sedans, and SUVs; and the company has gone public. Established in 2006, SolarCity is a solar energy company that obtained a $280 million investment from Google. It managed to have its initial public offering (IPO) six years after launch and has been a leader in natural energy research. Among these three entities, SpaceX has definitely garnered the most attention.

"Currently, not all parts of a rocket are reusable. Each flight cost a billion dollars. But the rocket we developed returns to the site where it was launched. And it can be ready for relaunch within a matter of hours. It is reusable. If we can reuse the rocket, the overall cost is greatly reduced."

Elon Musk had already asked a perplexing question to space scientists: "Has anyone ever analyzed why space rockets cost so much money to develop?"

He said studying physics was the source of his capability to pursue and integrate design, technology, and industry.

"We start by delving into the fundamentals of materials, without any conjecture. Our thinking is a bit different from the way most people tend to interpret things. When you want to do something new, you have to approach it with physics. It is intuitive."

He has achieved technological innovations no one ever thought of by looking at technological advancement as non-linear, tearing down existing practices, and changing his way of thinking.

Elon Musk's perspective showed growth at a TED talk held in Vancouver, Canada in 2017, four years later.

"People are mistaken when they think that technology automatically advances. It only develops further when a tremendous number of people work extremely very hard to make it better."

This might be just a rumor so it might be dangerous to leave this as it is. Can we just say "Until then, many in the media had depicted him as a tough CEO, saying that employees would get to see their families more often only if the company went bankrupt." But I was more impressed with his passion.

Either through luck or destiny, I wound up going with some KT employees to visit SpaceX in Hawthorne, California, six months after I watched his talk. It was for KT's launch of the *Mugunghwa 5A* satellite. I thought that I may have a chance to bump into Elon Musk, but I didn't set up a separate schedule for such a meeting. He is quite known for not taking the time to meet even with a prime minister or global CEO. Rumor has it that he was nicknamed "Iron Man" not because he was like Iron Man in the movie, but because he was good at making rejections without any facial expression.

We are running together to turn what we imagine into reality

The person who greeted us in October 2017 was the SpaceX Chief Operations Officer Gwynne Shotwell. She studied Mechanical Engineering and Applied Mathematics at Northwestern University, worked for a military space engineering project, and is an important figure in SpaceX's history. Elegant and considerate, she has served in her position at SpaceX since 2008.

The meeting went smoothly, with everything prepared adequately in advance. The *Mugunghwa 5A* satellite was to replace the aging *Mungunghwa 5* currently in orbit and was expected to expand the range of coverage from Southeast Asia to the Middle East. The launch schedule was set for the end of October.

"If you don't mind, he'd like to see you in his office."

COO Shotwell approached me while other employees were getting ready to leave. We were told before the meeting that Elon Musk might stop by to say hello, but he didn't. His invitation for a one-on-one talk in his office was unexpected. Glancing at my watch, I said okay. I was totally unprepared for the unscheduled meeting. Still, I couldn't pass on such an opportunity to share ideas with a "living icon of innovation." I quickly organized my thoughts.

I considered two topics for the brief time I would have with Elon Musk, then Shotwell guided me to his office. We reached his office after walking down a hall with satellite photos of Earth and Mars, which are also symbolic of him. His office isn't like the ones we commonly see in Korea. His desk is on one side of an open space he shares with regular employees. My first impression was a rather cold feeling, revealing one who does not waste his breath.

"Dominating the world's automobile market with autonomous electric vehicles is Tesla's main objective, isn't it?"

I broke the ice. Any conversation should be initiated with the listener's interests. An accident related to a Tesla autonomous driving vehicle was a social issue at the time. I had directly witnessed autonomous driving in Japan and Korea, but my experience as a mere consumer wouldn't intrigue him. That was why I chose "5G technology that completes autonomous driving" as a topic we might discuss. It was a topic that could be shared by both an engineer and a manager. I noticed his face was starting to show some curiosity.

"5G is most important for making autonomous driving work. KT was the first to declare a working 5G model and is setting comprehensive standards for the technology. We are preparing everything for a demonstration at the PyeongChang Winter Olympics."

At that time, KT was already running simulations to make 5G-based autonomous driving a reality. I was talking about seeing buses, minibuses, and passenger cars autonomously driven at the same time and how items were delivered by drone to an autonomous vehicle. That was when Musk asked what effect 5G would have on the realization of autonomous driving.

Braking is the most important consideration when driving. The brake must be controlled at an exact point. The response time for a 5G-controlled autonomous driving vehicle is faster than that for a human-controlled one. The system responds in one-tenth of a blink of an eye, ensuring the safety of vehicular occupants. His face brightened even more at my answer. I was encouraged by the change in his expression and continued talking.

A demonstration of an autonomous vehicle and drone delivery at the PyeongChang Winter Olympics

"The most fundamental aspects of safety and precision control in the autonomous driving infrastructure technology is to make the possibility of GPS errors extremely small. Currently, the margin for error is within tens of centimeters, but KT has the positioning technology to reduce that to a few centimeters.

If you'd like to see these things for yourself, please visit the Pyeong-Chang 2018 Winter Olympics. It is the world's only platform for running and testing autonomous driving. It is a perfect testbed equipped with 5G and basic infrastructure. What about watching the Olympics while people from your company cooperate with our engineering team to demonstrate autonomous driving?"

As he was checking his schedule, I brought up the second topic that might interest him.

"You can innovatively reduce energy consumption if SpaceX or the Gigafactory is equipped with KT's smart grid."

Tesla received investment from Panasonic and established the Gigafactory, a large-scale battery plant, in Nevada in 2016. Preparations were completed to begin mass production, and then Tesla announced it would build a second large-scale Gigafactory. Improving energy utilization at these factories has a very positive influence on both operational efficiency and environmental preservation.

I told him that I learned how to raise energy efficiency by maximizing energy production and minimizing energy consumption when I worked as the National CTO. I added that my acquaintance with global experts led me to develop the microgrid solution (a smart grid of local independent power networks where electricity is supplied and consumed independently through self-production, consumption, and exchanges) that optimized how energy was used through analyses based on AI and big data. KT possessed an advanced technology that had already been demonstrated. Elon Musk responded that it is a very interesting and creative idea, and said he wanted to look at the data.

We talked about two topics and half an hour already passed. I was getting ready to leave after this short meeting he squeezed in his tight schedule, when he told one of the employees, "Take Dr. Hwang and the other executives on a tour."

SpaceX is filled with new technologies, and it is also where they man-

A photo of the author and other executives at SpaceX in October 2017, standing in front of the first rocket to return from space

ufacture rockets. They are known for not giving tours to outsiders. Even clients are no exception.

I felt Musk's kindness through this offer. I thought it was a cordial reception for guests from far away and a gift for someone with whom they would build the future.

The inside of SpaceX was quite special. This was the first time I had ever seen a place that builds rockets as finished products, even though I had visited countless venues over the past three decades. It was massive and had a different working environment than regular manufacturing sites do. The layout consisted of several separately completed sections, and they gave us a tour of each one. COO Shotwell gave us an explanation by introducing the engine and software segments in order. Under tight security, she proposed we take a photo in front of *Artificial Satellite No. 1*, which had returned from space.

When I returned to Korea, I received a message from Elon Musk that he wanted to visit us during the PyeongChang Winter Olympics. However, a month later, another message from him said that he couldn't make it because of Tesla's opening ceremony for a factory in Shanghai. Both of us said it was a shame that our second meeting had been canceled.

Possibility is what we create

On my flight back, I looked at the photos I took with my phone while organizing meeting materials. The group picture we took in front of *Artificial Satellite No. 1* and the photo I took with Elon Musk caught my eye.

In it, we were shaking hands in front of photos of Mars and Earth, which symbolizes SpaceX. Looking at the display on my phone brought a smile to my face.

"What does it mean to meet an innovator?"

After the meeting at SpaceX, the author poses with Elon Musk in front of photos of Earth and Mars at the entrance of his office

Life at industrial sites is always stressful and wearisome. Developing a future technology with no clear answer or path forward is like marching in darkness. I have traveled the world first as the CEO of a semiconductor maker and then as CEO of a telecommunications service provider, weighed down by the constant need to develop diverse new products and technologies every year. It was a lonely and solitary journey.

However, there have been some sources of strength that have allowed me to endure this difficult process. First is the conviction that we will inevitably reach the future of our dreams. This faith picked me and my research team up when confronting technological limitations had us down. Second, I believed we were not alone in shaping the future. The innovators I met were like sweet rain in a drought. They ignited passion in our hearts and made us feel how meaningful our challenge is.

Knowing this, I always keep one thing in my schedule for no matter how busy I get: visiting college campuses to communicate with young people. I spent the last three decades going back and forth between the laboratory and schools. I thought it was part of my duty to talk about my real-life experiences in the field and global success stories to encourage young people to dream about taking on new challenges. When I stand in front of others from the engineering community, I encourage them to make a strong foundation for a "technologically-strong Korea" and let their juniors know the importance of science and technology.

However, these days, I feel conversing with young people is not always enjoyable. I'm distressed when I see young people, who should have big dreams and be prepared to take on challenges, unable to free themselves from the fetters of reality. Most of the questions I receive after delivering a lecture in Korea have been about "career path" and "employment." It is very contradicting from questions I get from students in prestigious colleges overseas, who ask about "majors" and "vision."

In today's environment, information is powerful, and convergence is easy to do. Our society is witnessing the most developed civilization since the birth of humankind, where rockets are launched into space and automobiles are fueled by eco-friendly energy instead of gasoline. However, so many people do not recognize this as an opportunity. You must indeed solve everyday problems, but you can't draw a big picture if you are deeply buried in your daily life.

Every year, I receive good news from those who are working collectively to open up the future. In February 2018, SpaceX reached its goal of creating a "rocket that returns to its launch site." Falcon Heavy, which took off from the Kennedy Space Center in Florida, successfully landed back where it had been launched, instead of being dropped in the ocean. The possibility Elon Musk mentioned in 2013 had become a reality. In August 2020, astronauts who stayed at the International Space Station for two months returned aboard a SpaceX capsule that splashed down in the ocean. A parachute on capsule softened the ocean landing, reducing the impact and enhancing the soundness of space travel.

"I don't think of the possibilities for success when I start to tackle a problem. However, I find a way while solving it. The possibility is something that we create."

I want to pass on once more to young people Elon Musk's message about facing bold challenges and creating a new future.

05

Only the paranoid lead tomorrow's growth

| Andy Grove |

If I'm asked to name figures who influenced me the most in my 20s, I can answer without hesitation that they are William Shockley and Andy Grove.

William Shockley is the developer of the transistor and a Nobel Prize winner in Physics. His accomplishment in developing the junction transistor in 1951 was recognized and led to his receiving the Nobel Prize in 1956. Meanwhile, he assembled a talented team by founding the Shockley Semiconductor Laboratory with the support of Beckman Instruments Inc. Among those in the group were Gordon Moore and Robert Noyce, who later founded Intel.

But they both couldn't stand William Shockley's difficult personality and high-handed managing style, so they decided to leave the laboratory. Shockley later called Moore and Noyce, along with some other colleagues, the "traitorous eight." They went on to establish Fairchild Semiconductor, which became the leader in transistor manufacturing, and Andy Grove

The three Intel founders (from left to right): Andy Grove, Robert Noyce, and Gordon Moore (creator of Moore's Law).
Source: Wikipedia

decided to join them after finishing his doctorate degree.

Moore and Noyce established Intel after being excited by IBM's creation of third-generation semiconductors. Andy joined them as the third founding member in 1968. He became the CEO in 1979 and was at the helm of the company for 25 years, until he retired as Chairman in 2005.

I personally like Andy Grove more than William Shockley. In the 1990s, he published an autobiography titled, *Only the Paranoid Survive*, which drew public attention. He believed that we should remain alert, in a constant state of hypertension, in order to be receptive to fundamental change. It was a great joy to read a book by a high-tech company manager who has both keen observation and judgment. Naturally, it allowed me to rethink the legacy he left in my life.

He wrote *Physics and Technology of Semiconductor Devices* when he was young, and the book was simply like a bible for me. I was a senior in college when I read it, and for the first time I decided to devote my life to semiconductors. I couldn't take my hands off the book, and it got so worn out I had to buy it three times.

Given this situation, words cannot express how I felt when I actually got to meet him face to face. To have a conversation with him while I visited Intel for consultation as a Stanford researcher was an experience of a lifetime. I learned about his adversities and life philosophy, as well as his ideologies as a manager through books and various media. Thanks to him, I learned that hardships, challenges, and growth are all interrelated, as if on a continuous line.

Andy's question to Gordon Moore regarding the difficulties as a manager prompted their company's growth to reach new heights, and that gave me many things to think about while I was in management.

"What would happen if we got kicked out and the board brought in a new CEO?"

Founded in 1968, Intel contended for victory in the memory semiconductor business. Intel was unrivaled in the memory market for a decade after releasing its first memory chips in 1969. In the 1990s, the company grew into one of the world's largest enterprises. However, it wasn't like that in the early 1980s.

In 1985, Intel fell into serious trouble after a Japanese company broke into the market with low-priced chips. Andy Grove agonized as the CEO of a company in crisis. The situation went unresolved for a year. Unable to find a way out of the gloom, he went to Gordon Moore and asked, "If we get kicked out and the board brings in a new CEO, what would that new CEO do?"

Gordon Moore was six to seven years older than Andy. He was smart, calm and, above all, a deep thinker. Gordon Moore, which his rock-solid character, blended perfectly with Andy Grove, who was hot-blooded and filled with energy. Moore's answer was what Andy expected:

"He would get us out of the memory business."

Andy Grove mulled over Moore's answer. In 1982, Intel was the world's second-largest memory chipmaker. By 1986, it had fallen to sixth place, and the business was in the red. It was the first time they had suffered a loss since the company went public 15 years earlier. The situation was clear.

"Then how about walking out this door together, come back and do it ourselves?"

Finally, Andy decided to let go of the DRAM-based memory business and stake his company's future on the growing "microprocessor" business. Everyone was coming to understand semiconductor circuits make up the central processing unit in a PC, but it was an unknown field back in the day. Most importantly, PC distribution had not been so widespread before. Taking the risk, Andy decided to abandon the technology that had kept their company going for fifteen years and face a strategic turning point.

Letting go of the memory chip business forced Intel to close seven factories in 1985 and 1986 and lay off 7,200 workers. However, that choice opened the door for Intel to become the top player in the semiconductor business.

Intel invested 30% of its revenue in the development of next-generation microprocessors, and signed contracts to supply its microprocessors to IBM and PC makers. This is how Intel's decision to take on a great challenge resulted in a great success

Only those who mull the problems intently can ask the right question

I met Andy Grove around 1988 when he was reorganizing his company and growing the business with IBM as a client. I was tasked with designing the transistors for Intel's Pentium chipsets, so I visited the Intel headquarters twice a week. Silicon Valley, where Intel was headquartered, was like a "breath of fresh air" for me. I observed intently how the semiconductors I was researching were actually being used in the industry. Then, I ran into Andy Grove at the cafeteria and greeted him.

"I bought your book three different times when I was still in Korea. I can even remember what sentences are on which pages."

He continued talking to me while leaning on his office door. He was known to be very strict with his time allocation, and simply getting that much of attention and kindness from him was enough to move me deeply.

At the time, I thought his attention and goodwill were just "a consideration for a fan from the Far East." I was aware that he was a Hungarian immigrant to the US. No matter how open the field of science and technology and no matter how casual the culture of Silicon Valley was, it was still the 1980s. One couldn't just dispense with the deeply-rooted American sentiments. I thought that maybe he felt some sort of sense of identification with me, since neither of us had been born in the US. In just over a decade, the organization I led became Intel's full-fledged rival.

After coming back to Korea, I heard about Andy's publication of his autobiography (the book I mentioned earlier) in the US.

Reading books about Intel and Andy Grove were a source of renewed joy for me. For example, I learned through stories he wrote about Intel how the book I considered my bible had been created.

It was in 1967, when he was working at this first workplace, Fairchild Semiconductor. Frustrated by his company's leadership, he planned an "auxiliary task." Instead of submitting his resignation, he decided to put all his energy into writing a book about semiconductors. And that is how a college textbook, which was almost unknown to the public, came into this world. It was the book I purchased three times. Later, the book became the "best way for Intel to attract the right people." It is said that the book became a

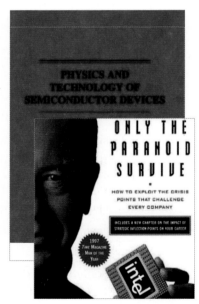

The covers of Andy Grove's *Physics and Technology of Semiconductor Devices* and *Only the Paranoid Survive*

must-read classic among engineers, and talented professionals voluntarily knocked on Intel's door to work with the great author.

Besides, there were stories about Andy that I wasn't aware of. His childhood was quite shocking.

I thought that he was an immigrant from Hungary. However, strictly speaking, he was not an immigrant, but a refugee.

He was Jewish, and his Hungarian name was Andras Grof. He was frail as a boy, suffering from scarlet fever and middle ear inflammation. The Second World War broke out right when he had started elementary school. The German government's pursued policies that persecuted Jewish people, and his family inevitably became both victims and scapegoats.

His father was pressed into military service and went out to the battlefield, where he was arrested by the Russian army. Meanwhile, while his mother spent her time going into hiding with her son and then escaping Hungary to avoid the danger of being slaughtered. To Andy Grove, war and death were immediate and vivid realities. After the Second World War had ended, his father was allowed to return to his family, yet life did not change, and they continued to face danger. When Hungary became communist, his relatives were arrested by the secret police and disappeared.

Despite all these twists and turns in his life, he still managed to finish college in Hungary and then by himself sought asylum in the US. The American education system allowed him to attend school free of tuition, but he had to keep working part-time to cover living expenses. Strong and passionate, he graduated with top honors from UC Berkeley. He anglicized his name, got hired by an American company, and lived his life as an American. He had never talked about his childhood in Hungary before publishing his autobiography.

After reading about his life growing up, I had this reasonable suspicion that he might have shown kindness to me because I was a Korean. It is only my assumption, but to a person who experienced the crisis and devastation of war, it's not a surprise if he felt a sense of kinship with someone from Korea.

As a manager, Andy was considered to be extremely strict, unlike the American management style. He always arrived in the office at 8 a.m., and wasn't flexible about the time he left the office. He wasn't authoritarian, but emphasized that the members of his organization must remain alert and move decisively for the company to survive. He constantly exposed himself to risks, too.

In fact, he had resisted going into the microprocessor business. However, he rigorously thought the matter over and then posed the appropriate questions both to Gordon Moore and to himself. They say he had always liked having debates with other employees. He let anyone openly criticize and rebut his ideas. Despite trial and error, his indomitable spirit to overcome challenges and struggle grew Intel into a leading company.

Augmenting the power to create a better world

I feel both nervous and excited whenever I approach a podium. This is even more the case when I am about to make a declaration for shaping a new future. People are more focused when you tell them something they have never heard before. However, I get even more nervous when I come down from the podium, because that is when the real rally begins.

I spoke at the Seoul Digital Forum, which took place at the Walkerhill Seoul hotel in May 2006, declaring that the IT era would be succeeded by the "era of fusion technology (FT)." This event took place four years after my announcement of Hwang's Law, when I made a bold prediction about technology going forward.

Back then, flash memory had come on the scene, and conventional data storage media such as photographic film, videotape, and compact discs were disappearing as multimedia mobile phones and laptops, which provided TV and Internet access, were entering the market. The accelerated convergence among digital devices based on advancements in semiconductor technology was expected to be followed by the convergence of advanced technologies. My assertion was rather early in the mid-2000s that information technology (IT), biotechnology (BT), and nanotechnology (NT) would converge, and that the FT era would arrive. However, I could see the FT era opening up, led by the consumers of mobile and digital products.

The convergence of IT, BT, and NT, three key technologies in the 21st century, presaged technologies on an entirely different level from those that simply combined functions or products. Convergence among large industries would generate new value for improving the quality of people's lives. My announcement that computers, networks, and life sciences would eventually merge to create totally new products and industries was reported as the headline on the SBS TV 8 O'clock news and created a sensation.

I asserted once again that fusion technology would come during a keynote speech at the IEDM conference in San Francisco on December

The author as a keynote speaker at the IEDM conference in December 2006 and the author's IEEE Andrew S. Grove Award.

11 of the same year. Using a theoretical basis and detailed cases, I told the international audience of my prediction that a different and greater opportunity would soon arise. On this occasion, I also talked about the completion of a OneNAND chip version, the world's first fusion semiconductor, as well as a 512M one DRAM, the second fusion semiconductor, which incorporates both DRAM and SRAM on a single chip. The OneNAND was designed to address operational speed and memory capacity problems plaguing mobile phones, and this design was enhanced by the Flex-OneNAND, the third fusion semiconductor. All fusion memory technology was provided under license from Japanese companies in 2007, bringing the era of technology fusion into full swing. For me, fusion technology began with the fusion semiconductor.

On that day, I received the Andrew S. Grove Award, named after the prestigious researcher whom I had admired since I was young. This award from the IEEE, the world's top organization in the fields of electrical and electronics engineering, has been presented since the year 2000 to those who have contributed innovative development in semiconductor-related areas. Eminent individuals from semiconductor circles, including professors at Stanford University and MIT and Intel's CTO, participate in the selection of winners.

"Today I accept this prize as encouragement for me to take on new challenges in opening up new mega-trends for the future."

In my acceptance speech, I expressed my special appreciation by sharing the anecdote of how Andy's book inspired me to devote my life to semiconductor technology. I also spoke of my resolve to keep striving to change the world through new technology.

The thrill and exhilaration I felt from being the first businessperson from East Asia to receive this globally prestigious award only lasted for a few days. The burden of that comes tomorrow was heavier and weighed me down. The only thing left for me to do was work tirelessly to turn my declaration into reality. Making a wonderful world is surely an exciting yet difficult task

Questions from a paranoid person nurture your competencie

The lessons I learned from Andy Grove can be summarized in one sentence: Only those who ask questions can find the answer and make it happen.

"Paranoid," the term Andy frequently used, isn't entirely a good word. Being obsessed with something can take us in the wrong direction. However, this paranoid attitude is actually important in the professional world. Importantly, the ability to concentrate systematically and constantly is very helpful in problem-solving.

Actually, I often encounter such paranoid questions on the management front lines. I looked at those questions as challenges. When I reached the point where I could answer those questions, crisis moments turned into opportunities, and I felt that my capabilities had improved.

Business sailed smoothly in 2006. After the release of the OneNAND, fusion memory sales were in the trillions of won (billions of dollars). I unveiled the world's first notebook PC with 32GB SSD of flash memory at the Samsung Mobile Solutions Forum in March. Then in May, I declared the advent of the FT era at the Seoul Digital Forum. I heard a report that Sony, Toshiba, and Fujitsu were following us and coming out with their own laptops supported SSD by flash memory. Results were starting to show after years of hard work.

Meanwhile, I was busy participating in investor relations (IR) events outside Korea. These company briefings required me to answer questions from investors and defend myself from their attacks, so I had to be fully prepared. My first order of business was clarifying our corporate vision for the future in order to persuade the investors. I had to temper myself on many occasions while giving presentations about our company during overseas IR roadshows between 2001 and 2007.

In those days, our performance was better than ever, and one day, I received a call from Capital International, a major shareholder of Samsung Electronics. Capital International was a large investor that once held over ten percent of all the issued shares of Samsung Electronics. Chairman David Fisher enjoyed holding meetings and was fond of listening to the CEOs of invested companies discuss market conditions and changing trends. He and I became familiar over several years through the IR activities, and we were close enough to stay in touch with one another privately.

I had an appointment to visit his office. After expressing his gratitude for the rise in Samsung's stock value, he went straight to the point.

"You are now running in first place. But there's no guarantee that you will keep the first place."

He asked how I would stay ahead of those chasing us. I would've been in trouble if all I had done during the meeting was to give a greeting and express my confidence of being the top player.

"As I told you before, we have a nomad's spirit. Until recently, we were mostly a DRAM maker, but we changed our focus to flash memory, then to fusion memory, and now to solid-state drives. As a result, preeminent companies such as Apple and Nokia have become our clients."

Chairman Fisher's expression softened at my explanation. And I didn't just stop there.

"But what is more important is our organization. As sales increase, profits grow, and the organization gets bigger. This is inevitable. However, I will not tolerate a lack of communication. Our engineers can talk to me whenever they want. I'm always open to them. Our decision-making process is also very simple. This is why we are able to stay ahead of those who are chasing us."

More specifically, I used the expression "flat organization." It was a simple explanation that our organization had fewer organizational levels than the average company does.

After listening to my answer with his eyes closed, Chairman Fisher hit the right armrest with a smiling face and said, "You pass."

That's how I passed a moment of crisis.

I received numerous questions during the IR briefings. Semiconductors always aroused keen interest from the audience. It was a field that required huge investment and generated large profits. Investors also had to remain on their toes because the market fluctuated from supply and demand imbalances.

Highly competent investors were like "the paranoid one." Their questions cut like a sharp sword. They frequently asked about the future outlook. And I had to have a strong shield ready to counter their blows. What mattered were having a clear strategy for making the company stand out from the rest and securing market share. To answer their questions, I armed myself with a strong portfolio of differentiated products and strategies for penetrating new markets that would drive new growth. In the end, I convinced many investors with our vision of where digital convergence would lead in the future.

Questions from paranoids gradually strengthened my capabilities as a manager, in the same way a shield gets stronger as it blocks the blows of sharp swords.

Transformation is innovation

Another question remains in my memory. It came when I visited the Harvard Business School in October 2018. The topic of my talk was "KT

Corporation in the New Energy Market." Harvard students and even those from other universities came to listen to me at Haws Hall. I felt sorry that many of them couldn't find a seat. Still, I had to begin the lecture.

When I was working as a Samsung Electronics consultant, I went to MIT to meet Professor Ernest Moniz to learn about future technologies. He served as the founding director of the MIT Energy Initiative at the time and was a top energy expert who later served as Secretary of Energy during the Obama Administration. He argued that energy would be the most important industry for national competitiveness. He stressed that the microgrid would become an innovative system that enables energy production, storage, consumption, and trading.

In the lecture, I introduced the "KT-MEG (Micro-Energy Grid)," an energy control platform developed by KT based on the Korea Micro-Energy Grid (K-MEG), which we developed when I served as the National CTO. The concept of this new technology was quite simple: minimize energy consumption through AI-based analysis of consumers' energy-use patterns. In other words, using information technology to reduce energy consumption.

I personally found this presentation to be easy to deliver. But this was only natural because I had already conducted a number of case studies while I worked for Samsung Electronics, and it was already my third lecture at Harvard after I had become the KT chairman. I delivered a special lecture on "The Power of Networks" at Memorial Hall in 2016, and another special lecture in April 2017 entitled "Korea Telecom: Building a GiGAtopia," as it was registered as a case study of Harvard Business School. I felt good about the lecture. However, some students

The author giving a lecture on the energy case study at the Harvard Business School in October 2018 and the textbook.

did not feel favorably toward a manager from a foreign country.

"Why does a telecommunications company like KT involve itself in the energy business?"

A student asked me this question when I was about to wrap up my lecture. The question had a keen edge, but I was kind of excited. Because I had an answer for it.

"In Korea, we have strong competition in telecommunications services. However, if two telecom service providers are equally as good while only one lowers energy consumption by 30%, which one would you choose?"

Customer data connected to the KT-MEG platform exemplify the effects of new technology. KT-MEG is the first energy platform that predicts the optimal results for any energy production, storage, consumption, and trading activity. The application of KT's e-Brain alone reduced energy cost by 10-20%. Replacing obsolete facilities raised the cost savings to 40%, and that figure goes up to 75% when the energy management system and automated control are added.

The e-Brain, KT-MEG's AI analytics engine, forecasts energy consumption and production based on machine learning, then optimizes energy production and trading. It doesn't produce energy itself, but it slashes energy consumption by enabling consumers to use less or no energy at all. Ultimately, fossil fuel consumption is lowered, which helps address environmental issues.

As Professor Forest Reinhardt of Harvard Business School introduced my lecture, he said he was impressed that KT, which is strong in ICT, entered the unrelated energy management market. He added that KT's swift attempt to link competitiveness advantage to a different category of industry will give great inspiration to students.

A few years earlier when I started the KT-MEG, which I was so proud of, I had also asked myself the same question the student asked me.

"What does KT have to do the energy business? How could you do it well?"

I soon found the answer: transformation is innovation. As such, a disruptive business model of a communications company's energy business was completed.

Let's go back to Andy Grove's story. In 2009, I invited Professor Robert Dutton of Stanford University to the War Memorial Opera House in San Francisco, where we watched Donizetti's La Fille du Régiment together. That day, Prof. Dutton told me, "I came here before to watch Wagner's Die Walküre and ran into Andy and said hello." I recalled Andy Grove whom I met at Intel.

Andy experienced the war and struggled to survive, and as a manager, he asked the most important questions based on the time, place, and circumstances to find answers and overcome crises, turning challenges into victories.

That was his life. When he published his autobiography in 1996, Andy Grove made it public that he was suffering from prostate cancer. He also suffered from Parkinson's disease three years before he stepped down as chairman in 2005, and his condition considerably worsened. Still, he never stopped taking the questions and listening to his employees despite his failing health. He is remembered as a tough leader.

"Did he live life as a paranoid?"

I think he did. Now, we are living in an IT environment, but he was the only who led an IT company from the beginning, when the term

"IT" was still unfamiliar. Without "paranoia," he wouldn't have been able to safeguard Intel for such a long time in an industry where countless companies appeared and disappeared

Now we are living in a world different from the world he lived in. We can't just simply respond to upcoming changes. The capabilities of a "paranoid" is required when looking towards the future and improving oneself.

Asking questions is the most practical way. Repeating the process of asking and answering questions like a paranoid will equip you with your own vision for the future.

Writing Korea's History
of the Memory Semiconductor

Dynamic Random Access Memory(DRAM)

A memory chip used as the storage device in computers.
The DRAM consists of one transistor and capacitor; power consumption and cost are both low, so these chips are widely used in high-capacity storage devices. As the DRAM is used in high-speed memory, the data stored inside is erased when the power source is shut off.

These chips are supplementary components that can use and erase data quickly while the computer's CPU is performing calculations. Changes in the PC industry trigger broad price fluctuations, limiting DRAM market growth. The DRAM was first developed by Intel in 1970, but now Korean makers hold a 70% share of the global DRAM market.

Static Random Access Memory(SRAM)

A memory chip used for the computer's cache and in communications devices. SRAM preserves any stored memory as long as the power is kept on. The level of integration is about a quarter that of the DRAM, but the data processing speed is at least four times faster.

Flash Memory

There are two types of flash memory: NAND, which prioritizes density, and NOR, which focuses on speed.
NAND flash is a non-volatile storage device, meaning the stored data are not deleted when the power goes off. Each transistor constitutes a cell, and the device is used for storing text data, music, and video files. Products

132

supported by flash memory can be made smaller and consume less power. The portability of smart phones, digital cameras, and MP3 players equipped with NAND flash memory is convenient, but the power supply is limited Initially the larger and faster NOR flash devices were preferred, but the market began to go for NAND flash from 2004 because of its greater storage capacity. The use of NAND flash spread quickly as demand for data storage volume grew with the introduction of 5G and AI. The growth in demand is being accelerated with the increased use of high-performance solid-state drives.

2002

Fusion Semiconductors

• OneNAND

OneNAND integrates NAND flash, SRAM, and software on a single chip. This fusion semiconductor provides the advantages of both NOR flash's fast reading, and NAND flash's fast writing, while the level of integration is also high. OneNAND rapidly replaced NOR in the market because it writes data 48 times faster than NOR flash can, and the chip is only one-third the size of a NOR flash device.

Since the advent of 3G networks, NAND became the mainstream device for mobile phones, where only the NOR flash had previously been used. Samsung began supplying NAND devices to Nokia, which had the largest share of the global mobile phone market at the time. The company began to develop OneNAND, a fusion semiconductor with both NOR and NAND properties, to support the market switchover from NOR to NAND. As a result, Samsung Semiconductor edged out Intel to took over first place in the flash memory market in 2003. The OneNAND is acknowledged to be the world's first fusion semiconductor.

In 2005, Samsung's fusion memory began to be supplied to Apple and was used on the iPod Nano, MacBook Air, iPad, and iPhone. From 2006, NAND flash quickly took over the flash market (10% in 2000 to 80% in 2007).

• OneDRAM

OneDRAM combines SRAM and DRAM. This is the second fusion semiconductor that integrates DRAMs used in CPUs for communication and multimedia functions in mobile devices, elevating data processing speed and reducing power consumption.

Mobile DRAM

   This DRAM uses less power than its counterparts in personal computers. It originally targeted smartphones and tablet PCs, and its application subsequently was expanded to include laptops with solid state drives. The key technological function is to minimize power consumption for maximum usage time with a limited power supply. In 2002, Samsung Electronics completed the world's first 64M and 128M mobile DRAMs, which were supplied to Nokia and other major mobile phone manufacturers. Samsung came out with a 256M version in 2004, followed by a 512M model in 2005. All of these have been used in Apple products.

Units: M (mega)10^6 ; G (giga) 109; T (tera) 1012; B (byte) = 8b (bits)
1 Mbyte (MB) = 1024 KB
1 Gbyte (GB) = 1024 (MB)
1 Tbyte (TB) = 1024 (GB)

Solid-State Drive(SSD)

   The solid state drive is a storage device that uses NAND flash memory. Once commercialized, the SSD quickly replaced the hard disc drive, which had been used as the storage device for PCs, servers, and other equipment. The hard drive uses magnetism to record or delete data on the disc. The mechanism impedes reductions in overall product size, weight, or power consumption. Hard drives are also vulnerable to external shocks. The solid state drive, by contrast, consists solely of semiconductors, and operates far faster than the hard drive can. The size, weight and power consumption of the SSD are all reducible, and the device strongly resists the effects of shock. In 2006, Apple equipped the MacBook Air with a 32GB SSD. Subsequently, 64GB 128 GM, 256 GB and 512 GB version were developed and commercialized. Solid state drives are currently available in capacities of 2TB, 4TB, 8TB, 16TB, and 32TB.

Charge Trap Flash (CTF)

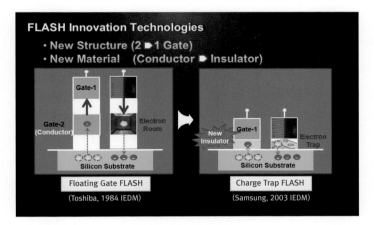

FLASH Innovation Technologies
- **New Structure (2 ▶ 1 Gate)**
- **New Material (Conductor ▶ Insulator)**

Floating Gate FLASH
(Toshiba, 1984 IEDM)

Charge Trap FLASH
(Samsung, 2003 IEDM)

This new technology addresses the problem of cell interference that occurs when storing charges in conducting or non-conducting spheres. The floating gate technology developed by Toshiba had been used for thirty years with NAND flash devices, but it was plagued by cell interference problems as chips became denser.

CTF stores charges in a new kind of insulation that consists of a thin, complex material instead of a conductor. This groundbreaking technology addresses the interference problem at the source and enables 3D cell architecture to be realized, resolving issues related to semiconductor development going forward, including ultra-miniaturization, very high capacity, and very fast performance. Samsung Electronics owns this proprietary technology and related patents, in step with the New Memory Growth Model, which focuses on the superb price competitiveness of the high-capacity NAND flash.

The CTF was first developed by Samsung Electronics and led flash-related proprietary technology and has still been applied as transistor density reaches the 10 nm processing node. Through technological development that lasted over five years, the 30 nm CTF 64G NAND flash (24 layers) was completed in 2007. As of 2020, devices with as many as 172 layers have been developed.

Challenge

Chapter 2

Start First
to Become Great

01   Never stop
asking questions

| Carly Fiorina |

Asking questions is one type of "behavior" that I believe is important. One needs a good deal of energy, passion, and courage to ask even a single question. Once I became a leader I often told the employees to "ask questions as often as possible and don't be afraid to ask."

I would frequently hear, "Well, I'm an introvert and I get nervous in front of people and can't think of anything to say."

Whenever I meet people who admit to having this problem, I tell them, "It's the same for me." When we ask questions, we reveal something about ourselves to others. That makes us even more uncomfortable. However, if one avoids asking questions for this reason, he or she won't be able to grow. To this I say, "Those with passion will always do what they must, regardless."

Having interacted with global leaders both in Korea and abroad for three decades, I often marveled at how they all seemed to share the same traits. The most noticeable of these was that they all loved their job.

Even while following a great vision, they remained faithful to the present, yet were curious about what changes the future would bring. Because of this, they knew how to listen but were also fond of "asking." Time and again, I witnessed their passion being expressed in an outpouring of questions.

Asking questions is the first gate we must pass through on the road to success. If you are searching for a way to express the passion in your own heart, you must never stop asking questions.

It all began with a question

During a conversation or presentation I focus on the speaker, but at the same time I am always thinking, "What question could I ask?" Listening while formulating questions keeps me focused on the other person and helps me understand the speaker's logic in my own language. By combining all this activity, I can then expect a sort of "networking effect" when I ask a question.

I think people instinctively want to give the right answer when someone asks them a question. To do so, they concentrate on their counterpart even more. This is because they can only provide an appropriate response once they have determined what their counterpart understands about the situation. From that point on, they develop an "interest" in the questioner. This interest serves as a "connection" between the questioner and the responder, which then becomes the starting point leading to networking.

In December 1985, while working as a research associate at Stanford University, I attended the International Electron Devices Meeting

(IEDM) held at the Washington Hilton Hotel. Even in those days, the IEDM was a global conference with some 4,000 researchers and engineers participating, and the presentations in various fields went on for three days after the keynote speech. I went to the semiconductor and memory section to hear the presentation of a paper by Dr. Fujio Masuoka, who was then working as an engineer for Toshiba, the top memory semiconductor company at that time.

Dr. Masuoka had gained fame in the previous year of 1984 by inventing flash memory, "a type of non-volatile storage medium to which data can be written and erased, even with the power off." However, the attention it won him was not so much at that time. Flash memory was optimal for mobile devices as it consumed less power and enabled high-speed reading and writing, but it was still the 1980s. It was difficult to come

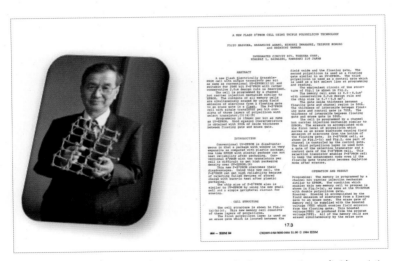

Dr. Fujio Masuoka, the first person to announce flash memory theory (left), and the paper he presented at the IEDM (right).

up with ideas, not only about the market, but for products as well. Still, I had intense interest in new technologies and future markets, and therefore I shared the feeling that this technology had great potential. I really wanted to meet Dr. Masuoka in person.

"I enjoyed your presentation, Dr. Masuoka. However, if future technological developments lead to flash memory being reduced to the submicron level, wouldn't the electrons become more active (in reference to Dr. Shockley's hot electron theory) and provide better performance?"

During the Q&A session after the presentation, I asked this rather aggressive question.

I was pointing out that if future technology reduced the semiconductor fabrication process to the submicron level, we might then expect a greater effect than what was theoretically expected at the present time. I believed also that the possibilities from such technological developments should be reflected in semiconductor design.

Although he is a professor at Tohoku University and has a global reputation, back then Fujio Masuoka was working as an engineer and was slightly over 40 years old. Evidently caught off guard, Dr. Masuoka answered briefly, "That seems to be a good idea."

As the session came to an end and people started to leave, I went up and greeted Dr. Masuoka. He replied to my question once again, and we made small talk after I introduced myself.

We had a conversation on how he developed floating gate NAND flash memory for the first time. In 1988, after Dr. Masuoka's invention, Intel recognized the potential of flash memory and began commercial development.

Of course, my interaction with Dr. Masuoka was of great help to me as well. The information I gained about flash memory would later become a theoretical cornerstone in my development work on charge trap flash (CTF, see page 137) at Samsung Electronics. Eliminating the "floating gate" structures that added complexity to the process was a huge task. The endless questions and ideas birthed at that time motivated me many years later to develop CTF.

What if I had not found the courage to ask questions at the IEDM? What if I had not interacted with Dr. Fujio Masuoka? I must admit; that one single question was the beginning of many things.

It takes passion to ask questions

Thinking back, I was probably the only engineer/manager who liked posing questions to partner companies. I was practically obsessed with wanting to know what our clients' demands were, and where the market was heading. And that's why I always met with our clients' CTOs. Our sales division staff wanted me to meet CEOs and purchasing department executives, but I knew who among my counterparts could answer my questions. I needed to hear from the CTOs to read the technological tea leaves and be prepared for the future before anyone else.

It is not an exaggeration to say that the development of "mobile DRAM," one of Samsung Electronics' most successful products in the mobile era, began after a meeting with the CTO of a client. The partnership between Samsung Electronics and Nokia remains strong to this day ever since the former began supplying flash memory to the latter in 2002. I was very fortunate to have had a conversation with Nokia's CTO about a smartphone developed by that company.

"Nokia 9000 Communicator," the first smartphone developed by Nokia.
Source: Wikipedia

Say the word "smartphone" and most people will think of the Apple
iPhone, which was released in 2007. But the iPhone wasn't the world's
first smartphone. In 1993, more than 10 years prior, IBM introduced
the world to "Simon." It had a 3-inch resistive touchscreen and various
functions such as sending and receiving emails and faxes, a memo pad,
and games. However, it failed to become popular because it combined
a huge $899.00 price tag with being inconvenient to use. Having
witnessed this, Nokia then released a smartphone called the "Nokia 9000
Communicator" three years later.

During my visits to Finland, I engaged in lively conversations with
Nokia's CTO. At the time, Nokia employees were using the Nokia 9000
Communicator and continuously monitoring it. In my own opinion,
it looked just like a pencil case. The product consisted of two panels
attached to each other, with the top panel serving as the display screen
and the bottom as a QWERTY keyboard. It was too big and heavy for

use as a mobile device, and thus inconvenient.

So, I discussed ways to improve the product's convenience with Nokia executives in charge of technology. Nokia was aware that the battery supporting the CPU was the cause of the product's heavy weight and large size, yet they didn't have a possible solution. Intuitively, I detected that low-power DRAMs would be required, on top of a low-power CPU and operating system for mobile devices.

On my flight home, I struggled thinking about product development ideas and eventually came up with the name "mobile DRAM" to develop existing DRAM chips for mobile products. I recalled the Zakura Meeting with Chairman Lee Kun-hee and his question about whether there was a future for DRAMs. I responded to him by saying, "DRAMs will evolve into mobile DRAMs, which will then become an even bigger market." Team organization took place at lightning speed, and a few years later in May 2004, we developed the world's first 256M mobile DRAM, which was then loaded on Nokia mobile phones. In January 2005, we developed the 512M mobile DRAM which was used in Apple smartphones.

I continued to have these active exchanges with CTOs, and they later enabled me to recognize changes in organizations and clients and discover potential needs and demands. Experiences such as I have described happened repeatedly, and resulted from the entirety of my passion being poured out in the form of questions.

Carly Fiorina's weapons—questions and listening

"Dr. Hwang, as you may already know, we are transforming Hewlett-

Packard (HP) into a global IT corporation. We believe that our future lies in networks and networking. What do you think we should focus on most?"

Whenever I begin to "organize my thoughts for a question," the first person who always comes to mind is Carly Fiorina. She was recognized as the most influential woman in the business world by *Fortune* magazine for six consecutive years.

From my first encounter with her, I realized I had many things in common with Carly Fiorina by the way she bombarded me with questions. To start, we were about the same age, and we both shared the experience of studying and working on the US West and East Coasts in our youth. Now, we were both dedicating ourselves to working for IT firms and dealing with global companies as clients. However, what gave me the greatest sense of kinship was that neither of us began our career under the glow of fireworks.

Carly Fiorina printed her first set of business cards with American Telephone & Telegraph (AT&T) at the age of 25. Soon proving herself extraordinary, she rose quickly through the ranks to become that company's first female executive at only 35. Only ten years later, she was chosen as the CEO of Hewlett-Packard while still in her mid-40s.

I first met the illustrious Carly Fiorina soon after she became the head of HP. In 2004, after being appointed president of the Semiconductor Division, I headed to Palo Alto in Silicon Valley to visit some of our major clients. At the time, Dell, IBM, and HP were the main clients of Samsung Electronics, and overall, their combined orders accounted for well over 30% of sales for the Semiconductor Memory Business Division. Maintaining a cordial relationship with clients was one of the primary tasks of the Semiconductor Division president.

Dressed in a vividly colored suit, Carly greeted me, along with several other executives in our group, in the CEO's office at HP headquarters. As the head of HP, a company with sales totaling nearly $84.4 billion, she was charismatic and confident, but her manner of speech was candid and straightforward. It was clear from her questions that her interests were highly diverse.

Many Silicon Valley leaders in those days tended to show a lot of interest in technological details. However, Carly was curious about the effects of technology on human beings. She wanted her organization to show as much competence as necessary in terms of focus, speed, and aggressiveness, and there were unique facets to her insight.

Through several other meetings with her, I was left with admiration and curiosity, and I wondered, "How could she have such insight for someone who is not an engineer?" After further reflection I concluded that her academic background in history and philosophy at Stanford University may have been responsible. As a former engineering student, I just figured that all liberal arts majors were about the same. However, while reading Carly's autobiography *Tough Choices*, published in 2006, I realized that her insight came from her unique life history.

Carly Fiorina's father was a famous law professor, so she spent her childhood traveling around and living in different places. She went to elementary school in three different states (New York, Connecticut, and California), spent junior high in the US and England, and high school in Africa and two US states (California and North Carolina). Frequent moves might have been confusing for her as a child, but she had her own solutions.

Her mother was her role model and showed her "how to adapt to new environments."

"My mother always asked her guests questions, and she was always interested in their answers. I just did the same thing."

"Questions and listening" became weapons she frequently used whenever she encountered an unfamiliar situation.

"When I'm in a new environment, I use the same strategy. I ask a lot of questions and read as much as possible so that I can evaluate the answers."

Just like me, Carly Fiorina stood in the continuum of change, and for both of us, "questions" were an important part of the process of determining direction. Questions guided us both in many ways and gave us answers.

Everything is possible

During a trip to Edinburgh, Scotland for a Samsung Electronics IR session, Carly called me on the phone. HP had just ordered a large quantity of semiconductors for a new server they were installing. She requested that I make sure their order, despite its sudden timing, did not fall behind schedule. I asked how she was doing, and she said that she was on a private plane heading back to the US from Europe. I felt a sudden urge to joke around with her.

"Carly, I have just received a call from heaven. How could I, a mere mortal on earth, say no to a queen who has called me by her own hand?"

We laughed together for quite a while as we held the phone.

Official meetings also played a significant role in allowing us to maintain our friendly relationship. In 2004, Carly visited Korea to attend the World Knowledge Forum organized by Maeil Business News Korea. Under the theme of "Partnership for Renewed Growth," renowned figures including Carly Fiorina, former Japanese Prime Minister Yoshirō Mori, Economics Nobel Prize winner Robert Alexander Mundell, and former Italian Deputy Prime Minister Gianni De Michelis, were all in attendance at the same venue.

As I exchanged greetings with the other speakers, I once again met Carly, who this time had short blond hair and was wearing a black suit. She had been designated as the first keynote speaker, following former Korean President Kim Dae-jung, who delivered the opening address. I came after Carly.

A speech by Paul Kennedy, Yale University history professor and author of the global bestseller *The Rise and Fall of the Great Powers*, brightened up the mood. Only a few minutes into his talk, the previously serious and solemn atmosphere changed.

"Today I learned about the spirit of the Great Admiral Yi Sun-sin, thanks to Dr. Hwang. I think that the spirit of challenge and risk-taking

The author chats with Carly Fiorina before giving a keynote speech at the World Knowledge Forum in 2004.

will be essential in future industry, including IT. As it so happens, I'm going to be talking about "risk management" today. My subject matter may pale a bit by comparison, but I'll continue anyway since that's all I have prepared."

Employing humility and wit, Paul Kennedy appealed to the audience for understanding before delivering yet another speech about risk.

Earlier that day, I had made a speech emphasizing the importance of risk-taking using Admiral Yi Sun-sin as a model.

Admiral Yi developed the potential of the turtle ship, which neutralized the enemy's main advantage of rifles and swords. He then defeated the enemy's massive fleet of 120 battleships with only 12 ships of his own at the Battle of Myeongnyang Strait. His main strategy was persevering through crises and "risk-taking." Even when faced with desperately dangerous times of crisis, he endured and fought onward. I also, by not settling on individual successes but accepting risk and pressing forward instead, was able to create new product lines and new markets, from DRAMs and flash memory to mobile DRAMs and solid-state drives.

I emphasized in my speech that Korean and global companies alike needed to arm themselves with the spirit of risk-taking and avoid fear of failure. Though it has been 10 years since I left Samsung Electronics, I take great reassurance knowing that Samsung Electronics Semiconductor is still achieving remarkable results with four main products (DRAMs, mobile DRAMs, NAND flash memory, and solid-state drives).

When I returned to the head table after finishing my short speech, Carly, who had just finished her speech before mine, welcomed me back by saying that she was impressed by my talk about risk-taking. As we continued chatting, she said, "Now I understand the secret behind Samsung Electronics'

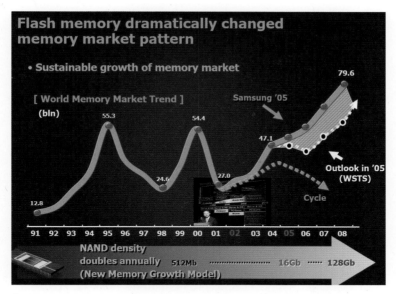

Sales trend for memory semiconductors over 20 years (influence of flash memory resulted in upward curve starting from 2004)

stable sales growth in semiconductors after fluctuating so much along with the Olympic cycle." Despite her unsparing praise, the highlight of the day had in fact been her keynote speech.

Carly Fiorina spoke on the subject of "change and adaptability."

Emphasizing the fundamental changes to modern society from three different aspects (advent of the digital age, technology at the heart of change, and vertical organizations' transformation to horizontal integration), she cited Darwin's theory of evolution, saying, "it's not the strongest of a species that survive; it's those that are most adaptable to change." Her conclusion that only companies with strong adaptability would survive in the future was very convincing.

The next day, Carly Fiorina's speech was quoted in articles by several newspapers. I recalled HP's slogan, "Everything Is Possible," as I was reading the newspaper. After becoming the CEO of HP, Carly Fiorina launched a global campaign under this slogan. I felt that no one epitomized this slogan more so than Carly Fiorina. In fact, many people around that time considered her a role model of success.

The first female awardee and first foreign awardee

In 2004, Carly Fiorina received the Medal of Honor from the Electronic Industries Alliance (EIA) of the United States. The award is often called the "Nobel Prize of the IT industry" and has been given every year since 1952 to the person who contributes the most to the development of the US electronics industry. Bob Galvin of Motorola, Mark Shepherd of Texas Instruments, and Thomas Watson of IBM are among the previous recipients. Carly Fiorina was acknowledged for being an innovation leader and contributing to the transformation of HP from a computer and printer company into an IT company.

At the awards ceremony in Washington in May, she said, "Use us more!" However, her acceptance speech wasn't quite as newsworthy by comparison to her being selected as the first female recipient of the EIA medal. Most news outlets gave more coverage to the fact that a female CEO had received the same award given to HP co-founder David Packard.

Up until then, I had no idea that Carly had been evaluated differently as a leader because she was a woman, even though I hadn't met any other female leaders before her. Only after reading articles about her accepting the EIA medal did I understand the distress and difficulties she must have had experienced to reach that position.

In the following year of 2005, I stood on the same stage where Carly Fiorina had stood. There I heard the news that I was "the first foreigner to receive the EIA Leadership in Technology and Innovation Award." It was only a few months after I had heard that for the first time in 53 years the EIA would extend the range of recipients to include entrepreneurs from around the world.

The news spread like wildfire that "the first foreign recipient of the EIA award was selected after the previous year's first female recipient." I headed to Washington DC under a spotlight of attention.

At the awards ceremony, held at the Ronald Reagan Building, EIA President David McCurdy briefly explained why I was selected.

"Dr. Hwang predicted the expansion of the mobile and digital market many years ago, and exerted strong leadership in the development of the world's semiconductor industry. His achievements resulted in innovations in the global market and IT companies, bringing about revolutionary changes."

I also delivered a brief acceptance speech, just as Carly had, in front of more than 150 people from the political and financial communities.

"The digital revolution that resulted in dramatic changes in the economy, society and culture was made possible by semiconductors. The rapid development of semiconductors is accelerating the transition to a mobile and digital society. The future is created, not predicted. I will continue to devote myself to technological development."

My acceptance speech also failed to receive much attention other than the fact that I was the first foreign recipient. It was then that I realized

The author receiving the EIA Leadership in Technology & Innovation Award in 2005 with EIA President David McCurdy.

how Carly Fiorina may have felt that she was treated like a "stranger" just because she was a woman. But of course, this was not the full extent of the inspiration I experienced while I was in DC.

Leaving the joy and emotion of winning my award behind, I prepared to return to Korea the next day to take care of impending tasks. While in the lobby of the Mandarin Oriental, waiting to check out and with my award in my luggage, a collection of national flags fluttering against a blue sky in front of the hotel caught my eye. In the middle of them, one national flag was particularly recognizable. I went outside and glanced up at the Korean flag, watching over me from the sky above.

As I was appreciating this familiar sight, one of my subordinates asked the hotel employee as he checked out why Korea's national flag was in the middle among the other flags. The employee answered, "We hung the

Korean flag in the middle because we heard that the EIA award winner was Korean." I felt deeply moved upon hearing that answer. It made me feel that there isn't a greater award than seeing my own country's national flag flying proudly in a faraway land.

Ask questions, and never stop

Carly Fiorina said she had never had the goal of "outdoing men" when she worked. She just faced reality, took one step, and then another, as she moved forward. Eventually, she reached that place which other people might refer to as a "position surpassing the limits."

The same was true for me. Like anyone else, I prepared, looked for opportunities, and realized achievement. However, in hindsight, I played a lead role in elevating a country viewed as a semiconductor backwater into a country that is now considered a global power in semiconductors.

Many people want to know the secret of success. They believe that successful people have something special. I was also curious about that as I met numerous global leaders, including Carly Fiorina. However, I failed to find that "special something" in them. Everything else looked quite normal when compared to the marvelous success they achieved. It was when I focused on their similarities, rather than their differences, that I figured out what made them successful.

Socrates said, "The highest form of human excellence is to question oneself and others." Wise questions indeed have the power to change yourself and your organization. To young people waiting for their own beginning I would give this advice: "Start asking questions, and never stop."

02

Boldly declare it
and see it through

| Steve Jobs & Tim Cook |

People like novelty. Thus, it is common to think that consumers will be enthusiastic about something new. However, that is just a great delusion. People are not open-minded toward new things. Rather, they sometimes show stiff resistance at first.

Most people who have taken on the challenge to creating something new are discouraged by reactions like "It's not that great" or "That's not as good as I expected..."

I also have laid out various concepts that the world had never seen, from Hwang's Law (2002) to the advent of the FT (Fusion Technology) era (2006), Smartopia (2011), GiGAtopia (2014), and the opening of the 5G era (2015). The process has definitely not been easy, and people's reactions have caused me considerable stress. I'd rather hear someone say, "Is that even possible?" Many would tell me, "You're like an insightful prophet," and then expect me to fail.

In fact, all new things only succeed after going through a certain period of failure. A time of persistent effort is necessary before even minor successes are assessed properly. However, every moment has been valuable to me during the past 30 years. I have led change by making bold declarations and then seeing them through. This is how world-changing technologies are realized.

The fiercely passionate ones and the partners who embrace them

While writing this book, I thought about what inspired me to do exciting but difficult things. I tried to recall figures who impressed me with daring declarations and challenges. I thought about the people I met over the past three decades while working for Samsung Electronics for twenty years, as the National CTO for three years, and as the CEO of a telecommunications operator for six years. But there was one person that no one could beat. The eccentric and meticulous person of wild passion—Steve Jobs.

Steve achieved great success as the founder of Apple, but he also went through bitter failure. He experienced the disgrace of being ousted from his own company (forced to submit an official letter of resignation to Apple in September 1985). He had started a business at the age of 20 and found himself jobless at 30 years old. He then drifted for a time before resolving to raise the banner of challenge.

This was how NeXT and Pixar were born. The former was a high-performance computer manufacturer, while the latter creates 3D animation with computer graphics. Crises persisted as consumers shunned NeXT computers because of their high price, and the Pixar co-founder left the company because of conflicts with Steve Jobs. However, *Toy Story*, which was released during the 1995 Christmas season raked in nearly $200 million in the US. And NeXT, which had to lay off about 280 of its employees (more than half of the workforce) in 1993, earned revenue by selling off its operating system and then was acquired by Apple in 1996. In 1997, Steve Jobs returned to Apple as the CEO, receiving an annual salary of $1.00. He launched the iMac in 1998 and then methodically built up Apple's ecosystem.

Steve endured moments of crises and then demonstrated his potential for turning crises into opportunities. His willingness to take on challenges, strong tenacity, and final victory inspired many managers. He passed away on October 5, 2011. Upon hearing this news, I sent an e-mail to Tim Cook, Steve Jobs' successor and Apple's CEO:

> "A man who changed the world has passed away. We will never meet a man like Steve Jobs again. I miss him. Please accept my sincere condolences to Apple for losing a great CEO."

I maintained a longer relationship with Tim Cook than I had had with Steve Jobs. When I became the president of Samsung's Memory Business Division in 2000, Tim was Apple's senior vice president. He silently oversaw the company's management while Steve was focused on product development. I frequently met Tim to determine the volume of semiconductors for use in Mac computers.

Back in those days, Apple's share in the PC market was about 5%. The preeminent players were Dell, HP, and IBM. However, Apple requested that we supply them under the same conditions as those major clients. I got the Sales Department to adjust the transaction conditions for Apple, considering the company's name value as well as the trust I shared personally with Tim Cook. Tim consistently accepted the same quantity of chips even when other clients did not as a result of price fluctuations. This convinced me that he wouldn't let go of our cooperative ties when times were difficult.

Steve Jobs had the insight for new products and tenacious resolve to move things along, while Tim Cook would quietly tolerate situations, consider the needs of others, and maintain his loyalties. In my opinion, the combination of the two different leadership styles were extremely beneficial to Apple.

Steve appointed Tim as his successor when his health deteriorated. In 2009, Tim Cook became Apple's acting CEO, and in August 2011, when Steve Jobs retired to become the chairman of the board, Tim came to the front and became the CEO of Apple. Many people couldn't imagine Apple without Steve Jobs. Some said, "It's over for Apple." Many expected that Apple's strong position could not be maintained under Tim Cook's leadership.

But I had another opinion. Steve believed in Tim because they were different. Tim Cook took care of Apple and paid attention to details. His leadership style focused on cooperation, which was essential for clearing the hurdles of the Fourth Industrial Revolution and the Second Generation Management. I personally supported Tim, and I was excited to see how he would lead and transform Apple.

He immediately replied after receiving my e-mail of condolences. He thanked me and said he would be glad to see me whenever I visited the

The author visiting Tom Cook's office upon invitation when he was the National CTO in 2011.

US. I was busy as the National CTO at the time, but I had an upcoming business trip to the US. I replied, saying that I would be traveling there in a couple of months and that we should get together then.

Remembering Steve Jobs

Upon Steve Jobs passing, a news magazine asked me to write a tribute, and a Korean publisher that was preparing to publish the Korean edition of his official biography, *Steve Jobs*, requested me to write the foreword.

Steve left a message when he was alive: connect the dots. The meaning of this message was that every experience and thought are solutions to difficult problems. While struggling to write my remembrances and book recommendation, I was surprised to discover the dots that connected us.

The first dot was the Macintosh that I used as a research associate at Stanford University. In the late 1980s, the Macintosh was a must-have item in the US, even more than today's iPhone. I remember its exact price: $4,999. I had to save a few months' salary as a research associate just to buy it. Its high price inspired the coining of the term "Apple Tax."

After consulting with my wife, I bought the Macintosh SE/30. Although it was expensive, I was so grateful to the creator of this computer. The unprecedented, convenient user interface and various typefaces made writing papers enjoyable.

The second dot was Stanford University. It is safe to say that Steve Jobs and I were walking around the Stanford campus during the same period. He was already a man of fame. After completing the development of the Apple computer in 1976, he released the Macintosh in 1984. The Mac TV commercial was designed with George Orwell's 1984 as the motif, and it was run that year during the Superbowl, which is notoriously expensive. The advertising campaign garnered a tremendous response. As mentioned above, he was fired from Apple in 1985, but before long he had taken over NeXT and Pixar and was back in business.

During 1989, he would visit the campus each time he was to deliver a lecture at the Stanford Business School. Later, he met Laurene Powell, his future wife, at the Stanford Business School. Just how far was my laboratory from the Stanford Business School in 1989? I reminisced about my younger days as I longed for a special friend who passed away.

The third dot is music. Steve often emphasized publicly how Bob

Dylan was his role model. I also loved music. I was not only into classical music, but I enjoyed various genres including modern music. When the iPod was released in 2001, I was not just a music fan but also an engineer. My intuition told me that the product could be better. I imagined how it could be when supported by the flash memory I had developed. I sent him a prototype equipped with the flash memory, which led to our meeting in person.

In November 2004, I received a call from Steve, who was preparing to release of the next-generation iPod. At the time, Samsung Electronics was getting ready for MP3 players, digital cameras, and USB drives equipped with flash memory. Apple was an innovative player in the personal computer area, but its market share was a mere 3%. Then the company broke into the digital consumer market with its iPod and created a sensation.

The cover of *Steve Jobs* and the author's notes for its foreword

As I mentioned earlier, my very first appointment with Steve Jobs was canceled because of problems with my flight. But I later heard that Steve had called Park Yong-hwan, then the head of Samsung's US subsidiary, to complain strongly.

"The only people I have ever invited to my house in Palo Alto were two heads of State!"

He vented his displeasure at being unable to meet with me. He said that he even had his wife standing by at his private reception hall and that I should have rented a charter plane if my commercial plane was unable to fly. Listening to that story assured me that I had been handed a strong chance to win.

On December 6, I devised strategies in my head to ease the tension as I rode in the car from San Francisco International Airport to the Apple Headquarters in Cupertino. When I arrived at the Apple Headquarters, I was lost in thought about how to lead the negotiation as well as what volume of our products they would want at what price.

I entered the meeting room where Steve Jobs was waiting for us. As soon as the door opened, I saw him sitting there with a smile on his face.

My first impression was that he was exceptionally intense. He greeted us with a cheerful smile, showing me that he also had great charisma. We laughed as we talked, with Tim Cook, who was the chief operations officer, and John Rubinstein, the senior vice president of Hardware Engineering, also present. However, there was definitely tension in the air.

When the time came for negotiation, Steve unreservedly revealed his stubborn and demanding character. He was also very thorough. He specifically talked about how the products worked, how they would be used, and what changes they would lead.

I had many chances to see clients from all over the world while working for Samsung Semiconductor. I met countless people of outstanding talent, but Steve Jobs was at another level entirely. He understood management and technology, as he was both a dreamer and a doer. From the moment we signed the contract, he asked constantly about the main parts that would be applied to the next-generation mobile devices. He fervently wanted to know the direction in which technological development was headed and technological strengths, including memory performance and speed.

However, as I mentioned before, the negotiation wasn't concluded on the first day. Both parties only agreed on Samsung Electronics supplying flash semiconductors to Apple. The next day my traveling companions and I climbed aboard a plane bound for Korea.

A few days later, I had an unexpected visitor. Tim Cook visited me in my office unannounced. He called my office only after he had arrived at the airport. I hastily canceled my afternoon schedule to receive him. The meeting without Steve Jobs was peaceful and amicable.

"By the way, Dr. Hwang, Steve will call you soon."

About ten minutes later, my secretary told me that Steve Jobs was on the line, and I took his call in the next room. He briefly said hello and went straight to the point.

"Tim flew all the way to Korea to see you despite his busy schedule. I hope that things will work out this time. I especially want you, Dr. Hwang, to look after things."

The phone call ended with his gentle and delicate request. When I came back to the meeting room, Tim asked, "What do you want us to do for you?"

I told him about an idea I shared with Vice President Lee Jae-yong while I was on my business trip in the US. I said that we would review the quantity and price with the stipulation that Apple would exclusively use Samsung's AP for the next-generation iPhone. Tim Cook answered definitely, "We will positively consider it."

When our negotiation was over, I looked at Tim while he was getting up from his seat and made a friendly joke:

"Tim Cook, is that all?"

He stared back at me dubiously. I told him that since Apple would soon hit it big with our semiconductors, Apple should at least give Samsung a gift. He giggled and said, "I will give you a reward." He left while saying that they would definitely give something in return if things go well.

While finishing up my tribute to Steve Jobs, I recalled a question that he had often asked, "Dr. Hwang, until when do you think Hwang's Law will be valid?"

I often answered, "Longer that you might suppose," to Steve, who was concerned over such matters as the CTO.

People assessed Steve Jobs in many different ways. Some say he was unreasonably demanding and boastful; others say they had been victimized and betrayed by him. However, the Steve Jobs I met was a trustworthy businessman and an entrepreneur who responsibly pressed ahead with a business with a rich IT ecosystem.

Merely saying that he was great is an understatement. Humanity owes him a substantial debt. Wouldn't the best way to commemorate his life be to follow in his footsteps and finish the job of making a world of seamless communication between people and technology, which he dreamed of so much?

A quantum leap is possible even in times of crisis

Although Steve Jobs had passed away, I continued to devote myself to seamless communication between people and technology. I became the chairman of KT three years after I wrote my tribute to him. In May 2014, four months after my appointment, I took the stage at KT Square for a press conference where I revealed KT's future vision.

I attracted much public attention as I declared the KT vision of becoming the "Global No. 1." Our goal was to be universally recognized as a proud industry leader by securing the most innovative and competitive services and competitiveness among the world's telecommunications operators. To this end, I presented our new image of the future, which we call "GiGAtopia."

GiGAtopia is a world in which gigabit-capable infrastructure and services enable the ever-increasing interconnection between people and things, as well as the convergence of various industries. My strategy was to seek a new driving force as we revitalize the ICT ecosystem through converged services that make life safer and more convenient amidst those changes. In the mid-2000s, with the mobile era in full swing, KT's stature was shaken within the industry. Wireline telephone revenue, once the cash cow, fell sharply each year. The media focused more on questions like "Could KT normalize operations?" than on such questions as "What should KT be aware of and what kinds of changes should be made?" Some went so far as to say: "They don't need Hwang's Law. They need Hwang's Magic."

I made a win-or-lose play called GiGAtopia to overcome KT's crisis. Of course, the decision to face this challenge wasn't easy. As I had predicted in 2006, before we had smartphones, the fusion technology (FT) era, where everything could be done on a mobile device, would arrive. Then, as the National CTO, I suggested Smartopia as the vision for Korea's national R&D projects. Along the way, I was able to lay the groundwork for GiGAtopia.

While working as the National CTO, I was invited to be a keynote speaker for CeBIT's global conference, the world's largest ICT fair, to be held in Hanover, Germany in March 2011. In line with the conference theme, "IT Enables a Smart World," I declared to the world Korea's vision of creating a global "Smartopia." This neologism combines "smart" with "topia" and refers to a world that goes beyond convenience, providing comfort based on the convergence of IT and other industries.

"Recently, with the paradigm shift from technology-centered to human-centered, the strong demand for HumaniTech becomes very apparent, where every technology is being rearranged to put people in the center. Smartopia is a world where various devices in and of themselves build optimal environments for the humans around them."

The Smartopia era is the time when devices that predict what people want even if people do not manually operate them (in other words, devices that can think for themselves) will appear one after another, and a constant dialog between those devices and humans can be maintained. One might say that seems plausible in our 2021 way of life. But back then, I was criticized by some, saying that it sounded like a sci-fi movie.

As the National CTO, I emphasized the convergence of the Cloud, big data, AI, and IT, which are key technologies for Smartopia. I insisted that if those converged technologies are integrated with existing industries, technological innovation could advance several steps forward. As I was preparing for that future and seeking new revenue sources for the nation's future, I didn't know I would become the head of KT and spearhead the convergence between IT and other industries.

At the beginning we were frustrated at every turn. The GiGAtopia strategy ran into considerable opposition within the organization. The ultra-high-speed internet market was already saturated, and fierce competition caused sales to plummet. The common opinion was that the ultra-high-speed internet was already fast enough, and that there would be no demand for even higher speeds. However, I was convinced that a gigabit-capable internet would be essential not only for creating a new market in the internet business but also for preparing for the upcoming evolution of the ICT industry.

The circumstances were similar to those when I announced Hwang's Law in 2002, when the IT industry was going through its worst period. Plummeting DRAM prices forced Samsung to downsize operations. Despite the opposing views, I announced the New Memory Growth Model, predicting that demand for memory chips would explode and that PC-centered growth would shift to a focus on mobile devices. Those who were somewhat doubtful only acknowledged the paradigm shift from a PC-centered market to a mobile-centered one after the fact.

If Hwang's Law envisaged the mobile era, then GiGAtopia was the prediction for a new era where gigabit-capable infrastructure and services would lead to industrial convergence. I tirelessly sought to persuade my employees and encouraged the development of new technologies in order to make my declaration a reality.

In October 2014, gigabit broadband connection was commercialized nationwide, marking a quantum leap in internet speed, which had been at a standstill since 2006, for more than a decade. The era of communication at gigabits per second came out of wireline services industry, and the net value of the gigabit broadband connection would reach an aggregate of nearly $1 billion over five years.

The "GiGA Internet" strategy has allowed KT to rejoin the ranks of domestic telecommunication service operators with at least 1 trillion (about $840 million) won in annual operating income, and it has taken global competitiveness to the next level. The company has proved that developing the driver for future growth and upgrading technologies can enable a quantum leap even in times of crisis.

Be daring and see it through

Steve Jobs always said that you don't reach completion when you have no more to add but when you have nothing left to take away. I really like this idea from Steve Jobs. He was very good at both driving innovation with his big picture and adding perfection to details.

Steve wrote the digital revolution creation myth, but when one looks back on the course of his life, it is difficult to say that he was the sole creator of it all. He did not invent all Apple products from start to finish.

Steve Jobs did understand the power of graphic interface, and he designed the Macintosh, but he publicly said that the source of its conception was "inspired" from Xerox. Even the concept iPod, which carries thousands of songs, was not invented by him. The MP3 technology and player were first invented in Korea. The iTunes platform for downloading music was created by transforming a source program that Apple acquired. My question is: How did Steve make it happen while others could not? It is because no one else but him could combine ideas, art, and technologies to shape the future. Steve Jobs encouraged talented people to make the best use of their skills to produce creative products. He was very good at igniting people's passion.

"Declaration" is the method that both he and I have used. It is like starting the engine so that colleagues and those who are curious about the future can embrace a vision and cultivate the future.

At MWC 2015, held in Barcelona, Spain, I gave a keynote speech titled "5G and Beyond, Accelerating the Future." I declared in that speech that 5G was not just about a fast network; it was a technology that could change the future of humankind with a platform based on ultra-high connectivity and ultra-low latency. I added that we would realize 5G to usher in a new era for humankind."

However, many people were not sure about my assertion that 5G would be the ultimate network that resolves the issues of speed, capacity, and connectivity in an era of ultra-high connectivity and that it would lead us to another level of growth and spark changes in life. Global telecommunications operators at the time anticipated that the actual emergence of 5G would be available in 2020 at the earliest, considering the rate 5G technology evolution. Not many of these companies were interested in 5G at a time when even 4G had not been brought fully up to speed.

Only Japan and China were preparing to embark on a massive R&D campaign and investment to showcase 5G services during the Tokyo 2020 Olympics and Beijing 2022 Winter Olympics, respectively.

Japan organized a 5G task force under the Ministry of Internal Affairs and Communications, and China has been preparing to show off the technological prowess of Huawei, the country's foremost IT company. Our taking over the lead in the 5G project and getting some of the world's top companies to take part represented was a great adventure and challenge.

In order to demonstrate the possibility of realizing 5G, I declared that we would present the world's first 5G pilot service during the PyeongChang 2018 Winter Olympics. My aspiration was to enable Korea's communications technology to make the leap to the world's top spot by making the PyeongChang Winter Olympics the world's first 5G Olympics. This is the same approach Japan took to further its position as an electronics powerhouse after broadcasting the 1964 Tokyo Olympics in color via satellite for the first time in the world.

I became extremely busy after delivering that speech. I couldn't do it on my own.

First, we commercialized the GiGA LTE, the pre-5G technology; then, I organized a 5G Special Interest Group (SIG) with some of the world's top device and chip manufacturers such as Nokia, Samsung, Ericsson, Intel, and Qualcomm. I had great debates and discussions with employees within the company to check the details and progress related to technologies, services, and global cooperation. I emphasized that we should not settle for doing well ourselves but instead collaborate with global partners, and that technological developments should be followed by publishing in academic journals and filing for patents.

KT opened the PyeongChang 5G R&D Center in Umyeon-dong, where global communications companies, device manufacturers, and related SMEs could test the 5G technology whenever they wanted. At the end of the whole process, we succeeded in developing the standards for 5G-SIG in June 2016 that would be used in PyeongChang, and in making the historic "5G First Call" together with Samsung Electronics in October.

I had additional chances to speak at the MWC, heading for Barcelona again in 2017 and 2019. With two more keynote speeches on "The World's First 5G Commercialization" and "Now a Reality, KT 5G and the Next Intelligent Platform," I had publicly announced the three steps in the 5G process: challenges, commercialization, and realization.

There are as many as 800 telecommunications operators around the world, and every one of them wants to attract global attention and show off advanced technologies. According to foreign news reports, the MWC

The author declaring the commercialization of 5G in his keynote speech at the MWC in February 2019.

selected me to deliver three keynote addresses related to 5G because it acknowledged that 5G was the key to future technology, and thought highly of Korea's IT technology.

The future we planned is becoming a reality worldwide. Of course this result was accomplished by the collective hard work of many colleagues.

The spark that makes a wonderful world

After we commercialized 5G, I met a good friend again at the 2019 World Economic Forum (WEF). Only 100 select members from around the world were invited to the International Business Council (IBC) event on the first day. There, I saw Tim Cook, and during the break, we naturally greeted each other. It had been eight years since we met in his office at Apple in 2011.

A few months after exchanging e-mails over Steve Jobs' passing, I was on a business trip to the US as the National CTO. My itinerary had visits to various global companies in Silicon Valley, including Google. Apple was, of course, on the list as well.

I jokingly asked, "Tim, where is my reward?" as he greeted me at the CEO's office.

He smiled at my joke and gave me a hug. We briefly reminisced on the memorable meeting we had had with Steve Jobs. As soft-spoken as always, Tim said, "We are looking forward to your continuous support, Dr. Hwang." At the time, Apple's iPhone wasn't available in Korea yet. Tim Cook must have had many concerns over this, but he didn't mention anything about it

The author meeting Tim Cook again at the World Economic Forum's IBC meeting in 2019

I left his office saying that I was grateful to him, the Apple CEO, for sparing me his precious time. He walked me out of his office, unsure of when we would next meet.

It was at the WEF's IBC meeting where we crossed paths again. We cheerfully greeted one another and took a photo together. We looked like two old veterans with graying hair.

"Dr. Hwang, I heard of your remarkable activities in 5G. What will the 5G market look like in the future?"

True to form as a CEO in the IT industry, he asked me about changes in the communications market. I answered with emphasis that existing communications services were focused on the B2C domain, but that 5G would stimulate innovation in the B2B market. I added that Samsung

Electronics would release a 5G phone within a few months, so Apple should also quickly make one of their own. To this he replied, "Apple will also adopt the 5G technology for its next-generation phones." Apple eventually adopted 5G for its model two generations later.

We had only been talking briefly when they announced the end of the break. We had to say farewell and were about to return to our respective seats. Tim grabbed my hand and said, "I'm really grateful for your support since our development of the MacBook. Apple has also performed well thanks to your help." I was deeply touched and sincerely told him, "You have also been reliable and supportive of me."

As I retired, I looked back on my relationship with Steve Jobs and Tim Cook, focusing on our encounters and the lessons I learned from them. More than twenty years have already passed since we first met. It has also been almost ten years since Steve left this world and Tim became the CEO.

Steve Jobs and Tim Cook had distinctive dispositions and management styles, yet both were successful in leading Apple to the top of their industry. Despite being different, they shared the courage to face challenges and the endurance to face hardships. One is described as being fervently passionate and the other is characterized as being silently tolerant, but they were both good at taking on high-risk challenges and seeing them through.

"You and I are creating the future."

This is what I felt during my encounters with Steve Jobs and Tim Cook. Our meetings always sparked a flame in my heart.

I hope my colleagues feel the same way. As an engineer, a leader and manager, I spent a lot of time boldly declaring my visions and paving the way forward. Although I'm now a retiree, I want to continue sharing this spark with someone who will be a part of making a more wonderful world.

03

Don't be afraid of
being a digital nomad

| Marc Benioff |

I guess I have a special connection with Japan. My decisions to go to work for Samsung Electronics and to take the position as the National CTO were both made while I was returning to Korea aboard flights from Japan.

I was born in Korea not long after the Japanese colonial period, so Japan was a country like a "mountain that had to be crossed." I was firmly resolved that we would not be outdone. Therefore, I learned to speak Japanese, benchmarked the country, and constantly paid attention to the things they had but we didn't. Young people nowadays may take my words as the rantings of an old man, but the word "patriotism" was like a magic spell I could not shake. In my youth, unadulterated passion swept over me, and I would not hesitate to abandon my ambitions for success or wealth if it was for justice—symbolized by the word "nation." To be an unpatriotic person would be both something both mortifying and terrifying.

I journeyed to world-renowned research centers after stepping back from the front line of Samsung management, and the Ministry of Trade, Industry and Energy (MOTIE, formerly the Ministry of Knowledge Economy) offered me the position of National Chief Technology Officer (CTO). Many encouraged me to accept the offer, but I declined it repeatedly saying that there were many more qualified than I. As a result, I had to hear some people even question my patriotist for rejecting such a great opportunity to serve the nation. Others sought to dissuade me, saying I should not get involved in government work. I recalled what I said the day I left the Samsung Advanced Institute of Technology (SAIT) without any promise of return:

"I'm leaving to search for the stuff to fuel our future. Let's meet again after all of you here have worked diligently to progress further, and I have done so somewhere else."

Frankly speaking, I had no plans at the time. Within a few short months, however, I started to study technologies while visiting the east and west coasts of the United States as well as traveling to Japan and Singapore. I met with world-renowned scholars for over two months, gathering one by one the things necessary to keep Korea moving forward. I was grateful to everyone who spared me their time and energy, and I pledged to apply without fail what I had learned for the future of my country.

Either coincidentally or inevitably, I then received the offer to work as the National CTO. I wondered if there would ever be a better opportunity for me to use. Once I realized I could go to a newly established government organization and sort out all the things I had learned and experienced, I calmly braced myself and accepted the proposal.

The unwavering nomad spirit just as it is

The day I decided to accept the position as the National CTO, heading the planning group responsible for identifying the revenue sources to drive the nation's future, I remembered my life from 20 years earlier.

I left Stanford University and returned to Korea in 1989. Having stayed at Stanford as a researcher for more than four years, the decision to go to work for a corporation was not easy to make. After finishing my doctorate, I refused to work at prominent corporations and settled in at a university research center. However I wondered whether I could adapt well to corporate life, which moved to a different tune than academia did. The stress of adapting to a new environment was tremendous.

And then I began to take on a new challenge 20 years later. More than a few doubted whether I would be up to the tasks at hand in the new environment known as the government after pursuing a career in the corporate world. Yet, I gladly accepted the life of a nomad, where I could develop uncultivated territory and constantly improve myself. With mixed feelings of excitement, trepidation, expectations, and concerns, I pondered the kind of future I would be facing. I truly felt I had the "nomad spirit," both past and present, always seeking out and moving into new realms to create new things.

To be honest, I felt a bit confident. I had performed well by applying the "nomad management" approach on the corporate front lines since the 1990s, far before it became popular. Growing as a manager after moving from a research center to a private corporation, I believed I could achieve new accomplishments if I applied my knowledge on technologies, businesses, and client management in government.

And since then, I worked intensively for three years. I used two strategies to find drivers for the future, distinguishing large companies from small and medium-sized enterprises (SMEs).

First, all business activities should be converged, centering on IT among large companies. I expected that connecting IT with other industries such as automobiles (autonomous driving) and shipbuilding would lead to the development of fusion technologies for the future.

Second, with respect to the SMEs, hidden champions* should be discovered and supported. Large companies make up 75% of Korean industry, an unbalanced structure that is rare in the rest of the world. Many small but robust SMEs must exist, as in Germany, for this sector to grow. I ultimately tried to reform the industrial structure to create hidden champions.

To this end we announced "National Vision 2020" and organized the Overseas Advisory Committee, led by Harvard Prof. George Whitesides, who had served as a consultant for multiple US presidents. For a year, I was busy making full use of what I had learned from global scholars while running the Office of Strategic R&D Planning. I also became the first Korean to deliver a keynote speech at CeBIT, the world's largest digital expo. A source of great strength for me was my conviction that nothing is impossible if approached with pure passion.

However, my life as a nomad did not end at that time. In 2014, I was

---

* **Hidden champion**: a company that is not well-known to the public but actually dominates the world market. Generally, such companies possess unique patented technologies or technologies that enable monopolistic production. In some cases, they rank first to third place in global market share. There are more than 2,700 hidden champions worldwide, among which some 1,300 are in Germany, 370 in the United States, and 220 in Japan.

The announcement of "National Vision 2020" at an event organized by the Ministry of Knowledge Economy's Office of Strategic R&D Planning in 2010.

named the chairperson of Korea Telecom, and worked on operational innovation as the CEO for the next six years. From a university research center to a private corporation, from a private corporation to a government institution, and then back to a private corporation... This journey resulted from my accepting the nomad's fate, always looking for new soil to cultivate then moving on after transforming it into soil that is productive in a different way.

"Create what you want it to be, not what it is."

Several CEOs come to mind when talking about the nomad spirit. I have met many people privately and as a business manager, and have learned much from them. They also motivated me to write this book.

One of them is Marc Benioff, the CEO of Salesforce.

Our first encounter was at the 2019 World Economic Forum. On the first day, the WEF's International Business Council (IBC) staged an event to which only 100 selected members from around the world were invited. I was a new member back then and sat behind Mr. Benioff. We greeted each other before the meeting started, and his piercing eyes were saying he already knew who I was.

Actually, I didn't know him very well at that time. I had only learned of his company, Salesforce, from *Blue Ocean Shift*, a book written by W. Chan Kim and Renée Mauborgne in 2017. In the book, Salesforce was introduced as a company that innovatively addressed difficulties in the traditional software market such as products that are very complicated, expensive to purchase and maintain, and difficult to install.

Marc Benioff recruited three people to help co-found Salesforce and developed a customer relationship management (CRM) solution available online through a monthly subscription. Salesforce was established in 1999 and grew into a company with annual sales of $1.3 billion within 10 years. For the fiscal year ended on January 31, 2021, annual sales were over $20 billion, and the workforce numbered around 54,000. Salesforce has been listed on Forbes' "The World's 100 Most Innovative Companies" and *Fortune's* "100 Best Companies to Work For."

Marc Benioff's unique management philosophy stressed the need to not think of something as it is but as you want it to be. Cloud services are common business models these days, but things were different in the late 1990s, when he started his business. His business model was to provide customers with access to software by paying a monthly fee and allowing them to terminate the service at any time. This was unimaginable in those days, as people were forced to lay out large sums to buy software. Clients who used software along with the Cloud service enjoyed remarkable cost-savings. Thus Benioff's company was pointed to as a best practice of the "blue ocean" strategy.

As many know, the concept of the blue ocean is the antithesis of the red ocean, a fiercely contested market. Marc Benioff packed up and left the existing red ocean approach to software sales, moving to a blue ocean in which software was sold online. He could have done well in the red ocean, but he boldly departed from it. His nomad spirit made the move possible.

One of the impressive aspects of his career was his declaration of "The End of Software." This meant that Salesforce was not the typical software company. Indeed, he used "The End of Software" as his corporate slogan to highlight how his company would innovate the software industry. Salesforce was one of the companies that made its way to the untilled land of the Internet.

How could anyone calmly resign from a secure executive position at Oracle and advance into undeveloped territory? However, he decided to let go of his vested rights and start out anew in the wilds. As a consequence, his domain expanded endlessly in digital space.

I was not able to engage in lengthy conversation with Marc Benioff at the WEF. Nevertheless, I had the impression that he dealt with people without concerns over their status and accepted his counterparts with an open mind.

He approached me during the break and told me he was interested in 5G and had looked into it. He said my speech earlier reaffirmed its importance and then thanked me. I answered by inviting him to come to my office if he ever found himself in Korea. A few months later, he really did come to visit my office.

Initially, Marc Benioff's liaison officer contacted me and said that Mr. Benioff was scheduled to participate in a 20th anniversary ceremony in Japan and then head straight back to San Francisco in his private jet. However he wanted to visit KT in Seoul. I answered that he would be welcome anytime.

The next day, he came to my office with a bright yet serious expression on his face. Greeting them like old friends, I took him and other Salesforce members who were with him on a tour of our 5G facilities and demonstration site.

When we came back to my office, Benioff noticed my photo with

The author with Marc Benioff during a tour of KT's 5G facilities and contents in April 2019

Steve Jobs. He said that he also had a special relationship with Steve, and shared his story of how he started his business.

Marc Benioff first met Steve Jobs while working at Apple as an intern when he was in college. However, the first company he chose to work for after graduation was Oracle, where he went truly on a roll. He was selected "Rookie of The Year" in his first year and was promoted to Vice-President of Marketing within just three years. He stayed with Oracle for 13 years. Establishing Salesforce in a small apartment studio in San Francisco in 1999 was somewhat unexpected.

A few years after he founded his company, he showed the demo of Salesforce to Steve Jobs and asked for a piece of advice. Steve told him he needed to grow his company tenfold within two years and build an application ecosystem. In addition, the encounter with Steve Jobs inspired Benioff to create AppExchange, the industry's first business software marketplace. Three years after the meeting, Salesforce's sales reached $300 million, and its size tripled.

I had met with Marc privately twice, and we met again at the summer IBC event and realized that we had become quite good friends. I was feeling some jet lag because before heading for Davos, I had participated in the Global Entrepreneurship Summit (GES) in The Hague to deliver a keynote speech entitled "Industries of the Future: 5G, Why the Hype." The GES is organized by the US Department of State in collaboration with the host country, and is attended by global venture companies and major figures from the host nation. It is like the US version of the Davos Forum. Marc told me he listened to my speech at the GES, and asked how Secretary of State Mike Pompeo had invited me. Our conversation went on for a while as we took a great liking for each other.

I suddenly got curious and asked if his annual Dreamforce event had something related to 5G.

He then asked if I could lead the session and I replied that if my friend asked me, of course I would have to go. However, I didn't expect to participate as a panelist in an event scheduled to take place in just a few months.

Although it is not widely known in Korea, Dreamforce is the world's largest international conference, with over 170,000 participants from around the world. It is a global event with sessions fully booked within two to three days after their public announcement. Salesforce, a B2B company, takes a full year to prepare, leveraging its competencies to the maximum to attract public attention and create potential clients. As a rule, the session plans are finalized six months in advace for an event of this scale.

Marc is known as a dynamic CEO with powerful drive. He immediately took out his phone to call the person in charge of Dreamforce. And just like that, a new stage for 5G was set up for the VIP session and my itinerary for a trip to San Francisco was confirmed. That November, I led a talk about the present and future of 5G at the Yerba Buena Center for the Arts, the same place where Steve Jobs unveiled the iPad.

Dreamforce was grander and more splendid than I had expected. Marc Benioff made himself available after the event for main guests and took me on a tour of the Moscone Center. The exhibition hall had hundreds of global companies displaying their products, including Volkswagen, equipped with Salesforce's solution. It took an hour just to tour a single floor. Marc Benioff in his signature energetic style, introduced me to the CEOs of global companies.

The author listening to Marc Benioff's explanation of the exhibition after delivering the keynote speech at Dreamforce 2019.

Marc would ask them, "Do you know him?" Some answered, "He's Mr. Semiconductor" or "He's Mr. 5G."

The next time I met Marc Benioff was at the 2020 WEF in Davos. He prepared a unique, igloo-shaped exhibition hall, where he received guests from around the world. As always he happily greeted friends and showed how much he enjoyed visiting with them. He grabbed my hand

and invited me to sit with him for a meal at the head table.

His curiosity and passion for 5G was also as strong as ever. Our conversation started with his question, "How do you think 5G will advance going forward?" Although our conversation ended quickly, it was both delightful and meaningful.

Lack of experience is no longer a weakness.

Experience gives us a sense of stability. We learn what we're good or bad at through experience. This is why many say that experience is the best teacher, and I agree with that assertion to a certain extent.

However, I also believe we should go beyond the realm of experience when we talk about insight. Realizations come most often in situations one has never experienced before.

When I first met Marc Benioff, I was reminded of the time when my team completed development of the world's first 265M DRAM in 1994. I encouraged researchers by saying, "We must transform ourselves from being fast followers to first movers."

I launched the 256M DRAM development project in early 1992, even though the 64M DRAM had not yet been completed at the time.

The matter of greatest concern for companies was to bring the 64M DRAM to market, and the members of my 256M DRAM development team were mostly beginners with very little experience in semiconductors.

At the time, I never considered that we were simply in an inferior position. At any rate, we were walking a new path we had never gone down before, so I believed it was appropriate for us to take on challenges using approaches never tried before. Perhaps ambition and confidence are most brilliant for those who are not mired in preconceived ideas. Thinking like this showed that a lack of experience was no longer a weakness.

More than 70 of our top team members immersed themselves in research around the clock. The young researchers were filled with pride and passion as we pioneered a way never taken before. New approaches, new tests, and incessant challenges were all possible for them.

In April 1992, after two years of hard work, we succeeded in designing a 256M DRAM prototype, and developed the commercialized version in August. That was when my belief in them proved me right.

Meanwhile, we announced that we had completed the world's first 64M DRAM. However controversy erupted as another Korean company announced they had just developed one, and reports were circulating that Hitachi in Japan had made the same claim at the VLSI Symposium. The title of being "the world's first" was diluted in the process. On the other hand, considerable time had to pass after we announced our development of a 256M DRAM before any other chipmaker could talk about their accomplishing the same thing

We supplied samples of our 256M DRAM to Hewlett-Packard in December of that year. Immediately after that a Japanese economic newspaper wrote an article about "Samsung's development of the world's first 256M DRAM," an official acknowledgment of Korea bypassing Japan in the semiconductor field. The day we announced its development was coincidently August 29, Korea's "National Humiliation Day" (i.e., the anniversary of Korea's loss of sovereignty to Japan on August 29, 1910).

Despite such an achievement, I constantly pledged that we would "never be complacently satisfied with becoming No. 1 in DRAMs." And

A Japanese newspaper article on Samsung's development of a 256M DRAM (Jan. 26, 1995). In the article, there are words such as "winning with technologies and not price," and "surpassing Japan in semiconductors." In the photo (top right), the author is shown handing a commercial sample of the 256M DRAM to an HP executive.

I continued to press forward tirelessly on the development of new products. From DRAMs to flash memory, to fusion memory (OneNAND), and solid-state drives to mobile DRAMs, I had to continue my race to create new products as well as new markets.

"Taking on challenges is also a habit."

This is what some of my acquaintances sometimes tell me. The reason? I made "Nomad Spirit" my official slogan from the time I was a division chief. I never hesitated to take on new challenges in my position in management, and I continue to emphasize this sentiment while searching for new industries after reaching retirement age. Some are worried to see me still working so hard outside the corporate milieu. However, I am not the only one with this mindset.

The author with Marc Benioff at the 2020 World Economic Forum.

The Marc Benioff I know is a WEF board member with an excellent power of command at meetings. As a corporate leader, he has an outstanding ability to read the market. Add to this his enterprising spirit, which allowed him to leave the much talked-about the red ocean to create the blue ocean. He shares the same feelings that I have had for the last 30 years while developing business items or when switching organization to enter unknown territory. I believe that Marc Benioff, an admired CEO and innovation icon, has also reached his current position on the basis of his nomad spirit.

Awaken the nomad's way of survival, which is embedded in your heart

"Where can I find the necessary "insight" on the digital era?"

Let me answer this question by looking back on my experiences.

I like reading books—history books in particular. Admiral Yi Sun-sin, Sima Qian, and Genghis Khan are well-known figures, and I've avidly read their biographies several times. Not only did I want to remember their achievements, but also I also desired to capture the messages they left behind.

"The nomad spirit" is a precious message that I discovered in a book about Genghis Khan. When I learned history in school, the Mongol Dynasty established by Genghis Khan was labeled barbaric. However, Genghis Khan and his empire were described differently in different books that I read later on.

Nomads had horizontal and open cultures. Booty was equally distributed, while engineers were viewed highly and even appointed to office. Genghis Khan had an information-oriented mindset and was good at collecting and understanding information. He founded a multi-ethnic and multi-religious empire, but he had no difficulty in ruling because he got people to live in harmony and unity. By contrast, people in sedentary societies thought in vertical terms, were obsessed with rank, and often absorbed in bureaucracy and struggles over vested rights. This caused me to disagree with the chauvinistic claim that sedentary societies alone caused human civilization to sprout.

"Future technology should be nomadic." This sentence from a paper that was published in an academic journal in the 1980s further entrenched my beliefs. Semiconductors, IT, and other future-oriented industries must not settle for just one technology, but rather search out customer needs, then quickly make what is needed and migrate accordingly.

Creating the future with the nomad spirit

After I was promoted to president of the Memory Business Division, I more aggressively pressed for the "revival of the nomad spirit." "Mobility" and "the Spirit to Face Challenges" were what I emphasized at the worksites. We must not become complacently stuck in one place but rather be constantly changing and pursuing new things. That is because once we achieve the top spot in one area, our position will quickly disappear if we build a fortress to try and protect it and do not move on to other objectives.

"A running horse does not stop for horseshoes."

A nomad is not complacently satisfied with past accomplishments. We can learn much from our experience, but we cannot go forward by lingering there. This is even more the case in the digital era. Insights based on the past will inevitably become invalid in short order. Our insights for the future must be constantly upgraded as we look ahead and transform ourselves.

I am often amazed working with young people. When I share my vision and ask them to work in harmony, most of them make astonishing results beyond expectation. The results are not directly proportional to their abilities but rather depend upon how much they face challenges with open-mindedness. Everything becomes possible when we awaken the nomad's way of survival that is dormant in our hearts. Being flexible, having little to lose, being receptive to new things, quickly understanding information, and listening to others carefully—these are traits of young people. To this list the nomad business strategy is complemented with a proper mix of offering a vision, being very quick, sharing returns, actively communicating, being information-oriented, using strategies from *baduk* (game of Go or a board game in which two players seek to surround the most territory with "stones"), and having the desire for new technologies.

Digital nomads will play a more active role in the future. As someone who has been working in the field for more than 30 years with the nomad spirit, I can say for sure that boundless territory remains that we can dominate in the new world referred to as digital. As the value of experience decreases, don't lament over your limitations. Instead you must advance with the "nomad spirit."

04 When things get tough, focus on what you're good at

| **George M. Whitesides** |

There are always two sides to everything; pros come with cons, and gains are attended by losses..

The same is true when it comes to taking on new challenges. Just when things are going well and the road ahead holds only the promise of excitement, "fear" raises its ugly head. More than a few "challengers" who stood on the starting line have experienced this ambivalence.

The most commonly heard advice for challengers comes in the form of phrases like "stay positive," or "just do your best." Sometimes though, it helps to get advice that's a little more concrete.

"Focus on what you're good at."

Not only people, but technologies too are good at certain things and not so good at others. In the case of a machine that contains technology, the proper approach is to remedy its weaknesses so that its full capabilities are revealed. Human beings, however, need simply to focus on what they are good at rather than cling to something they cannot do. A challenger should not adopt the half-baked attitude that "I'll just work on my weak points and give it my best."

Instead, a challenger needs the will to say, "I'll use my strengths and get good results." Furthermore, the challenger must sharpen his or her abilities to a fine point, until they become a spearhead that can pierce through fear.

Do your best as the pursuer today to come out ahead tomorrow

The larger an organization is and the farther you go down the organizational ladder, the fewer the decisions that can be made.

When I took my first step as head of the device development team at Samsung Electronics, my first task was to fuse myself with the existing organization. Since I had turned down the secure executive position they offered me, and joined the company as the head of research, I was determined to get along well with the staff and put down roots in the organization.

But at the same time, I had another more personal goal, and that was to turn the organization I was now a part of into a world-class company. Japan in those days had many engineers who possessed expert knowledge on top of a strong artisanal spirit, while in the US, horizontal organization and free discussion enabled technological synergy.

By comparison, Korea was not only lagging behind technologically; our engineers tended to get stuck in a corner with the technologies they were given. Technological development and organizational change—it was now my goal and main ambition to catch these two rabbits at the same time.

However, so soon after my appointment as a mere team leader, there wasn't much I could do.

In reality though, the power of inertia was extraordinary. In a meeting with the president and executive staff members, I frankly voiced my opinion that we should have a discussion with the heads of other departments and hear their views, but bringing about change so quickly would not be easy. It is essential particularly with big projects to cooperate and communicate among departments, but my hands were tied by the rigid organizational culture.

I was troubled due to the disconnect between my ambitions and reality. "What is the most effective resource that I have?"

What researchers felt they lacked and desired was information on the technological trends and strategies of their top competitors. As a researcher, I had a high level of competence in learning advanced technologies and the ability to actively network with many engineers. The fact that I often visited Japanese semiconductor companies while working at Stanford University and still maintained good relations with them was an invisible asset I possessed. Moreover, I had been regularly publishing journal articles and building relationships with overseas researchers..

In 1990, one year after I joined the company, I wrote a letter to a number of overseas semiconductor companies and conference representatives. First, I proposed a "Technology Exchange Meeting" to Japanese companies. Because of its geographical proximity to Korea and strong technological foundation, Japan was the best target for benchmarking. To the

Stanford University campus (Source: Wikipedia).

Japanese, however, Samsung Electronics was a weak presence as it only ranked tenth in the semiconductor industry. The top two players, No. 1 NEC and No. 2 Hitachi, did not really welcome this idea, saying that there was not enough "room" to share.

I then mobilized the connections I had built up at Stanford and Intel. As a senior researcher at Stanford University, Japanese companies had approached me for industry-academia collaboration. The relationships I formed with them turned out to be of great help.

"Samsung Electronics has only just entered the market from a technology standpoint; however, they have a surplus of vitality in their young, excellent workforce and they are also boldly investing in technology."

To begin with, it was important that I pique their curiosity and show there was indeed room for exchange. As soon as the Japanese companies started showing interest, I proffered once again that technology exchange could provide fresh stimulation for them. Due to my persistent overtures, the Japanese eventually agreed to meet.

On the one hand, while we were out searching for companies to benchmark, our researchers were working hard internally to strengthen their basic skills. At first, I suggested holding relaxed weekly meetings to study the latest technology trends. However, the process of compiling recently published academic papers, conjecturing, and discussing them was too intense to be called "studying." It was tiring, but these technology discussions, which often stretched into the wee hours, soon proved effective. Gradually, the researchers' perspective started to broaden, and they began to open up more towards each other.

I flew to Japan with a group of researchers who now had a greater thirst for technology. We began technology exchanges with the Hitachi Central Research Laboratory starting from 1990.

Our researchers were astonished in the meetings which lasted all day and covered a variety of areas. Japan's technological prowess was formidable.

After the meetings, researchers from both countries got together for din-

The Hitachi Central Research Laboratory in Kokubunji-shi.

ners that went late into the night. And even after returning to our accommodations, we didn't want to waste time sleeping. We pulled all-nighters going over what had been discussed that day. For these Samsung Electronics researchers, who had just jumped into semiconductor development for the first time, the notebooks they filled up were great stimulation. Thanks to their ceaseless efforts in benchmarking Japan's advanced technology, we were able to quickly close the technology gap. These technology exchange meetings with Japanese companies continued for ten years.

Incidentally, these semiconductor technology exchanges were the first such meetings that Samsung Electronics ever held with a leading competitor.

For me, the meetings served as one of two wheels that accelerated our catching-up process. The other wheel was our participation in international conferences. I encouraged our researchers to submit articles to the world's three main semiconductor conferences, the International Electron Devices Meeting (IEDM), the International Solid-State Circuits Conference (ISSCC), and the Symposium on Very Large-Scale Integration (VLSI). The door was opened for us in earnest when I was named as a committee member for the VLSI and IEMD.

In 1990, at the VLSI held in Japan, I met Lewis Terman who was then with IBM and was also the chairman of the IEEE, the world's largest professional association of electrical and electronics engineers. I had known him since we first met at Stanford University. I expressed my interest in becoming a judge at the VLSI and he asked me to first send my resume. I included in it the title of my journal article that had won 2nd place at the VLSI, and ten other titles that I had published in *IEEE*

Transaction on Electron Devices and *IEEE Transaction on Electron Devices Letters*. I was selected to serve as a judge in 1991 following a review by the board of directors.

At the time, the VLSI conferences were held alternatingly in the US and Japan in accordance with the semiconductor agreement between the two countries. The panel was also composed of 15 judges from the US and 15 from Japan. However, Japan had absolute superiority in the semiconductor industry as demonstrated by its advanced technology, the enormous number of papers published by six Japanese companies (Hitachi, Toshiba, NEC, Mitsubishi, Fujitsu, Matsushita), and its dominance of the semiconductor market. Naturally, the examination process was conducted in Japanese since the VLSI was being held in Japan.

As a committee member, I suggested changing the official language to English for fairness in the examination process. In the name of the judging committee it was also decided to use "US and Far East Asia" instead of "US-Japan.".

Back then, the Japanese members of the judging committee were less than fluent in English. By thoroughly reviewing the submitted theses beforehand and uncovering their key points, I was able to ask questions about them in English which helped me to lead the conference. Doing so instantly reinvigorated the atmosphere of the committee meetings. As committee members, we were expected to thoroughly review about 100 academic papers two months prior to the final judging. For me, it was a good chance to study and learn new information on advanced semiconductor technology.

I pushed our company's researchers to actively participate in the article review process. It provided an opportunity for them to gain an international perspective and learn relevant knowledge. I helped the researchers who were inspired by this process in preparing their own academic papers. My colleagues and I used to board airplanes carrying bags full of academic papers.

While the two wheels of technological exchange and conference participation turned, new winds of change were stirring within the organization. An atmosphere of discussion and collaboration began to set in. Once a topic was provided, researchers and regular employees alike would jump in to discuss it regardless of their job titles.

We were able to make rapid progress on the challenges we took on because we started with areas that we were already good at. It did not take long to see results.

In 1994, we started our first project and succeeded in developing the world's first 256M DRAM, and it only took two and a half years. It was a great achievement that beat out the leading semiconductor companies in Japan and the US by a full year. In the process, Samsung Electronics filed 129 patent applications with 49 of them being filed internationally. It represented the first time that the pursuer became the frontrunner and holder of the most advanced technology.

At international conferences up until that time, IBM, Intel, and NEC were the leaders and had the best technology. In only a few years however, Samsung Electronics became the technology leader at the international conferences.

Among researchers, presenting a thesis at an international conference meant an opportunity for patent sales. The most authoritative conferences in the industry were battlegrounds of fierce technological competition among the top semiconductor companies. Participating in these conferences played a significant role in Samsung's technological leadership.

Doing better in what you are already good at is better than innovation

Looking back, I believe that I have learned a lot from experience. It took me a long time to absorb the words "focus on what you are good at" as truth. For this reason, I believe there is a better person whom I can use to explain this idea.

That person, Professor George Whitesides of Harvard University, reminded me to focus on what I was already good at during the most confusing and difficult time in my life.

Earlier, I mentioned that I had traveled around meeting scholars overseas after resigning from being the president of the Samsung Advanced Institute of Technology in 2009. My pilgrimage in search of a future direction of work began in May.

Prof. George Whitesides is someone who truly deserves the title of University Professor, which in 2004 had only been given to three other Harvard professors. At Harvard University, they have a unique title known as University Professor, which is not used by other universities. This honor is only bestowed on professors who have been recognized for their wide-ranging contributions in research and other work.

Professor George Whitesides specializes in chemistry, but he owns around 50 patents in various fields including biology, materials engineering, and chemistry. In addition, he has unique, real-world business experience as a

The author in a discussion with Professor George Whitesides at the Global R&D Forum in 2011.

co-founder of 12 companies related to his areas of specialty, with a combined market capitalization of $20 billion. He worked as a technology advisor for the Obama administration and was later on scientific advisory boards in India and Taiwan.

According to a description from Professor Hongkun Park of the Department of Chemistry and Chemical Biology at Harvard University, Professor Whitesides was viewed as humble and easy-going despite his stature and reputation. Having seen the professor, who was then over 70, actively engage with much younger professors in their 40s, I could completely agree with Professor Park's description of him.

In our first encounter, Prof. Whitesides talked about the nanotechnology and biotechnology industries as an expert in both fields. In particular, he had unique insight on commercialization of the latest technologies.

"If you are targeting the billion-plus population Indian market, try developing a low-cost health diagnostic kit that can be used by a country with a population of 300 million."

His argument was that countries lacking medical professionals should be supplied with technologies that enable remote diagnosis and treatment through simple tests. He was always full of practical and realistic solutions.

After returning to my hotel room, I wrote a long report on the professor's proposals for new sectors including water resources, CO_2 preservation, energy, and healthcare. I still have the materials from that day and keep them as precious mementos.

I contacted Prof. Whitesides right after accepting the job offer as Korea's National CTO.

At the time it was well known that I put a great effort into recruiting a team of international scholars for a national advisory group. While organizing the group, which comprised eight individuals from abroad and nine from Korea divided into five subcommittees, I struggled over whom I should choose as chairperson. That's when I thought of Prof. Whitesides. The advisory group was made up of outstanding scholars in their respective fields, including two Nobel laureates. However, I had particularly high expectation for the chair. I needed someone with deep understanding of academia and the real world, and who also had the experience to predict the future of Korean industry.

Despite his busy schedule, Prof. Whitesides responded that he would like to contribute his time and energy for Korea's future development. Later in June 2011, he volunteered to be a keynote speaker at the Global R&D Forum together with Professor Hermann Simon of Germany.

The author and Professor George Whitesides at the Global R&D Forum in 2011, trying out a blow mouse connected to a Galaxy tablet for people with disabilities.

My second encounter with Prof. Whitesides was well before June 2011. I had visited his lab again, in November 2010, as I experienced a sense of urgency after becoming the National CTO. I went there to interview him on his insights into Korea's future business prospects.

While on a tour of advanced R&D facilities in the US, I was able to obtain a lot of information on the latest innovations in areas such as smart cars, novel drugs from natural substances, the energy industry, and solar cells. It all looked like gleaming jewelry to me. I was more than eager to adopt new technologies and ideas for Korean businesses, to find promising areas in which they could perhaps become future market leaders.

I asked the professor how each of these technologies could be developed in Korea. His answer was simple:

"Instead of searching for areas that have large growth potential, look for the areas that Korea is already good at."

His advice meant we could achieve better results by focusing on areas in which we excel at rather than by looking for something in areas completely unfamiliar to us.

"Korea possesses such advantages as outstanding technologies, investment capacity, infrastructure, and highly educated human resources. At the same time, your country has difficulty in innovating well. I believe it is wise to focus on things that Korea can do well."

What he pointed out was not wrong, given Korea's situation. I, too, knew that Korea's strength was in applied technologies rather than in innovative basic technologies.

Various factors are at play for technology to be applied successfully to a business. The roles that culture and capital play are just as important as technological expertise. In the US, many businesses have been created within a system affiliated with universities. A prime example would be Silicon Valley, which is supported by excellent human resources and technologies from neighboring universities. In addition, venture capital investments flow smoothly. Japan also utilizes trained personnel to create quality-driven competitiveness. What about Korea? Korea has a large number of highly skilled workers who can learn fast and make good products.

Innovation is a process of creating remarkable outcomes, but it is not something that can be achieved through a single factor. I have emphasized convergence since the early days of the IT industry. However, convergence necessitates two or more technologies that have already reached a considerable level of advancement.

"You cannot build smart vehicles just because you are good at telecommunication services and automobile manufacturing. You need technologies for built-in components and controls for the overall traffic system. There are industries that Korea excels in. You need to converge these industries and first seek possibilities in the major areas."

Everything Prof. Whitesides said is correct. I arrived at the conclusion that we must create a new industrial catalyst by integrating information technologies into industries where Korea does well such as the automotive, shipbuilding, semiconductor, and telecommunications sectors. With this, I could finally string disparate pieces of the puzzle together such as K-MEG, and graphene, and start to zero in on the target.

Some people may think that anybody could say the things that Prof. Whitesides had suggested. However, anyone who has tried to take on a challenge directly would know the true value of his words.

You don't have to be special to do things others are doing or things that take much money to accomplish. However, this is merely a struggle over who will come in second or third place. The most efficient innovation takes things already being done well to a still higher level. For this reason, challenges must begin with what you are good at as business gets more difficult and the business climate worsens. Starting from where Korea excels was also the right step for Korea's future.

Believe in possibility and potential, and exceed the limits you've set for yourself

While serving as the National CTO, I considered my basic framework to be that all industries must ultimately converge around IT so they can generate the means to drive future growth. Thus I inevitably became interested in the telecommunications industry with its IT-based infrastructure. I embarked on the "new challenge" everyone knows about after my three years as the National CTO. This challenge meant two things to me:

First, I wanted to replicate in telecommunications services, a major sector serving the general public, the same kind of global success experienced by the semiconductor industry, which is a business selling to corporate clients. Semiconductors and telecommunications are both related to IT, but they target different customers. I believed expanding my B2B experience into B2C would be an important challenge and experience for me.

Second, I wanted to achieve outcomes by applying Smartopia, which I had promoted during my tenure as National CTO, in the real world. Smartopia was an important plan for converging telecommunications services with other industries to provide Korea with the impetus for future economic growth. I eagerly wanted to keep this project going through achievements in the field.

However, in reality, it was an arduous journey that everyone, including myself, realized was full of difficult and challenging tasks.

"Please create a company that allows us to ponder what we able to accomplish."

"I want to build an attractive company that I can recommend to my family, friends, relatives, and juniors."

Make it so I can tell my children to "please study hard and then join an excellent company like KT."

I started working at KT and then spent many a sleepless night after reading comments like these posted on the company website.

In hindsight, my body felt tired when I worked as the National CTO, but I was never heavy-hearted. Even though it was a very important job, the more I worked, the more I felt that the future was unfolding in front of my eyes.

However, being the head of KT was different. I had more than 60,000 employees relying on me around the country. The first month after my appointment was the time when I was supposed to put the organization in good order, yet we were hit by a series of bad news. The public gave us the cold shoulder, and we suffered our first revenue deficit in the company's history. Employee morale plummeted. As expected, the advice that I needed at the time was, "Focus on what you're good at."

"We must examine whether we are overlooking known problems in the name of customary practice, doing work solely for appearance's sake, or neglecting customer needs with stopgap measures and departmental self-centeredness. We need to fundamentally change our attitudes and ways of working. If we, as individuals, fail to recognize our mistakes and work on areas of improvement, these kinds of actions will persist."

"There is nowhere to hide any more. In our present state, one more mistake could mean we have no future. Now is the time to become resolutely determined and take on innovation. Let me say this clearly: no more will we tolerate words without responsibility, planning without execution, willful negligence, and slipshod work because that is how it has always been done."

"KT is a national company that held the top market position for a long time. Let's take pride and be confident as KT employees, and let's achieve the highest performance in our field. Let's bring our passion together and make KT No. 1."

I sent out this memo, which resembled a declaration of war, to all the employees and then started to address tasks that required attention inside and outside the company.

KT was a company that had clear strengths. However, instead of focusing on its strengths, the company's business was expanded recklessly to the extent that the strengths were no longer strengths. A classic example of this was the strategy to "get away from telecommunications and expand aggressively." At the time of my appointment, KT had 53 affiliates. First, I cleared away the affiliates that performed poorly or were experiencing capital erosion. Then, I provided support for telecommunication services, our mainstay business, and aggressively nurtured it by establishing new affiliates or incorporating outside units into the group to cover areas that could elevate the group's overall competencies.

Next, I informed everyone inside and outside the company in no uncertain terms the directions in which we were heading. In May 2014, I announced our corporate vision to be "Global No. 1," laying out GiGAtopia to the world.

The important thing for us to accomplish was to regain our leadership position in telecommunications services, our area of strength. In addition, our aim was to become the top in the global market, something beyond our known world. To this end, we had to awaken internally our "No. 1 DNA," i.e. our potential for reaching the top spot.

Up to that point, the market for Korean telecommunications service operators was restricted to the domestic arena. Companies would get what they paid for in the contest over speed as 3G and 4G technologies came out. This fostered a widespread belief that "there was nothing new anymore." Competition intensified by the day, and people in the field were complaining loudly about how tough things were. Looking at the big picture, however, we were unable to free ourselves from our myopic point of view. No matter how excellent the technologies we developed or improved upon became, we lacked the will to deploy them. So they usually wound up being buried away or crammed into a laboratory file.

"KT is a company that maintained the top market position for ten to twenty years. How much R&D had been done? So let's go find something new among the things that we can do well."

As far as I know, KT's R&D was definitely the best in the country. The company's strengths were a long technological history and tradition as well as a talented workforce. If these areas were cultivated well, we could set our eyes on becoming the global No. 1. That was the hope I had.

I frequently visited the research center in Umyeon-dong. I shared opinions in meetings with engineers who put their heads together. Nothing we discussed was trivial. The researchers, who were shy and hesitant at first, started to speak forthrightly. I listened carefully and spoke sparingly, resulting in discussions that were both productive and creative. And there, a new future was created for KT. Complex technologies that became the standard for the world's first commercialized 5G, a mobile phone security platform, an AI speaker with voice recognition function (GiGA Genie), an energy management platform, and a global epidemic prevention platform (GEPP) were introduced to the world.

People think innovation is limited to shifting from existing paradigms. However, based on my experience, that is only a half of innovation. The other half is trusting the possibility and potential within ourselves.

Both individuals and organizations are aware of the things they are good at to some extent. However, a limit is also created insofar as it is difficult to get even better at something we're already good at. Innovation is achieved when we go beyond our limits, and this is only possible when we believe in the possibility and the potential within ourselves.

The start of KT's quantum leap was "focusing on what we're already good at." First, we achieved innovation in telecommunication services. The next step was to put effort into "doing better in areas where we already excel." This was the process of converging telecommunications, television, artificial intelligence, and security. This was made possible because everyone went beyond their limits.

Nothing is easy, but it is not as hard as you think

A few years ago, I heard that Prof. Whitesides wrote a tribute in *Science* magazine. It piqued my interest, and I read it. The tribute was to John Roberts, an honorary professor at the California Institute of Technology. This is the summary of Prof. Whitesides' message:

I did my post-graduate study in John Roberts' lab in 1960s, and writing a thesis in that environment was quite a quandary. Although the lab was liberal in everyday practice, Professor John Roberts' lectures on writing were quite strict. He would cover theses written by graduate students with red ink, and return them. This process seemed to go on forever.

Prof. Whitesides is a guru in his 80s with unique insights. Reading about his struggles in writing and finishing a thesis in his younger days brought a smile to my face.

Some people may smile after hearing my inside story. Whenever I was on a business trip, I often got complaints like, "I could not sleep because of you." But I had my own reasons for doing what I did.

The first time I came to the US, I was a postgraduate student. And since I was working on my PhD degree, English still felt like a completely foreign language to me. To speak English naturally, I had to just try to speak as much as I could. I kept trying to read aloud, but fighting sleep was not easy, so I could not do it while sitting down. I still tend to walk around as I read the materials aloud over and over again, but, in most cases, I am not the only one in the room. My colleagues who were on the business trip with me said it was torturous. Listening to me read the English script out loud, on top of having to hear my footsteps, would have made it truly difficult for others to sleep.

I know someone else who is crazy when it comes to practice. Park Yong-hwan, then the head of Samsung's US subsidiary, once told me about his encounter with Steve Jobs. Steve had arrived at the Moscone Center to announce the release of Apple's latest product. According to the story, he did not go straight to the parking garage, but stopped his car outside the first floor lobby. He urgently called an Apple employee. He was looking for someone to park his car for him, so he could go and practice for the presentation. This was not a case of using power to boss people around. Instead he ditched his car in order to get in just a few more minutes or seconds to practice. I heard through multiple channels this account of Steve Job's practicing to make a presentation in front of executives.

Just like what everyone says—nothing is easy. Doing better than others in something that you're not good at is hard. But doing better in something you're already good at is also extremely challenging.

Surprisingly, when we're at the finish line, we find ourselves saying, "It was not as hard as I thought it would be." Many people I've met have also said that. People who experienced successes both large and small, and even the Norwegian explorer Erling Kagge, the first man complete a solo expedition to the South Pole, said the same thing.

Young people in this modern world say every day is a challenge. Then, how about for once try believing the words left by those who have walked a difficult path before? It is a matter of finding something that you're good at and then giving it one last go. At the end of the challenge, you will find yourself saying, "It was not as hard as I thought."

Declaration of Hwang's Law

Hwang's Law Declaration Timeline

1998	Organized the Flash Research Forum with Samsung Electronics' Wireless, Video, and Home Appliance Business Divisions
2000	Upgraded the meeting for flash application synergy to a regular meeting with the Wireless, Video, Home Appliance, and Semiconductor Business Divisions
2001	Organized several development teams (for 1G, 2G NAND flash) Attended the Zakuro Meeting organized by the Chairman (to refuse Toshiba's joint venture proposal)
Feb. 2002	Publicly declared Hwang's Law (New Memory Growth Model)
Apr. 2002	Met the presidents of electronics-related affiliates (reported on the future of flash memory) Collaborated with Nokia (expanded the supply volume for NOR flash; transitioned to OneNAND)
2003	Launched the Future Technology Team (CTF technology, etc.)
2004	Enabled Apple products (iPod Nano, iPhone, iMac) to switch from hard drive to solid state (flash memory) drive Expanded global marketing for flash memory by holding the SMSF in Taiwan (for six years)
2005-2006	Selected by IEDM as the best paper on CTF technology
2006	Developed world's first 32G CTF NAND flash with 40nm design rule
2007	Developed world's first 64G CTF NAND flash (24 layers) with 30nm design rule
2019	Started mass production of 128-layer CTF
2020	Developed 172 (176)-layer CTF

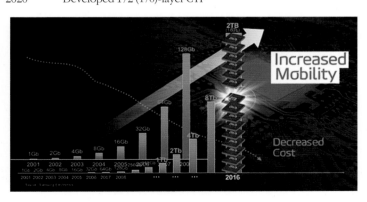

Comparison of Hwang's Law and Moore's Law

	Moore's Law	Hwang's Law
Made public	1965 Paper in *Electronics* magazine	2002 Keynote speech at the ISSCC
Main Content	The number of transistors in an integrated circuit doubled every 18 months for 10 years until 1975; revised to double every 24 months after 1975. PCs play the main role.	Semiconductor memory capacity doubles every year. Mobile devices and digital appliances play the main role.
Grounds for prediction	Predicting the 10-year exponential growth was based on the development trend from 1958, when the integrated circuit was first developed, to 1965.	Predicting the increase of memory capacity following the increase of memory demand after third generation communications was based on the simulation of future memory capacity of mobile devices; the theory has remained valid until the present, and is expected to work for at least 10 more years with 5G commercialization.
Substantiation and Modification	Proven through Intel's microprocessor technology: The period of application was longer than the initially suggested period, while controversy remains over technological limitations. The exponential development speed gradually slowed down with the advancement of technology: from doubling in 12 months, to doubling in 18 months, to doubling in 24 months.	Proven through the NAND flash development: 512M in 2000, 1G in 2001, 2G in 2002, 4G in 2003, 8G in 2004, 16G in 2005, 32G in 2006, and 64G in 2007. Application of the CTF technology in 2010, which led to the development of the 24-layer, and the 172 (176)-layer in 2020; continuous development is anticipated. The theory is predicted to remain valid with new applied fields, markets, and technological breakthroughs.
Application	PC-centered (specific devices) CPU processing speed	Mobile and digital consumer products (various devices) Memory capacity
Driving Force of Innovation	Technological innovation	Market demand and technological innovation in various fields (3D, new materials design) that support its market demand
Strategy	**Technology Push**	**Market Pull**

Passion

Chapter
3

Secure the
Best Weapons
to Win

01

Late movers have to be different

| **Exchange Meetings & Study Groups** |

People always seek to be No. 1, which is a source of distress for the late mover. The ones who jump into the business late are weaker than the ones already out in front, and resources are lacking, causing tremendous frustration.

Whether I was working for Samsung Electronics, as the National CTO, or at Korea Telecom, I never had a team that started out in front. Moreover, the leaders were always way out ahead of us. I had to start from behind, or try to lead a team that was already at the rear of the pack. So, I had no choice but to work harder.

Fortunately, I always had great colleagues. Whenever I insisted that we needed to take over the lead, they would put their trust in me and start running as fast as they could go.

"Technical Exchange Meetings, the Flash Research Forum, the Samsung Mobile Solutions Forum, the Medici Research Society, and the Gwanghwamun Forum."

I met many fine teachers and colleagues through these five gatherings, and to this day, I still get together with some of them from time to time.

Perhaps they worked even harder than I did to create new products, realize innovation and greater value, and develop new markets. Thanks to them, the organizations I led were able to proudly announce their presence by surpassing the market leaders when it was not thought possible.

I still remember those days of struggle as a late mover and can recall the faces of the people who worked with me.

Proving yourself

In February 2002, I was invited to be a keynote speaker at the International Solid-State Circuits Conference (ISSCC), which is held annually at the San Francisco Marriott Hotel. The ISSCC is also known as the "Semiconductor Olympics," as it is the largest conference in the semiconductor industry. The event is attended by more than 4,000 experts in related industries, including CEOs and CTOs.

"The semiconductor industry in the future will steer away from dependence on the PC market and develop around mobile and digital devices. In doing so, semiconductor memory capacity will double every year, exceeding the speed at which the integration level increases according to Moore's Law."

I had just announced the "New Memory Growth Model," also known as "Hwang's Law." As I came down from the podium after delivering my keynote speech which lasted about 40 minutes, I greeted two acquaintances. The first was Robert Dutton, one of my professors at Stanford University.

The author explaining the New Memory Growth Model, a.k.a "Hwang's Law."

From his seat in the front row where he had been listening attentively, he gave me a thumbs-up sign and stretched his arms out towards me.

He had a profound expression on his face, as if to say, "Did you really just say that?" His bewilderment was no surprise considering that half the audience was doubtful of the New Memory Growth Model.

The other acquaintance was Jensen Huang, a Taiwanese-American who is the founder and CEO of Nvidia Corporation. Instead of only making eye contact, he ran up as I made my way down from the podium and greeted me excitedly.

"Dr. Hwang, that was great!"

His greeting helped to relieve the built up tension I was feeling.

And then jokingly, he added, "It's nice to meet another Huang (Hwang)."

After earning his master's degree in Electrical Engineering from Stanford University in 1992, Jensen Huang went on to become a skilled engineer in charge of designing CPUs at two semiconductor companies, LSI Logic and Advanced Micro Devices. In 1993, he co-founded Nvidia, the world's first company specializing in graphics processing units (GPUs), and began building a reputation with the successful release of a GPU called the "NV3" (RIVA 128).

Down from the podium, I had gained confidence in my thinking that, "if my theory convinced Jensen Huang, a leader in the semiconductor industry, it won't be hard to turn my theory into reality."

I remember Jensen as someone who always greeted people warmly and with a big, hearty laugh. I had frequent encounters with him because he was both a CEO and CTO. He would always greet me with somewhat exaggerated gestures every time we met. Even the time I met him as a client after the ISSCC, he yelled out "Dr. Hwang" loud enough for everyone around to hear him, and walked up to me with his arms wide open. Big hugs were always a part of every meeting between us.

As time passed and Hwang's Law became an established theory, Jensen and I would talk about the ISSCC each time we saw each other.

"Thanks to your announcing the New Memory Growth Model, Dr. Hwang, my company was prepared for the memory chip era and was able to enjoy a lot of success."

While expressing confidence in his company, Jensen also showed his appreciation for my work. It is no exaggeration to say that Nvidia, Jensen's company, has been the greatest beneficiary of the mobile era. The market grew about tenfold as gamers moved from PCs to mobile devices.

Nvidia's achievements as a leading GPU manufacturer grew by the day, and Jensen would often ask me about the future of graphics and gaming devices while always paying close attention to my opinion.

My encounters with Jensen continued when I happened to see him again at the 2017 Mobile World Congress (MWC) in Barcelona. It was right after the declaration of 5G. Nvidia was set to take another quantum leap with its graphics chips, which are used in GPS navigation of autonomous vehicles. The fact that 5G would now accelerate the commercialization of autonomous vehicles represented a great opportunity for Nvidia. Needless to say, Jensen was more than delighted to hear the declaration of 5G at the MWC.

Looking back, it may seem meaningless whether one is a first mover or a late mover in a market. Jensen Huang established Nvidia when the concept of the GPU was unknown to the world. Obviously, his company was a first mover. Early on, however, the primary and secondary versions of the company's products were not successful because they were ahead of their time. Nevertheless, by getting into the market early and being prepared for gaming and other future business, Nvidia turned out to be a top performer in the GPU sector.

Samsung Electronics, as everyone knows, was a late mover in semiconductors. Nationally, Korea entered the industry 30 years after the US and Japan. But only ten years or so after jumping into the semiconductor business, Samsung became an industry leader that could not be ignored. Moreover, now that the first movers and late mover are all rubbing elbows at the top of the industry, judging by the results, they look pretty much similar.

If I had to choose between being a first mover who is way ahead of the pack and being a second mover who got off to a late start, I'd say that I prefer to avoid the "sorrow of the second mover."

When I was readying my speech for the ISSCC, the semiconductor market, specifically the memory market, was in the doldrums. In fact, the situation was so bad as to be called the "worst-ever semiconductor recession." Some even referred to it as the "decline of the memory industry." Among those who knew the content of my speech before I delivered it at the conference were people who had quietly warned me that, "this could be construed as a fanciful assertion that may end up having international consequences." The word "sorrow" is insufficient to describe how I felt as I pushed through that process.

This was also true in business. As a late mover, I was constantly proving myself every step of the way, and especially when I met with first movers in the market. I had to work much harder than the first movers to persuade them and be fairly recognized as a market player. In addition, if I had been alone on that path, I never would have attempted any of it, and I cannot forget the faces of my colleagues who shared those difficult times with me.

Surpassing "Japan as No. 1"

Even today, 18 years later in 2020, the New Memory Growth Model is still dominating the market. Moreover, the same confidence with which I told a group of students during a special lecture at Harvard in 2016 that the New Memory Growth Model was still in effect is still with me today, two decades after my speech at the ISSCC.

It was also immensely helpful to have my New Memory Growth Model reviewed by my colleagues from the Technical Exchange Meetings and the Flash Research Forum, who had been working with me for about a decade before and after my announcement of the theory. Starting out in the 1980s as a late mover in the semiconductor industry, we all struggled together until we became a first mover. We were all in the same boat.

As I mentioned earlier, the Technical Exchange Meetings (TEMs) were Samsung Electronics' first attempt at benchmarking. By the time I arrived there, a great deal of interest and investment was already being poured into semiconductors at the group level. However, the situation then at Samsung Electronics by global standards was severely inadequate. Although they had secured the interest, the investment, and a talented workforce, they were putting little effort into learning about global semiconductor trends and technologies. No one had considered reaching out to the leading manufacturers in Japan and the US, and little thought was given to the idea of benchmarking their technology.

Of course, this was not a problem unique to Samsung Electronics. Basically all companies were competing against each other. For this reason, "exchange" and "cooperation" were only possible when both companies had something to offer the other. There is an anecdote that in 1980, Samsung founder Lee Byung-chull requested cooperation in semiconductors from NEC Chairman Kobayashi Kōji, with whom he had a good relationship. Yet he was rejected. A first mover has no reason to waste time and energy helping a late mover.

Considering these unfavorable conditions, I used my personal network and contacted some Japanese companies. I picked out several doctoral-level researchers from within our organization and formed a team. The researchers were dumbfounded at the thought of interacting with a Japanese company.

"Dr. Hwang, how could you possibly know people working for NEC and Toshiba?"

Back then, the word "international" was more commonly used than the term "global." To researchers in Korea, the concept of a "global network" was still unfamiliar.

They listened with great interest to my stories about the exchanges I had with Japanese semiconductor companies while under Prof. Robert Dutton at Stanford University.

In those days, it was typical for the Japanese, who had the No. 1 semiconductor company with the highest competitiveness, to present papers at the ISSCC, the world's most authoritative conference on electronics, held annually in San Francisco, and then tour Silicon Valley. They also enjoyed attending seminars at Stanford University, which is the mecca of Silicon Valley. This was only natural because William Shockley, the inventor of the semiconductor, was still at Stanford University at that time.

Prof. Dutton, my professor, was the favorite semiconductor expert of the Japanese companies and they often called him on the phone at his lab. It was through these personal connections that everything started. Right before I came to Samsung Electronics, I visited Japanese chipmakers for two weeks at the recommendation of Prof. Dutton. I met with CTOs and research fellows who were referred to as chief engineers because they possessed the most advanced technology in their respective fields, and it was because of them that I was able to launch the TEM.

In the early stages when our sales were poor, we had TEMs with all six of the Japanese companies I had contacted: Hitachi, Toshiba, NEC, Mitsubishi, Fujitsu, and Matsushita. Every quarter, a team of seven or eight of our researchers visited one of these companies. Their favorite company to visit was Hitachi.

The Hitachi Central Research Laboratory is located in Kokubunji, a quiet city about 30 minutes by subway from Shinjuku Station in Tokyo. On our first visit, our researchers were all surprised at the dignified appearance of the laboratory, which is surrounded by a dense forest of old trees. Once there, we were introduced to the laboratory's founding philosophy since its establishment in 1942, which is "Creating New Technologies for the Coming 10 to 20 Years."

Hitachi's reputation in Japan was such that people would often say, "If the US has IBM, Japan has Hitachi." "Hitachi technology" is another phrase that is still commonly heard today.

One day, we were getting ready to leave after the second or third session of exchange meetings at the Hitachi Central Research Laboratory, and the laboratory's assistant director proposed that he show us the R&D development line for 64M DRAM, which they had announced at the VLSI Symposium in May 1992.

I was invited along with seven or eight of our researchers to go and see their fabrication ("fab") facility firsthand. The fab was in a special security zone and access was restricted. Upon entering we could easily see part of the development equipment and the layout inside the facility. We were also sufficiently experienced by that time that we were able to absorb something we had seen. At the same time, after viewing the advanced research facility we were also emotionally affected enough to say to ourselves, "We have just had the luxury of peering into the R&D facility with state-of-the-art technology." Lee Yoon-woo, the Managing Director at that time of the Samsung Electronics Semiconductor R&D Center, was keenly interested in the TEM and supported us in various ways. In March 1992, Samsung Electronics President Kim Gwang-ho and Managing Director Lee Yun-woo instructed me to organize a team to develop the 256M DRAM.

As the development began, the major players in the industry had already joined forces. A joint venture was formed in 1992 among Toshiba, the largest memory company in Japan; IBM of the US, the company recognized as the world's top computer company and as having the most advanced semiconductor technology; and Siemens, a German company representing the best of European technology. This event coincided with my organizing the 256M DRAM Task Force. Subsequently, Hitachi and Texas Instruments in the US also formed a partnership.

There were three major advantages that these allied forces had gained. First, they could now cooperate to overcome technological barriers. The technological barrier to design at the 0.25-micron level was quite high.

Next, they were splitting up the massive R&D investment required to develop the 256M DRAM. An astronomical amount of investment was needed as the development of 256M DRAM would have to be preceded by the development of expensive equipment. There was also less work for each member of these allied forces since they were dividing the labor.

Finally, they could now hold Samsung Electronics in check, as we were now rising to prominence in the semiconductor arena. In 1992, Samsung Electronics was ranked No. 1 in DRAMs, and in 1993, we took first place in the memory sector. Under such circumstances, Samsung needed a powerful spear to penetrate the siege strategy of our global competitors.

Only a few years after starting the TEM, I began serving on the committees of the VLSI Symposium and the IEDM. Furthermore, I shared hundreds of papers that were submitted to both conferences with our researchers and had them study these papers thoroughly. I also began in earnest to support our own researchers' submissions to the ISSCC, the IEDM and the VLSI, the world's three main conferences on semiconductors. These efforts garnered good results as Samsung Electronics made a name for itself as the company to present the most papers and win the most awards for them by the mid-1990s.

As the achievements piled up, the TEM continued to develop and gained further status with the unilateral transfer of technology. By the late 1990s, we were getting more requests for exchanges from Japanese companies. As our competencies improved, we reduced the number of companies with which we were having exchanges and focused more on cooperation with Hitachi, NEC, and Toshiba. Each of these companies had advantages in basic technology, DRAM, and flash memory, and this enabled the TEM discussions to become even more fruitful. The TEM continued on for another ten years.

Looking back, I remember people who raised objection by asking me, "Why do you have researchers writing papers when they're already busy enough developing products for business?" However, I would always argue in return:

"Conferences are not simply occasions for presenting papers. These events are at the forefront of international technology patents and standardization. Before a paper can be presented, the author must complete patent registration procedures. This is how you become a leader in new technologies and secure technological strength in new areas. It is also the highest level of strategy that an IT company can undertake."

Indeed, for late mover Samsung Electronics, this strategy produced optimum effect. By publishing papers our researchers were able to gain distinction, achieve the technological advantage and overtake the first movers, and get the upper hand in future markets.

In addition to CTF technology, countless other original patents that we created during that period are responsible today for our ability to overpower our competitors and be a technology leader. Our previous incarnation as a company that had to buy technologies and pay royalties no longer exists. It is my hope that Samsung Electronics will continue to collect royalties and grow as a semiconductor company without rival.

In little more than a decade, Korea surpassed Japan, the first mover of that time. Japan often quoted the phrase "Japan as No. 1" in various economic charts. But the use of this expression steadily decreased in the 1990s, for the country was outstripped by a late mover.

For instance, Samsung Electronics was first to establish the 8-inch wafer production line, and in 1994, we developed the world's first 256M DRAM. Late mover Samsung Electronics even took over 1st place in the production of flash memory, which was invented by Toshiba's Dr. Fujio Masuoka. And since the 2010s, almost all Japanese companies have disappeared from the global semiconductor market.

Preparing for the mobile era together

Looking back at the 1990s, Korean engineers had an intense desire to learn about advanced technology and culture, so much so in fact that they didn't need much encouraging from me. All I did was provide an opportunity for interaction with leading engineers, expose them to advanced research practices, and create an atmosphere conducive to research. They reacted to these external stimuli on their own.

Around then I realized that "creating opportunities for people to work together" is the best way to motivate them. After the success of the TEM, I organized several other groups where our people could put their heads together and generate results to further grow the organization.

The Flash Research Forum is an organization that is more directly related to the New Memory Growth Model.

At the ISSCC in 2002, the reaction of the roughly 4,000 people in the audience was divided. Although they nodded half in agreement at my New Memory Growth Model, some were doubtful and seemed to be wondering, "Can the memory market possibly grow at an even faster pace?" However, it didn't take long for them to confirm that the "New Memory Growth Model had precisely predicted the future."

The mid-1990's Japanese market, as I witnessed it, experienced an explosion of products that adopted semiconductors. By the time Samsung Electronics entered the semiconductor business, Japan was already a kingdom of not only semiconductors but also home appliances.

Their market was so large and dynamic that one could easily find all the latest home appliances by visiting Akihabara, a major electronics market in Tokyo.

Japan's population passed the 100-million mark early. They became a powerhouse of home appliance technology thanks to a culture that emphasizes artisanship, and high domestic demand. Japan was developing various types of flash memory for mobile devices and home appliances. I met with experts from Toshiba, Hitachi, and Fujitsu—which together with Advanced Micro Devices (AMD) founded a joint venture called Spansion—and I was continuously analyzing their technology.

Most semiconductors were going into digital cameras, but they were also being used in various digital home appliances. I also noticed the changes in the amounts of data used in emails and mobile phones. For example, text messages sent by email could have a size of only 10 KB, but this increased to 10 GB when attaching photos and videos. That meant a million times' more data. Naturally, I was then able to predict the rapid growth in the demand for flash memory.

In 1998, I was appointed head of the Semiconductor R&D Center and launched the Flash Research Forum. Gathering together executives from both the Semiconductor Division and the Set Division (i.e., finished products), we conducted workshops to research how flash memory would be used in the future in end-user products such as mobile phones, home appliances, and audio/video devices, and particularly, to study the market and technology regarding the role of flash memory in mobile phones, the core of the mobile industry.

The Flash Research Forum was also the embodiment of a philosophy that I stressed constantly, which was "cooperate from the start." I was in charge of the semiconductor business, but ultimately, semiconductors were meaningless until they went into devices that could be called products. The Set Division, however, needed knowledge of future semiconductor development to make products according to desired specifications.

The interaction between the Semiconductor and Set Divisions enabled them to answer mutual questions and deliver products that generated a high level of customer satisfaction. The result was a win-win atmosphere in which units that had moved independently were now eliminating barriers and resolving points of conflict.

In 2000, after I became president of the Memory Business Division, the Flash Research Forum was naturally disbanded as consultation on a higher level became possible. Early cooperation was now easier since I was able to meet the president (or CTO) of the mobile phone, home appliance, TV, audio, and video business divisions at Memory Business Division meetings.

For me, the Flash Research Forum and later exchange meetings were events that clearly demonstrated how semiconductors needed to develop in preparation for the advent of the future mobile era. As the volume of information rapidly grew, and functions, services and even devices converged through the innovation of multimedia and storage methods, I was able to see my prediction of "lighter, thinner, and smaller storage devices" come true. I also came to realize as we held more meetings among our business units that we needed new technologies and laws to represent the mobile era. It was clear that the further development of Moore's Law had physical limitations because the scaling of fabrication processes had increased IC density. I established a new theory stating that "with the transition from the PC era to the mobile era, the core component CPU will be replaced with flash memory and the speed of development will be faster and steeper than before," and I named it the "New Memory Growth Model."

Immediately, the new model presented a key direction for Samsung Electronics in developing flash memory and creating new markets. After my announcement of the New Memory Growth Model, Samsung began in earnest to spur the development of memory chips for the mobile era and created new technologies such as charge trap flash using new design technology with 3D structures. Moreover, Samsung Electronics went on to conquer the market as a result of having this core semiconductor technology, which played a leading role in the mobile revolution.

The author at the Samsung Mobile Solutions Forum in Taiwan in 2006 (with Managing Director Hong Wan-hoon at right).

Starting in 2004, Samsung Electronics began holding the Samsung Mobile Solutions Forum (SMSF) in Taiwan, the home country of several highly competitive mobile companies, to display its achievements on the world stage and gain an early foothold in the global market. Since the 1990s, I had been stressing the need to be ready in various ways for the advent of the mobile era. Samsung therefore launched the SMSF to lead the mobile era in the 21st century and establish itself as a "Total Solution Creator."

As the home of mobile and digital devices, Taiwan was a country with excellent product planning capability. It also had many SMEs that manufactured mobile devices. The SMSF served as an important event for promoting new flash memory solutions to these SMEs, who were also major Samsung clients, and as a "messenger country," Taiwan was as good as any other place for us to announce our mobile vision to the world.

Through the Total Solution Creator strategy, Samsung planned to produce hundreds of types of semiconductors for five main areas including mobile DRAM, flash memory, mobile processors, display driver ICs (DDIs), and image sensors to provide solutions for diverse customer needs. The strategy corresponded with the company's omnidirectional marketing approach of discovering new markets such as USB drives while also expanding the MP3 player market.

At the SMSF, I introduced flash memory to over 1,000 presidents, owners, and CEOs of Taiwan's representative IT companies while vigorously promoting Samsung Electronics and its products. Over the course of the SMSF's six-year run, the image of Samsung Electronics as a late mover in semiconductors gradually disappeared. Samsung was unquestionably the top player. The label it once had as a late starter had been removed. Managing Director Hong Wan-hoon (then president of the local subsidiary) oversaw the local preparation and direction of the SMSF, and also played a key role in establishing good relations with Nokia through SRAM when he was working at one our European subsidiaries.

Late movers have to be different

After announcing the New Memory Growth Model, and with the success of the TEM and Flash Research Forum as a foundation, I continued working to arrange meetings for discussion wherever possible. For I believed that exchanges, which are difficult to attempt within the existing organization of the late mover, must be stepped up to address current problems to prepare for the future.

I organized the Medici Research Society (MRS) when I was both chief technology officer of Samsung Electronics and president of Samsung Advanced Research Institute (SAIT). As is well known, the Medici family during the 15th century supported creative art projects across Italy, spanning the areas of music, fine arts, architecture, and philosophy. This patronage by the House of Medici shares much with the tradition of interdisciplinary studies. From a modern perspective I view this approach as being based on the spirit convergence.

It was my fervent hope that establishment of the MRS would serve as a catalyst for creativity at SAIT. I wanted to revive the tradition of the House of Medici, which bore some of the most beautiful and creative cultural achievements in history by bringing together experts from all walks of life to share their knowledge. More than 20 young researchers in their 20s to 40s and from various fields took part in the MRS. They engaged in frank discussion and exchange of opinion regarding their ongoing research, presentations, and new technology areas.

Despite my short time as SAIT president, the MRS enabled us to examine a wide range of advanced technologies broadly and deeply, including new future materials, 4G communications, biochips, and graphene semiconductors. In particular, we conducted a detailed investigation into biochip technology, which was closely related to the future of semiconductors. The MRS provided an opportunity to build an engine for future growth and eliminate barriers between business units while also enhancing technological synergies.

Meanwhile, the most impressive item we discussed was "graphene." I played a leading role in introducing graphene to the MRS and fully supported its research, although it was then a new and relatively unknown

Dr. Choi Jae-young and his co-authored paper published in *Nature*.

material.

The story behind it began the day after I was appointed Head of SAIT. I called Dr. Choi Jae-young into my office to ask him about the progress of his graphene research. His facial expression betrayed a hint of embarrassment, and he was probably curious as to why I was bringing up the subject of graphene when it was only a small part of his research.

"Ultimately I think graphene has significance as a semiconductor material. It is already known that its conductivity is 250 times better than silicon. I also think it's important to take over the market early since it's the new material of the future. I asked, "Have you by any chance sent your paper to

Advisory committee members of the R&D Strategy Planning Agency under the Ministry of Knowledge Economy, (from left) Professor Stephen Quake of Stanford University, Professor Philip Kim of Columbia University (currently at Harvard University), and Professor Hongkun Park of Harvard University

Nature?"

Even then, SAIT researchers were not actively publishing papers.

Upon hearing from Dr. Choi that graphene accounted for only one-third of his work, I gave him some additional personnel and encouraged him to prepare a paper. I also asked him to make an announcement of his agenda at the MRS. In January 2009, about six months later, Dr. Choi and his co-researchers published a paper in *Nature*, and from that point on, Samsung Electronics also began taking a serious look at graphene.

Within in a few years, Samsung Electronics had produced some outstanding graphene-related research achievements and earned a reputation as the company holding the largest patent portfolio for graphene technology. The paper published in *Nature* by Dr. Choi and his co-researchers is one of the most often cited works in the field of graphene. The basic patents registered during that period are also internationally recognized as among the strongest original patents related to graphene.

They are also being widely used in other industries. Later, Dr. Choi was appointed as director of the Samsung Graphene Center, and after retiring as an executive in 2015, he was hired as a professor of nanomaterials at Sungkyunkwan University, where he devoted his time to the future commercialization of graphene semiconductors.

My connection with graphene continued even when I conducted projects as the National CTO. My meeting Philip Kim, a professor at Columbia University who was awarded the Ho-Am Prize in 2008, turned out to be a fortuitous event. While heading the national advisory committee, I felt sure that we needed to include graphene on our to-do list as a future national growth engine. Although I was not successful the first year, I eventually got it selected as a national research project the following year.

Prof. Kim was a renowned expert on graphene and was nominated for a Noble Prize in 2010. After joining the national advisory committee, he assisted Korea greatly in taking a proper approach to graphene research. To this day, I feel proud knowing that Korea still has the most advanced proprietary technology and the most patents in that field. I look forward to the commercialization of the graphene semiconductor, which will enable Korea to continue leading the semiconductor industry.

I hosted the Gwanghwamun Forum during my time at Korea Telecom. When I became the CEO of that organization, I stressed the importance of R&D as well as technology differentiation. The common belief in the telecommunications industry is that marketing and distribution competitiveness must be strengthened because telecommunications is a service. However, I emphasized that KT would not be able to grow with its existing tools as the market had already been saturated.

The Gwanghwamun Forum was launched in an effort to answer the question, "How do we prepare for the future?" and was sponsored by the KT Economic Management Research Institute.

The Forum was held once every two months, with the participation of R&D experts in future growth engines such as energy, autonomous driving, augmented reality (AR), virtual reality (VR), electric vehicles, and big data. Two to three topics were selected for each session, and discussion for each topic began with a presentation by a KT executive, followed by 30-minute presentations by experts and a 30-minute discussion. For the seven to eight experts who spared their time, the Forum served as an opportunity to contribute to the future of KT, and for the more than 20 KT executives, it was a chance to acquire a technology roadmap for the future. As a result, KT took great strides forward in becoming a platform company for the network-based 5G era.

During my time running and managing various organizations, out of consideration for employee morale, I did not particularly emphasize that we were late movers. I did have however an inner determination to surpass the leader by experimenting and taking risks. But now that I think of it, experimentation and risk-taking are a privilege of the late mover.

Fortunately, all of my colleagues accepted the process of preparing something new as their destiny. Engineers, in particular, basically believed that nothing is impossible. There were several occasions where the impossible became possible based on the cooperation of experts from different fields. Putting together the characteristics of late movers and engineers made our preparation for the future much easier.

"Push yourself a little more."

I still ask myself, "How do we prepare for the future?" Whenever I miss the fields that I worked in, I would often recall the special lecture I did at the University of Cambridge in the United Kingdom.

In November 2002, I had lunch at T. S. Eliot restaurant, named after the famous poet, and gave a special lecture on the topic The Semiconductor Industry of Korea, to about 250 attendees in an auditorium at the Cavendish Laboratory, which has produced more Nobel Prize winners than any other research center in the world (30 winners as of 2022).

Alec Broers, the president of Cambridge at the time, was a Doctor of Engineering who majored in semiconductors and worked for IBM. I was greeted at the president's office in a magnificent building that showed its 400-year history.

On the table was a copy of the paper that I had announced a few months earlier at the ISSCC. At the time, I believed their high level of interest in engineering was only due to the personal preferences of the president.

"Two weeks ago, Gordon Moore delivered a lecture at the Cavendish Laboratory. There were so many people who came to listen that we had to open the doors of the lecture rooms on the second floor. I wonder how many people will come to listen to your lecture today."

Gordon Moore, a renowned figure who a former chairman of Intel, the world's top semiconductor company, was also known for "Moore's Law," and I thought to myself that my lecture couldn't possibly compare with his. I may have sparked some discussion with my own "Hwang's Law," but just how many students would come to listen to some business-man from the East?

However, as the time of the lecture approached, I realized I was way off the mark.

The doors to the lecture rooms on the second floor opened, and there were no empty seats as the rooms were filled with students. I wasn't entirely happy then because newspapers in Korea had reported that the students there were avoiding natural science and engineering.

In the UK, interest in natural science and engineering was somewhat stagnant by comparison with the US, Germany, and Japan. However, the enthusiasm among students who attended my lecture was extraordinary. I was amazed by their concrete and expansive questions.

As time went by, Korea became a widely acknowledged semiconductor powerhouse. However, the world's leader in semiconductor foundry is Taiwan. And recently, later movers including China and other memory

The author talking with Professor Sir Alec Broers, president of the University of Cambridge in 2002. (Left) Ra Jong-yil, the Korean Ambassador to the United Kingdom; (right) Managing Director Kim Ki-nam (currently CEO and chairman of Samsung Electronics).

chip companies have been fiercely racing to catch up. I couldn't just sit back and relax knowing this.

There must be students everywhere in the world who are filled with the same passion as the students I saw at Cambridge. In the global community, there are more people who became leaders after starting late than people who started out as leaders. Late movers should work harder than first movers to stand on their own and overcoming hardship and obstacles. As I always tell myself, "Push yourself a little more." I hope late movers today will keep this spirit in their hearts and continue to work hard.

The author preparing for his lecture at Cavendish Laboratory of the University of Cambridge in 2002. (Left) The author's lecture materials are seen on the lectern.

02   **If you fail,
try again**

| **David Navon & Robert Dutton** |

I think it was about ten years ago. I sought to learn which TV shows were popular among my younger friends in order to not fall behind the trends, and it turned out that the so-called "survival audition" (i.e., singing competition) programs were most watched. Apparently a lot of Koreans like such shows, considering how long they have remained on the air. The challenge, competition, and prospects of victory or defeat hold the audience in suspense.

All of us know it well. That only a handful of people make it through the auditions. Thousands of people end up losers on just a single TV program. Competition is like that. Only a few win; everyone else loses. Those who watch the process of winning or losing feel all sorts of emotions.

I also could not avoid the cutthroat competition while I was at companies and in government organizations for such a long time. I often enjoyed the thrill of victory, but I didn't always win. Fortunately I managed to stay happy. When I won, I was happy about winning; when I lost, I was happy to have the prospects of trying again. I was able to maintain my initial passion even while facing exhausting challenges.

But what made me able to do so well? Now that I look back, it was possible thanks to David Navon & Robert Dutton, two of the professors I had when I was young.

They say you make many mistakes or fail often when you are the most vigorous and upbeat. When I was young, I spent most of my time in the laboratory. I experienced mistakes and failures every day. My two professors, however, did not think it was a big deal. They believed in me and entrusted me with projects, and when I failed, they gave me a chance to do it again. Thanks to them, I learned to tolerate failure and became a leader who empowered subordinates without hesitation.

"Never mind!" no matter what the mistake or failure

One day while I was working on my PhD, I was shocked at the sight I encountered when I arrived at the University of Massachusetts laboratory. I threw down my bag and rushed to the computer. The printer connected to the computer was working when I had left the lab the day before. But the next day, a mountain of paper was piling up in front of the printer that was next to the computer.

The printers in those days were not as good as they are now. We shared a dot matrix printer at the lab. Instead of sheet paper, we had to use rolls of printer paper with punched holes on the margins. Dozens of pages could be printed out in a connected stream. Perhaps something was wrong with the program and the printer had just kept on printing overnight.

It seems like a minor mistake now, but at the time, it was a mistake that cost quite a large amount of money. I was heavy-hearted when I saw my professor. Professor David H. Navon's reaction was the opposite of what I'd expected.

"Never mind!"

He said it was okay. I immediately felt relieved and even got a bit choked up about it.

Prof. Navon was an older scholar, almost 60 years old, and a professor of Electrical and Computer Engineering. He was born and raised in New York, and fought in the Second World War. He joined Transitron Electronic (TE) in his youth and served as R&D director for over ten years, working on the development of the early transistors.

The author having a friendly chat with Professor Navon (second from the right) before the banquet that Chancellor John V. Lombardi (right) of UMass hosted on April 15, 2004.

He began his professorship at the UMass College of Engineering in 1965, and he already had an excellent reputation and research record by 1981, when I entered their doctoral program. Despite his stature, he was considerate and listened carefully to what young students had to say.

Prof. Navon put me on the project for making semiconductors with a gallium arsenide (GaAs) substrate. Silicon has always been the main material used in semiconductors, as it is inexpensive, nontoxic, and durable.

By contrast, GaAs is expensive, but its electron mobility is six times faster that of silicon. Thus, GaAs wafers are used in the aerospace, defense, and wireless communications industries, where speed is the lifeblood. Prof. Navon was keenly interested in the development of GaAs semiconductors; he drew me the big picture and left me to work out the research details. When I brought him new ideas, he always gave me positive feedback first, and then he added his thoughts on their modification. That alone was a source of great strength.

Shortly after I was put charge of the project, Prof. Navon drove me, riding shotgun, to Yorktown Heights, New York. We were heading for the IBM R&D Center (Thomas J. Watson Research Center). At the time, the Center was one of the top destinations for young engineers to visit at least once. A considerable number of global patents came from there. For that reason, IBM earned the reputation of holding the most patents among all US companies.

My jaw dropped in awe upon seeing the massive crescent-shaped structure at the end of a beautiful road, nestled among trees under the blue sky. I think Prof. Navon wanted to let a young engineer from East Asia witness the place where world-class technologies were being created. After touring around the IBM facility, I returned to the laboratory with high hopes for the future.

With Prof. Navon's attentiveness and encouragement, I was able to complete the doctoral program smoothly. Characterizing the process as "going smoothly" may sound a bit odd, but suffice it to say I did it "like any engineering student who takes the doctoral program." Of course, this was not an easy path to take. Over three years, I published one paper in *IEEE Transactions on Electron Devices*, a prestigious scientific journal popular among researchers, and two papers in *IEEE Electron Device Letters*. These were my achievements after putting all my passion into my work.

One of the rewarding moments over this course was when I gave a presentation with Prof. Navon at the Cornell Conference, a biennial symposium on semiconductors held at Cornell University in New York. Cornell had the only national laboratory for GaAs semiconductors in the US, funded by the US government. The conference held here was also sponsored by the government. Our paper was selected for the event, so we presented it in person. I was named the lead author, while Prof. Navon was listed as the corresponding author.

Prof. Navon possessed unique technology for computer-aided semiconductor design, but the only lab to implement this technology in the US was the MIT Lincoln Laboratory. He requested cooperation from the MIT Lincoln Lab, where he had once worked, and he assisted with the project execution.

He was delighted and proud when he found out that my paper had been selected by the Cornell Conference. Even in the US, not many professors present their papers at prestigious conferences. Government institutions, including the US Department of Defense, and global companies focused their support for research on those who managed to make presentations.

Prof. Navon helped me to receive research grants from the US

Department of Defense even after I left UMass. I owed him a lot and was always grateful to him. My paper's selection was happy news that slightly lightened the debt of gratitude I owed to him.

When I finished the doctoral program, I received job offers from Texas Instruments and IBM. However, I chose Stanford University as my next destination because Professor Robert Dutton at Stanford University's Department of Electrical Engineering personally contacted me and asked whether I would like to work with him on research. He also said he became deeply interested in my research after reading my paper published in *IEEE Electron Device Letters*.

I'd made up my mind to go to Stanford, but leaving the professor who supervised my doctoral course to go work with another professor weighed on me. My concerns were unwarranted, as Prof. Navon never showed any sign of disappointment. He was as bright as usual when he encouraged me to go to Silicon Valley, pursue the research I wanted to do, and dream bigger about the future.

Autonomy indeed is the greatest resource for motivation

I served as a post-doc at Stanford University for six months and then went to work as a research associate for four years. The school allowed me to work as a technical consultant for Intel for two years. I consulted for HP as well, but it was short-term, project-based work. Thus, it was my experience at Intel that influenced me the most. That was when I met Andy Grove at Building SC-9, the Intel Headquarters.

Prof. Dutton, who invited me to Stanford University, was a brilliant man who studied at UC Berkeley with Andy Grove, the CEO of Intel back then. His studies focused on integrated circuit processes, device and circuit technology, computer-aided design (CAD), and parallel calculation methods. He was engaged in academic society activities, publishing papers in more than 200 journals. This was why Stanford University hired him in 1983 as their youngest professor ever. Prof. Dutton was also actively networking within industrial circles. He consulted for various companies, including Fairchild, AT&T, HP, IBM, and even Matsushita in Japan.

I got along with Prof. Dutton as a true friend. Although we were separated by rank, we dropped strict formalities. He always invited my family to his family events, such as Halloween parties. He frequently asked me if I needed something or was experiencing any difficulties in my research, and if so me would help to resolve them.

My research at that time required a heavy-duty computer for processing graphics, and our lab had a computer connected to a big screen made by Texas Instruments. It was far too expensive to buy for personal use, so I would have to spend nights at school. Seeing this, Prof. Dutton let me bring the computer home. I brought the computer with the large screen home and was able to proceed smoothly with my research after I ate dinner with my family.

Prof. Dutton and I were headed in the same direction when it came to research as well. The paper we co-wrote in 1985 came in second place at the VLSI Conference, and we had the opportunity to present another paper at the IEDM Conference the following year. He suggested that I make the presentation and readily gave me the chance to rehearse.

One could say the process of getting used to practical research in Silicon Valley, the center of the semiconductor industry, was the ideal environment for a researcher. As I could perform a wide range of research with autonomy, I was filled with ambition and would not allow myself to slack off on any of the diverse research activities. Firsthand experience taught me that I needed basic research on major industry trends, and this understanding elevated my energy to nearly superhuman levels. Ultimately, writing a research paper is like a battle of ideas. I was able to spend time intensely immersed in my work, without being hindered by deadlines. This led to fruitful outcomes: I presented more than ten research papers at renowned semiconductor conferences and published ten more in *IEEE Transactions on Electron Devices*. Prof. Dutton's encouragement and advice were of a great help in all of this.

One of the very impressive things about him was his strong interest in Japan. He was among the few Westerners who could speak and read Japanese, and he would open up a book and ask me about Chinese characters when we went on a business trip together.

It was shortly before I decided to travel to Korea. Prof. Dutton was on his sabbatical, visiting Japanese makers of electric and electronic products. About six months into this, he called me to come to Japan, and took me to Japanese semiconductor companies for over ten days. We visited six companies in Japan that were all in the list of top ten in their field globally, and I gave a lecture at Osaka University. Talking directly with research center directors and top-ranked research fellows in technology fields allowed me to feel firsthand how far Japan had advanced technologically. Networking with them became extremely helpful for benchmarking during the Technical Exchange Meetings at Samsung afterward.

The age of voluntary madness:
your madness is our happiness

People say it is difficult to overcome the limits of experience. When I had to serve as a leader in an organization, I often used the skills I had learned from these two professors. I understood that mistakes and failures are part of the process, and I supported the persons in charge so that they could make full use of their capabilities. Above all else, I endeavored to create an environment in which employees could be made happy by "voluntary madness."

I was appointed president of the Memory Business Division in 2000, and early on I put great effort into the Management Briefings, as we began frantic new year at the beginning of the new millennium. Business had gotten so bad that we posted losses in some months, and we fretted, unable to find a way for a soft landing. Despite the busy and uncertain times, I strove to ensure that the Management Briefings were never left out.

At the Management Briefings, we discussed diverse issues, including clients, technologies, and strategies. I didn't choose any special or specific stories. Initially, Microsoft and Nokia were major clients for Samsung Electronics, and later on Apple joined the mix. I shared everything that I had heard to our engineers, telling it just as it was: the clients who showed were enthusiastic about our technology, the new technologies they were pursuing, and the areas in which we could cooperate with them.

Even the engineers who initially showed no interest had their eyes light up as they listened to what happed at Apple: "With Tim Cook and John Rubinstein in the room, Steve Jobs grabbed a marker and started to draw the products that Apple would develop in the next ten years

Berlin Philharmonic Concert

Samsung Electronics Management Briefing on semiconductors

on the whiteboard. Then, he told us the semiconductor functions and requirements that he needed from us."

The story about our visit to the Apple headquarters in December 2004 became widely talked about among employees. They said their hearts raced when they thought about how impressed major client companies were by our technologies and how global consumers cheered for our products.

I realized something simple from the difficulties caused by repeated mistakes and failures and from the crisis moments: business is not just about strategy, technology, and clients. It starts by having all organizational members share the same strategy, and by getting each and every individual to be resolute in overcoming the crises.

I sometimes liken managing a company to conducting an orchestra. If I were to describe the essence of corporate management in a word, it would be "harmony." Successful management is made possible by interlocking various factors with respect to corporate activities, such as business strategy, human resource utilization, customer relationship management, technological development, future investment, and financial management. Importantly, the tougher the conditions are, the less you can afford to neglect new technology development. To this end, you must risk failure, take up new challenges, and have the passion to dream about taking the bull by the horns. One of my assignments was make sure the fire kept burning in employees' hearts.

The Management Briefing was a precious time for all of us to feel that we were of the same mind. I held Management Briefings from 2001. I believed that I needed to concentrate more on technological developments and people as the IT industry saw a sharp drop in business activity and markets became increasingly difficult. I thought I had to share my vision and information with others. The 90-minute briefings continued once a month through 2008. These events allowed everyone in the business division to share the same vision and the latest information as well as to come together in solidarity. In an orchestra, everyone needs to get along and work together for the various instruments and performers to be in perfect harmony. Likewise, for an enterprise to achieve the best results, everyone in the organization must, from the get-go, open their hearts, communicate, reach consensus, and collaborate through all processes, to include research, development, and mass production.

Such efforts continued to be necessary when I was working as the National CTO. Korea's civil servants have excellent capabilities. They showed outstanding attitudes and expertise when we went on business trips together, or when they were discussing with renowned scholars from overseas. Scholars and engineers from around the world praised them, too. However, certain systemic difficulties arose in the communication process as well as in establishing and implementing the overarching vision. Problems persisted in an age-old bureaucratic organization.

I took on the task of tearing down the barriers among government agencies and improving unreasonable policies as we put together and implemented the "meta-plan," a comprehensive strategy for securing the nation's future revenue sources.

It was shortly after the iPhone 3G was introduced in Korea. As the popularity of Apple's second-generation phone soared, the Ministry of Knowledge Economy (MKE, now the Ministry of Trade, Industry and Energy) launched a project to create proprietary and software technologies that could outperform Apple. Software and materials were the talk of the town. However, the project proposal they submitted was unsatisfactory. It was lacking in many ways, perhaps because it was prepared in only a few months. The proposal didn't include any interdepartmental cooperation, and most of the projects planned were short-term. I put the brakes on the budget execution, and suggested that all officials from relevant agencies should get together to have an open discussion.

Sixty to seventy individuals gathered at the government building in Gwacheon. They included the MKE Minister and Vice Minister, sections and department chiefs, director generals, nongovernmental delegates in the software and materials divisions, and members of the National Office of Strategic R&D Planning.

At first, they seemed hesitant to speak at such an unfamiliar event; however, after they understood it was a venue for an open discussion, they began to show what they were capable of. Some were so passionate they even followed me into the hallway during the break to talk. Members of the Office of Strategic R&D Planning suggested that it would be a waste of money to develop software we could buy from India and insisted that the budget should be spent for things Korea definitely needs. The MKE, our mediator, listened to our opinions and closed the discussion stating, "Let's make a new plan as it is apparent that this one won't work."

While the plan was being revised, I raised my voice: "Why can't the different agencies work together? The projects should be performed by the MKE in partnership with other government bodies like the Ministry of Land, Infrastructure and Transport; the Ministry of Health and Welfare; and the Ministry of Science and ICT." Even competing corporations and countries collaborate, so it didn't make sense for government agencies to not work together as we ponder the country's future direction. After my

The author after the ceremonial pitch at the KT Wiz Park.

suggestion, a revised plan was produced, and the project proposal finalized after two to three months differed completely from the initial proposal.

I continued to emphasize listening carefully and empowerment after my appointment as the CEO of KT in 2014. I added some unprecedented events at KT such as the Management Briefing, Lunch with the CEO, and No. 1 Workshop. The old school approach was needed to completely make over the company atmosphere. Employees must feel they are getting emotional support if they are going to be willing to take on challenges and do their best. Communication in the form of listening to the employees face to face and responding to them was just as important as offering a vision and encouraging everyone to advance together.

One of the things that stand out in my memory was when I went to the baseball stadium in Suwon for the inauguration of the KT Wiz, the company-sponsored professional baseball team.

The game was with the Samsung Lions. Before it started, I went out onto the field wearing a catcher's mask and chest protector. A pregame event was held to celebrate the 130th anniversary of Korean telecommunications. The highlight was throwing out the first pitch. However, I was not the one throwing the ball; a newly hired KT employee did. I caught the ball while I had my face covered with the mask. When I took it off, 10,000 spectators cheered in surprise.

In my youth, my life was consumed with voluntary madness. I vividly experienced how madness was essential to our nation's prosperity when the company I worked for became the world's top chipmaker. On that basis, I was confident that things would work out well if I kept getting back up in the face of numerous mistakes and failures. I got this attitude from my teachers who tolerated my mistakes and failures and encouraged me.

When I became the leader of an organization, I wanted to give my organizational members and those who would become the next generation of leaders the gift of an experience similar to the one I had. Through my unprecedented throwing out of the first pitch. I wished to convey to the minds of senior management the message that I would tolerate and accept any result, whether it be a strike, ball, or safe hit, so long as we took on the challenges with everything we had.

Meeting again after 20 years

Although I thought of them from time to time and missed them, I was only able to get together with my two former professors after my hair had

A congratulatory playing of Arirang during the banquet after the award ceremony at the Massachusetts State House in April 2004.

turned gray. Almost twenty years had passed before we met again. Seeing them again was all the more delightful and heartwarming because I had been through so many challenges and failures in my life. I was also proud I could show a more mature version of myself after all the adversity.

In April 2004, a call from UMass informed me of the news that I would receive the Distinguished Alumni Award. There was a banquet at the chancellor's house the day before the award ceremony. There I met Prof. Navon and his wife again. We had a very friendly conversation together, as if the passing of two decades was of no account. Prof. Navon was still teaching future scholars even though he had been retired since 1987.

The ceremony for the Distinguished Alumni Award was held at the Massachusetts State House. The chancellor jokingly told me that Jack Welch, the General Electric CEO, received the same award only after he

Professor Dutton giving a lecture at the TAC.

was in his 60s, while I got it while still in my 50s.

I experienced a deeply moving moment during the banquet that followed the ceremony. The choir of about 40 UMass music students broke out in a song very familiar to me. It was the Korean folk song, Arirang. The audience of over 200 distinguished guests listened with pleased looks on their faces. The ceiling of the State House was quite high. I listened along with Prof. Navon to the resounding tune through the fourth verse. I couldn't hide how deeply moved I was.

About three months after I returned to Korea, I heard that Prof. Navon had passed away at the age of 79 after a short battle with a disease. I still cherish our unexpected reunion, which turned out to be our last.

I met Prof. Dutton again in Korea. I was solely in charge of hosting the Technology Advisory Committee (TAC) when I was serving concurrently

Professor Dutton giving the author a shoulder massage.

as Semiconductor Business president at Samsung Electronics.

Committee members included world renowned experts in various technological fields, such as professors at Stanford, MIT, Harvard, and UC Berkeley in the US, as well as the University of Tokyo and Tohoku University in Japan. The TAC was held over two nights and three days. All the 700-800 researchers at Samsung Electronics came to listen to the keynote speeches. After that the participants divided up to join various sessions that covered specific research areas and were led by global scholars. The event also had a three-hour panel discussion, for which I invited Prof. Dutton to be the moderator.

Our researchers were highly motivated by the opportunity to be in the presence of globally-renowned scholars in the semiconductor field and be able to ask them questions directly. I was also filled with emotion as I introduced young Korean researchers to Prof. Dutton.

I visited Stanford University again in 2009, after retiring as the Samsung Group CTO. At that time, Prof. Dutton massaged my shoulders and said, "You did a great job." He advised it would be important for me to spend some time recharging my energy after working for such a long time in industry.

Thinking back on what he said, my visits to Harvard, MIT, and Stanford to meet top global scholars was my "recharge time." That energy boost enabled me to perform more passionately as the National CTO and member of the KT organization.

Failing is also part of competency

"If you do it or don't do it, you'll have regrets either way. So you might as well just do it."

Those senior to us emphasize the importance of taking on challenges. Because at least you won't have to regret not trying.

When I got to be a manager, I felt the same way. Many organizational members would ask what to do or how to do it, but the key question is "how many times have you tried?" If you fail, you at least discover one way that doesn't work. It took me this long, but now I can surely acknowledge that failure is also part of becoming competent.

About two years into taking office at KT, I met Chung Eui-sun, the vice chairman of the Hyundai Motor Group (currently chairman). I grabbed his hand, recollecting the difficult days, and said, "It wasn't easy, but it's nice to hear that you managed well to succeed in your business."

When I was the National CTO, we focused on five categories for securing future revenue sources: (1) new industries (biotechnology, bioengineering, etc.); (2) mainstay industries (automobiles, machinery, chemicals, shipbuilding and construction), (3) IT (semiconductors, telecommunications, and software); (4) materials, and (5) energy (nuclear power). Electric vehicles were included in the mainstay industry segment. I visited automakers and encouraged them to move into EVs, which as a national project would receive government support. This was a huge initiative, with hundreds of millions of dollars earmarked from the national budget.

However, making an automobile without an engine was unimaginable for domestic automakers, and they were reluctant to accept the government's offer. In Japan, Nissan had just released the Leaf, and Toyota was about to come out with the Prius, but many in Korea felt strongly that it was still too early to produce electric vehicles domestically. I talked with the person in charge of the EV project several times to devise some way to carry it out. After repeated requests, we succeeded in getting Kia to join. Thus our hard work paid off, as this project was later acknowledged to have kick-started Korea's electric vehicle development.

Finding a project operator for EV production was not easy, and neither was securing the budget for it.

I've maintained a special affinity for graphene ever since I was the SAIT Head. Graphene is a thin, light and highly durable material that was first isolated by a Russian physicist. It has a wide range of applications, given its unique physical and chemical properties. For instance, graphene has 1000 times higher electrical conductivity than copper does, and 150 times that for silicon. It is 200 times stronger than steel and has twice the heat conductivity of diamond. Graphene satisfies every condition for innovation-faster speed, greater capacity, and smaller size. I learned about the potential of graphene from Harvard Professor Philip Kim, one of the world's top graphene experts, so I have continued to believe we must secure the technology early and use this material as future revenue source. When I became the National CTO, I went to one of the people in charge of the national budget at the Ministry of Economy and Finance. The answer I got from him was quite unexpected.

"Sir, can you produce the results in one to two years?"

That question left me dumbfounded for a moment. I replied:

"My duty is to create revenue sources for Korea 5-10 years in the future. It wouldn't be one of my responsibilities if it were a short-term project. That would be handled in the private sector."

"Then it would be a hard (read: impossible) to allocate the budget for that."

My first attempt failed just like that. I added some explanation about graphene's potential and how it would transform the nation's technological strength, but to no avail. That is how my string of bad luck started. The following year, a more serious situation arose.

"Then, why did you hire me for this position? Didn't you employ me to do benchmarking around the world, identify the technologies that would be needed five to ten years from now, and then recommend which technologies would be best suited for our country?"

At last, one of the budget people pulled me aside and told me the funds had been allocated:

"I know you are passionate about the future and requested a budget. It is less than what you asked for, but I arranged these funds at any rate. I'm sorry it took so long."

I accepted it with gratitude. This is a basic technology, the graphene projects represented just a small portion from the overall budget.

Nonetheless, graphene has become a driver for making Korea a powerhouse for materials. Korea's proposal was adopted by the International Electrotechnical Commission (IEC) as the global standard this year. We managed this by overcoming restraints imposed by the US, the UK, and Japan. The global market for graphene is forecast to grow from $100 million in 2019 to $1.5 billion by 2025.

Success is very rare without first suffering failure, and I, too, have experienced numerous failures. Despite this, I was able to reach my goal because failure never stopped me.

As we attempt to take on various challenges, let's recognize that mistakes and failures occur. Let's consider small steps forward as being important. Many leaders became great by treading such a path. This way is always open, so I hope young people who will lead the future of Korea will follow it.

03 Experience it: the power of science and technology that is ushering in the great transformation

| Klaus Schwab |

I'm an early adopter. When a new device comes on the market, I will visit the store, try it out, and buy it if I like it. Then, I'll show it off to the people I know. When I started my work life, I strove to be the first to use the new products we made and evaluate them from the customers' point of view. By doing this repeatedly, it got fun and eventually became a habit. My early adopter mentality became a resource that motivated me to grow in all areas of my life.

Life as an early adopter is advantageous in various ways. The days when only engineers get to explore and experience new technologies are now over. Whether you are a student or leader of a global company or country, knowledge in science and technology is necessary for reaching the place you want to be.

Thus, when I am asked a question like, "Do you have any habit that helps you look ahead to the future?" I often answer with: "Become an early adopter and experience it for yourself." Because being in the customer's shoes is the most important attitude a manager should have.

The aspirations of one starting out anew, not the requests of one leaving

"I started out here as a researcher, dedicated myself to R&D, and wound up in this current senior position. Looking back, I am deeply moved.

The research center is where unforeseeable dreams are inspired, and where those dreams are turned into reality. Researchers must have dreams and, above all, have the strength to affirm them. Don't build walls around yourself. Instead, you must always be interested in what your colleagues are doing and remain dedicated to creating new markets.

I may be leaving this place today, but wherever I will be, I will continue to ponder the new technologies that will become the future growth drivers."

This was what I said 10 years ago when I resigned from Samsung Electronics. I had been serving as the CTO and SAIT head. I will talk about this later, but I once formed a study group of young scientists in their 20s and 30s called the Medici Research Society, collaborating among people in various fields to foster talented people with flexible thinking.

I felt sad leaving the organization, but what I wanted more was to support the continuous growth of the researchers who remained at SAIT. After careful consideration, I closed my farewell address with the aspirations of a person who was starting over again, not the requests of one who was leaving.

Early in 2009, I enjoyed the longest vacation in my life after taking a step back from the front line of Samsung management. Up to that time, I had spent most of my time traveling overseas or running around Korea on business. Now, for the first time I took two weeks off to attend performances I liked and visit historical and cultural sites. I went to St. Petersburg, where I visited museums and tourist attractions during the day and listened to concerts or watched plays in the evening. The historical and cultural sites were mesmerizing. My mental fatigue melted away as I visited Leo Tolstoy's house and the restaurant where Tchaikovsky got infected with cholera.

However, my vacation did not go completely to plan. Even before my schedule became fully booked, I opened my laptop to write e-mails to global scholars and request meetings. I wrote that I wanted to meet and learn from them, not as a company CTO but as an early adopter of future-oriented technologies. Thanks to the long relationship we'd shared, they wrote back, welcoming a late bloomer who is enjoying his freedom in both mind and body. Importantly, Harvard University Professor Hongkun Park, with whom I had been in contact for a few years, arranged most of my itinerary with Harvard and MIT. He replied that I was set to meet with a Nobelist and a chair-professor at Harvard University, among others.

After receiving these replies, I started to prepare like one going on a business trip. I made detailed plans regarding the people I was to meet and the places I had to go. My schedule mostly concerned prominent scholars in technology fields and some of the world's most advanced research centers.

Early in May, I flew to the US East Coast, focusing on the topic of

Professor Park's office at Harvard University.

future technology trends. The countries and regions on my schedule continued to change, and the traveling did not end until the following year.

I started by visiting the research centers at Harvard, MIT, Stanford, and UC Berkeley, as well as promising companies in Silicon Valley. At MIT, they gave me a tour of the Energy Initiative, Media Lab, AI Lab, Materials Research Laboratory, and others; at Harvard, I looked around the Brain Science Institute, Bio Labs, Nanotechnology Research Lab, and Broad Institute, which had world's top authority in DNA sequencing.

I was able to spend about four weeks on the US East Coast, working at a professor's office with permanently preserved materials used by Nobel Prizewinners. Harvard granted me special permission to use the place after Prof. Park notified them of my visit to the school. I enjoyed the privilege and expressed my gratitude. Next, I went to the US West Coast to visit Stanford University, UC Berkeley, and venture companies in Silicon Valley. My former teacher, Prof. Dutton, let me use an office that was next to his, and I stayed there for four weeks. At Stanford University, I visited the Center for Genomics, AI and Robot Labs, the Global Ecology and Climate Solutions Lab, Geballe Laboratory for Advanced Materials, and 3D Semiconductor Device Laboratory; at UC Berkeley, I toured the Biomolecular Nanotechnology Center, Micro/Nano Electro-Mechanical Systems (MEMS) facility, and Wireless Sensor System Lab.

Last, I went to the Biological Resource Centre in Singapore, as well as biotech and environmental research centers in Japan. As I studied the latest technologies during the trip, it felt like I was back in my old days as a student. The freedom of not belonging to any company allowed me to explore novel technologies going beyond the confines of semiconductors.

Meetings and discussions with more than 60 renowned scholars left me an immense impression on me. During that one year of learning, I noticed that massive and fundamental changes had begun that were greater than the world could imagine. The question "What are the Korea's future growth drivers?" never left my mind.

However, amid the intense discussions, I often felt infinitesimally small. Previously, I had been proud to serve as a CTO of one of Korea's leading companies, and in that position to be a global trendsetter and to never have strayed from the center of new technology development. However, as I visited the research centers of interdisciplinary universities, I couldn't help but acknowledge the rather wide gap between them and us in Korea. In particular, I have this vivid memory of being let into the human genome analysis center with Harvard Prof. Park, the world's top

Head Stuart Schreiber of the Broad Institute, the world's top DNA laboratory, explaining DNA sequencing technology.

DNA laboratory jointly run by MIT and Harvard University. The facility is not open to the outside, and my visit was arranged with the special consideration of Head Stuart Schreiber of the Broad Institute.

Here, robotic arms complete the genomic maps of three to four individuals each day. Elsewhere at the time, creating the genomic map for an individual typically took several months to complete. Looking around a facility that works with the most advanced biotechnologies to investigate the causes of complicated diseases, and seeing research on personalized diagnostic tests, I became certain that the future would, after the semiconductor industry, be led by the biotech industry.

Despite feeling fatigued from being on the road for so long, my stream of consciousness went on alert. With my characteristic positivity, I had resolved to take another powerful step forward, and that was just at the time I was contacted about the National CTO post. After refusing the offer several times, I finally made up my mind and accepted the position, determined to make Korea a country with robust technologies going forward.

I thought that if I could link the successful track record brought by semiconductors to future-oriented industries and technologies, then new economic growth drivers could be identified and nurtured. That would create a second legendary achievement. I was determined to get young people to trust in their potential and dream of a better future and a better world.

Consequently, things learned while meeting freely with other scholars and visiting research centers served as a valuable resource for me while working for the National Office of Strategic R&D Planning and at KT. It helped me come up with ideas to map out a future direction submerged in a turbulent sea. Also, the energy that recharged me during my trip enabled for me to converge new technologies and make them commercially viable.

As I worked in the field for another decade, I realized directly that the era had ended where only scientists get to develop technologies and managers get to manage businesses. In the current environment everyone needs science and technology to survive. Now is the time when everyone must build their knowledge of state-of-the-art technologies and converge what they know with other resources in their lives. One can hardly obtain significant insight into life without experiencing new technologies.

Such awareness of reality isn't simply something I came up with alone. Those are also the words of Klaus Schwab, the World Economic Forum (WEF) founder. We overcame nationality and age differences to become friends.

An encounter with an ardent believer in
and early adopter of technology

My relationship with Klaus Schwab, also known as the "president of the global economy," started in 2017. I visited the WEF headquarters in Geneva, Switzerland, to give a presentation on KT's project to prevent infectious disease globally.

At that time, KT attracted public attention with its GiGAtopia strategy and "5G will be the power that changes the world" declaration. KT was making a quantum leap as a telecommunications technology company by leaving behind its old image.

I was truly excited about the meeting with Klaus Schwab. Klaus is widely known for founding the WEF in 1971 and developing it into an independent global organization. He has long endeavored to build a venue where global leaders can share agendas and have neutral and fair discussions. He introduced himself in several media as "an ardent believer in and early adopter of technology," and emphasized his firm conviction that technologies would contribute to the advancement and development of humanity. I was deeply impressed by his activities and philosophy, and I expected that his ideas would be similar to mine.

In 2015, two years before my meeting him, Korea celebrated its 130-year history of telecommunications. Being the KT president at the time, I announced that intelligent gigabit-capable infrastructure and information and communications technologies (ICT) would converge to

The author announces Korea would lead the Fourth Industrial Revolution during an event celebrating Korea's 130th anniversary of telecommunications in September 2015.

drive the Fourth Industrial Revolution (4IR):

"The convergence of ICT and businesses, which is giving rise to the Fourth Industrial Revolution, is capturing global attention. It was the steam engine that drove the First Industrial Revolution, electricity for the Second, and computers for the Third. In the same way, the convergence of ICT, with its strong network base, is forecast to become the new industrial driving force."

At that time, Germany started to talk about the connection between manufacturing businesses and ICT under the Industry 4.0 Project. However, discussions on the Fourth Industrial Revolution were not yet in full swing. Nevertheless, I spoke about how the Fourth Industrial Revolution, riding on the world's most advanced intelligent ICT infrastructure, would realize new industries and value by converging manufacturing, energy, finance,

276

The author shaking hands with Klaus Schwab after signing an MOU related to the GEPP at the World Economic Forum headquarters (person on the far right is KT's current CEO, Koo Hyun-mo).

automobiles, and other industrial sectors.

Four months later in January 2016, the Davos Forum was held at Swiss vacation destination of Davos under the theme Mastering the Fourth Industrial Revolution.

The Davos Forum lasted three days, and almost half of the sessions (140 out of 300) were related to the 4IR. The diagnoses and predictions for a new, unimaginable era based on the convergence of cutting-edge technologies—including robots, AI, and the internet of things (IoT)—caused a global sensation. Klaus Schwab's *The Fourth Industrial Revolution*, published in June 2016, became a bestseller in Korea as well. He was surprised at the great interest of Korean readers, saying that among the one million copies sold all over the world, 300,000 were sold in Korea.

As expected, our meeting was deeply meaningful, and we had a great conversation. Chairman Schwab welcomed my visit and fostered an upbeat atmosphere. He also attentively listened to our Global Epidemic Prevention Platform (GEPP) plan.

KT's GEPP is a global platform for preventing the spread of infectious diseases by using data roaming to track individuals who visit regions where an epidemic has broken out. The platform also provides people who have been traveling internationally with information on the infectious disease. If a pandemic spreads globally, the system gathers and analyzes data on visits to the affected regions by all mobile phone users. Then disease alerts are provided to the mobile phone users around the world and to national governments. To make this work, of course, global agreements must first be signed, which requires active cooperation from international organizations in various fields, such as the International Telecommunication Union (ITU; communications), World Health Organization (WHO; healthcare), and WEF (economy).

Klaus Schwab was enthusiastic about the idea. He gladly accepted my proposal saying that the WEF has allotted some budget for the solution of infectious disease prevention. Klaus asked me on the spot to take part in Davos Forum 2018 as a panelist and to introduce the GEPP during a session called Preparing for the Next Epidemic. I immediately accepted his offer.

Klaus treated me as a friend from that day on. Our age difference of fifteen years didn't stand in the way. We both had special affinity for future technologies and we're proud of being early adopters. We also asked each other about personal interests.

"Dr. Hwang, currently, there are discussions on Industry 4.0 (manufacturing) in Germany. What do you think about it?"

Born in Germany, Chairman Schwab obtained his doctorate in Economics at the University of Fribourg and a doctorate in Engineering at the Swiss Federal Institute of Technology. Afterwards, he received a Master of Public Administration at the John F. Kennedy School of Government of Harvard University. In 1972, he was hired as the youngest professor at the University of Geneva. Klaus had great affection for Germany, his native country.

I evaluated Germany's Industry 4.0, which was launched in early 2010, and explained that Industry 4.0 was not concentrated on manufacturing so much as expanding towards the digital transformation. I also suggested Korea should seek ways to develop various industries while the massive Fourth Industrial Revolution framework expands worldwide. Klaus agreed with me, saying that the convergence of technologies and industries is indeed the key to future technologies. Our first conversation lasted an hour longer than scheduled.

On the other hand, he expressed his particular fondness for 5G technology. Klaus was deeply impressed by KT's 5G declaration, the world's first, and told me he would add a section about 5G in the second edition of *The Fourth Industrial Revolution*.

After I returned to Korea, I received an e-mail from him attached with an English copy of his manuscript. He wrote, "I would be extremely grateful if you would examine the manuscript before I finally hand it over to the publisher." I thoroughly reviewed the manuscript with all my heart and soul. The second edition of his book now includes a section on 5G technology

What will drive the evolution of human life in the 4IR era?

In January 2018, I revisited Davos, Switzerland to participate in the Preparing for the Next Epidemic session and give more details about the GEPP.

MERS first hit Korea in 2015, with 186 confirmed cases and a death toll of 38. KT developed and applied the GEPP as a response to a second MERS outbreak in 2017. The GEPP helped prevent a disease spread, and no deaths were recorded as a result.

"If we apply the GEPP to developing countries with poorer hygiene and lower national competencies, it should lead to remarkable results. If the GEPP model is adopted worldwide, the use of smart technology can help protect people everywhere from epidemics." After hearing my impassioned speech, numerous global leaders said they were deeply

The author conversing with Bill Gates at the breakfast talk.

impressed by the GEPP project and that they would consider using the platform. Some countries did adopt the GEPP afterwards, and are active in providing the related support.

For instance, Bill Gates, expressed interest in the GEPP, calling it "creative and fresh." While sharing our thoughts before breakfast, I briefly explained the idea behind the GEPP, and he has showed a positive reaction from the initial stage of implementation. This encounter became the cornerstone that enabled KT to start a research project called "A Next Generation Surveillance Study for Epidemic Preparedness." The three-year, approximately $12 million study was begun in May 2020 with support from the Bill & Melinda Gates Foundation.

My relationship with Klaus Schwab and the WEF continued. He visited Korea in April 2018 after receiving an invitation from the President of Korea, and found time in his schedule to visit my office. Klaus told me how he felt when he watched the 5G technology demonstration during the PyeongChang 2018 Winter Olympics, and asked me to come to the 2019 Davos Forum. He said he wanted to invite me as a member of the International Bureau Council. The IBC consists of 100 international figures from political and financial circles, including the United States President, the World Bank president, and the International Monetary Fund chairperson. I was the first Korean businessperson to be included among the members, and it made me feel proud. Apple's CEO Tim Cook became a new member the previous year, and President Rafael Rief of the Massachusetts Institute of Technology was registered as a new member in the same year as I was.

In 2019, I participated in the Davos Forum as an IBC member. On the first day, there was an exclusive meeting for IBC members, and I attended as a new member.

The theme of the 2019 WEF, which celebrated its 49th anniversary, was "Globalization 4.0: Shaping a Global Architecture in the Age of the Fourth Industrial Revolution." However, the biggest issue among IBC members was the conflict between the US and China. In 2018, the previous year, President Trump participated in the forum, and was the talk of the town. It had been 18 years since a US president (Bill Clinton) last participated in the event.

However, President Trump caused embarrassment among the participants and audience when he delivered a speech emphasizing his America First policy, which was at odds with the Forum theme, "Creating a Shared Future in a Fractured World." Making matters worse, this happened just one year after Xi Jinping became the first Chinese President to attend the

IBC members at the WEF's Annual Meeting 2019.

Davos Forum in 2017. Then, the US-China conflict escalated in early 2019 because of the issue surrounding Huawei. The global company CEOs who participated in the IBC meeting predicted that 5G, the key future technology on everyone's mind, would also be a point of contention between the US and China.

Our discussion started with the question: What is the most important thing for Globalization 4.0? As the debate continued, the topic of 5G came up. However, when the conversation started to focus on the conflict between the US and China, I slowly raised my hand. It was time to correct wrong predictions and misunderstanding of reality.

"5G is a mobile communication technology that uses a very high frequency of 28 GHz. The 4G long-term evolution (LTE) uses a frequency below 2 GHz, and provides a slow but long reach. High frequency, on the other hand, has strong flatness, and provides a fast but short reach. In particular, the latter is characterized by a shortened latency of 2 msec compared to 4G that has a 20-msec latency, which means it can be applied to key industries of the Fourth Industrial Revolution, including autonomous driving and remote medical examination and treatment. It was KT that reflected 80% of 5G standards as the international standards in the lead consortium."

I explained Korea's technology in front of leading business and political leaders from different countries. KT not only showed the world images which were unimaginable at that time during the PyeongChang Winter Olympics the year before, it also perfectly reproduced the 5G pilot service. I reminded every participant of this fact, and announced that KT was ready to commercialize 5G, for the first time in the world, within two months. Next, I changed the subject to talk about what I

The 5G session at the Congress Center of the World Economic Forum.

really wanted to say.

"Let's go back to today's topic. We are talking about what we should do for the world, what is the most important thing, and how we could share economic benefits to many people, especially those who are disadvantaged.

The advantages of 5G are not limited to density and speed. We should also focus on its connectivity. 5G will change humanity as it connects everyone by delivering unbelievable data volumes at extremely high speed. The platform will also be provided for everyone at low cost. Thus, 5G will be the key technology that can address inequality in the world."

I continued with the following rationale:

"Billions of people still have no internet access, and humanity is faced with the task of solving this digital divide. The ultrahigh connectivity of 5G will be the foundation for distributing fairly the benefits from the Fourth Industrial Revolution. At the same time, its ultralow latency will make autonomous driving, remote medical treatment, and other such technologies work, allowing all of us to enjoy a safer and

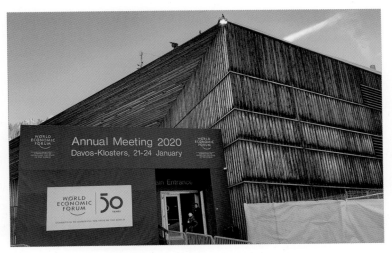

The World Economic Forum celebrated its 50th anniversary in 2020.

more convenient life. 5G is not only an important tool for the Fourth Industrial Revolution but for people who are financially disadvantaged. It will be a core technology for solving inequality in the world."

The thundering round of applause lasted for the longest time. President Benioff, who was in the front row, gave me a thumbs-up to indicate I had closed my impromptu speech well. Sunil Bharti Mittal, the chairperson of GSMA and founder and chairperson of Bharti Enterprises, was handed over the microphone and he added:

"I agree with Dr. Hwang one hundred percent. The impact and power of 5G is something we have never experienced before. I believe it will have an absolute influence on our economy."

Later, at the IBC meeting, they told me, "Thanks to you, Dr. Hwang, I could learn that 5G is one of the most important and urgent technologies for Globalization 4.0."

Emphasizing the importance of 5G for the first time in the world was a really memorable moment for me personally. After the speech, I was nicknamed "Mr. 5G" at the WEF. Marc Benioff started that nickname, which spread among the other participants at the event.

I expect I will continue to take part in the Davos Forum. I will go anywhere to introduce Korea's advanced technologies, and seek ways to contribute to the development of humanity through technological revolution.

Build up your experiences, for technology offers both challenges and opportunities

When I was active as a semiconductor specialist, I got many questions from young people who wanted to start their career as an engineer and climb the corporate ladder into management.

When they asked what they needed to do to prepare, I emphasized the importance of having solid knowledge and experience as a researcher in one's field. Competence is essential, of course. In addition, they need to be able to get along with others and be a team player. I have also worked on teams to study trends and build networks, and the experience has improved my communication and collaboration skills. These naturally equipped me with abilities necessary for a management position.

However, I received a different question while working as a professional manager at KT: "How can we learn future-oriented technologies and dominate them ahead of others?" I guess I had been a manager for so long they somehow forget the fact that I also used to be an engineer.

"You should understand what people thought of in the past, and what they think of in the present; how they are living their life now, and what kind of life they want to live in the future. It is the same when it comes to semiconductors and telecommunications."

When I was a researcher or manager, the people I first met with at client companies were the CTOs, not the CEOs or heads of procurement. I had to know about the technology that the client company was working on to understand their business interests and vision going forward. Then I would be able to offer them the solutions they needed to get there.

Importantly, CEOs must be able to precisely read market flow, so they are informed sufficiently to make the right decision at each inflection point of the market. To do this, they have to know consumer needs and pay attention to technologies and marketing. Among these requirements, they will only be able to make decisions with conviction at the right time if they can read accurately the technology trends and market pulse. In this sense, the fact that I started my career as an engineer was very advantageous for me. That allowed me to embrace experimentation and keep up with technology.

Many managers say the future of humanity depends on how we use the wisdom provided by science and technology. However, science and technology are greatly beneficial to individuals, too. No matter which field you devote yourself to, you cannot dismiss the influence of cutting-edge science and technology. If you think of technologies as "not a part of your business," you will have difficulty in gaining insight from great transformations like the Fourth Industrial Revolution.

At the risk of repeating myself, let me add that the scientific way of thinking and mindset are necessary regardless of the area you devote yourself to. Also, I hope that young people will go out into the world with a more positive and optimistic attitude toward science and technology.

The development of science and technology will continue to provide us with numerous challenges and opportunities. They have already changed our ways of life, our ways of working, and our ways of interacting with others.

Those who understand and predict the acceleration of innovation and the pace of destruction will realize the value of labor, which is more important than capital. Now is the time to ponder (life) from a higher dimension, one that prepares for the future through science and technology.

04

Passion will always be your pathfinder

| AI Tech Center |

March 2016 was an interesting month for me in many ways. First, was the Go (or *baduk* in Korean, traditional board game) match of the century between the computer program AlphaGo and the professional Go player Lee Sedol, with a 9th dan (the highest) rank. I watched them play five matches in a series continued over six days. The match between a human and an AI program based on Google DeepMind was intriguing in itself.

Unfortunately, Lee could win only once. In the last match, AlphaGo was pressured by the clock ticking down, and the game was close. However, Lee, who played black and was confident of a win, failed in defeat AI. The reality that AlphaGo's capabilities outperformed a human master was shocking in and of itself.

AlphaGo added fire to the global AI craze, which began when Amazon released the Echo smart speaker for the home two years earlier. Alexa, the AI platform loaded in Echo, may not be so impressive by 2020 technology standards, but it made headlines at the time because it understood users' commands and could control the internet of things. The advent of smart virtual AI assistants, previously only seen in movies, seemed to be at hand.

I used to subscribe to the Japanese newspaper *The Nikkei*, which carried an AI column day after day. "What Korea should focus on first is AI, second is also AI and the third is AI as well," Son Jung-ui (Masayoshi Son), the founder and CEO of SoftBank, told Koreans in 2019. However, I had already read this message in a Japanese newspaper three to four years earlier. I felt uncomfortable.

My interest in artificial intelligence started to materialize about ten years earlier. I was working as Samsung's CTO and head of SAIT director, so I met researchers from relevant fields to gain a comprehensive understanding of AI. After retiring, I was able to visit Harvard University, MIT, and Stanford University, and I discovered how unimaginably far the new technologies had progressed.

I came to appreciate the importance of artificial intelligence after I met Professor Victor Zue at MIT's Computer Science and AI Lab (CSAIL) in 2009. He is Chinese-American who majored in Electronics Engineering and Computer Science. His expertise in AI, especially in voice recognition, was acknowledged by his winning the Okawa Prize in 2012 and a prize from IEEE in 2013. Prof. Zue, who was working on the development of an easy and natural human-computer spoken language interface, showed me how voice recognition and AI technologies worked.

He explained that he was studying autonomous cars, (verbally) interactive GPS, and super-large screens, based on the vision that IT would be at the center in the future. He was also proud that his projects at the research center were wholly carried out in collaboration with global corporations, including Nokia, Microsoft, NEC, and Google. His list didn't include any Korean company. I asked why, and he said no Korean company had been interested when he knocked on their doors.

As I was leaving MIT, I felt chills down my spine. I felt ashamed and wondered what we were doing while these others were making strides ahead. It was the same chill I felt while watching the match between AlphaGo and Lee Se-dol. The introduction of AI was still one of my assignments.

My mind was racing when I visited the KT R&D Center in Umyeon-dong in mid-March 2016.

"KT will watch over Korean households."

My weekend visits to the KT R&D Center were an important slot in my schedule after I became the KT CEO. I directed the company to include tacitly approved technologies, i.e. technologies that could be developed going forward, in the R&D mix and to discuss them. I also called on the executives in charge of decision-making to participate in the meetings to encourage and support technology development. My involvement in this effort with my own hands and ideas brought results.

At the time, the Institute operated three laboratories, and our discussion participants ranged between 30 and 50.

I visited each laboratory in turn, listened to what the researchers had to say, and pondered with them the kinds of support needed.

"It's nothing."

This was on a day when the shock from the AlphaGo match still lingered in my mind. Researchers were hurriedly straightening up some documents when I opened the door. I asked them what was going on, but I didn't get the answer I wanted. Again, I said, "It's okay. Please tell me."

When Baek Gyu-tae, the laboratory chief who led the meeting, signaled with his eyes, one of the researchers started to say, "It's about using the voice recognition technology..." At that moment a flash came into my head. "Lab Chief Baek has finally done it!" A smile crept across my face.

Lab Chief Baek was one of the few AI experts at the KT R&D Center. In the 1980s, when the AI phenomena first emerged, he went to the US to begin a doctoral program in Computer Science. He obtained his PhD, returned to Korea, and joined KT in 1995. After he finished the studies, advancements in AI technology stalled for an extended period, and so public interest in the field waned. He weighed his options carefully and then he decided to come to KT rather than become a professor.

KT had few areas in which he could exercise his expertise. When internet protocol television (IPTV) came along, he was put in charge of media and his main task was to support that business. He spent more than twenty years so engaged, putting aside what he really wanted to do—AI-related work.

When I became the CEO of KT and exchanged greetings with the employees, I noticed that Baek Gyu-tae had a unique bent. Not only he was a rare AI specialist, but you could feel vitality from the glint in his eyes.

He was remarkably determined not to miss technology trends while confirming where the latest technologies were heading.

"It is my habit to get up at 5 o'clock in the morning. I watch TV and do some Googling to see the direction in which the world is spinning. Now the AI age is upon us. I see that with my own eyes.

Unlike others his age, who are typically preoccupied with getting a promotion or starting life after retirement, he still had this intense curiosity about the world and focused on how the technologies he had studied were changing. He worked harder than everyone else. His co-workers, subordinates, and superiors often called him a workaholic, which could both be a compliment or criticism. Others felt sorry for him as he still failed to become a managing director although he was past his mid-50s and had been working for longer than twenty years.

At the end of 2015, I called the lab chief, informing him about company's regular personnel appointments.

"Managing Director Baek, please do your best in 2016. Light your final torch at KT."

I had personally informed him of his promotion, one in fact, everybody had sought to dissuade me from giving. However, I stood firm, saying "I have a task for Managing Director Baek." As I congratulated him on his promotion, he said in a slightly excited tone, "I will really do my best." I felt his sincerity.

It took only three months for him to get something done. He quietly prepared an AI project, which was an assignment that had weighed heavily on me. He only gave an oral report, no formal presentation or manual, but I immediately understood the kind of device he was planning. I was sure that he would make it.

"KT will protect Korean households."

Managing Director Baek expected that global IT companies like Amazon, Google, and Apple in the US, as well as Baidu and Xiaomi in China would jump into the development of AI speakers. He also understood the AI speaker would do more than just communicate with the user and operate home appliances. He believed it would also converge with diverse industrial fields as an AI engine or platform and he stressed that KT should move fast before the American or Chinese AI speakers land in the Korean market and take over Korean households. I agreed with him 100%. To no surprise, it was like a meeting of two minds.

Heaven helps those who help themselves

Lab Chief Baek told me with full confidence that he would make the prototype in three to four months. I promised him full support.

At the early stage, we faced internal opposition, and the main reason cited for this was the fact we had not experienced much R&D success to date. They said that we had made countless devices based on new technologies and ideas, but consumers didn't pay attention to products made by a telecommunications service provider.

I emphasized that "the cutting-edge products consumers want are different." The AI speaker we were preparing was not a simple grafting of technologies to satisfy consumer curiosity. It would be a product that uses cutting-edge technology to open a new era. If we link IPTV, KT's strongest advantage, with the AI speaker, the synergistic effect would not be double, but twenty times greater. I also thought consumers wouldn't simply ignore a well-made product.

The second reason they were against the project was that we had never worked like this before. Upon hearing Lab Chief Baek's report, I ordered the various company units to work together from the early stages of development. Normally, once a new product is developed, the marketing people perform a review, followed by testing and modifications. Once the technology has been finalized, the design is tweaked, and parts are procured. Following the customary workflow, the product does not go onto the market for a minimum of 1-2 years and sometimes as long as 4-5 years. Should the person in charge delay the process while concentrating on other projects, the project in question could simply wind up buried. For this reason, I called on all the concerned units, from design and technology development to parts and procurement, to work together from the product planning stage. I persuaded them to ponder whey they needed to collaborate, and to realize that by cooperating, they would discover ways that they haven't seen before.

The third reason cited for opposing the project was that we didn't know enough about AI. However, I trusted Lab Chief Baek's expertise and passion. Lacking the experience, technology, and specialized human resources was our reality; but still I trusted his passion and believed it was worth giving it a go. In addition, KT might have been behind in terms of AI, but it had a preeminent position in big data, IoT, and both wired and wireless infrastructures. We were also able to use technologies that the KT R&D Center had been building up for the past twenty years, including voice recognition, natural language processing, and media curation. KT had another great asset: the various basic AI technology specifications.

I believed in Lab Chief Baek and the 128 researchers working with him, and I encouraged them. Fortunately, things went really well because of their consensus and strong convictions. We checked the prototype ourselves during the demonstration day in May, and everything went well; in July, we presented the prototype to our executives at the R&D Roadshow of the KT R&D Center. It was the first time for the executive members to see a completed version of GiGA Genie.

"We had four areas of consideration with the name Genie. First, was the pronunciation. We started the name with the Korean consonant (similar to the letter "j" in English) to make it easy to summon with voice commands. Second, Genie has interactive AI, which means it understands human speech and can execute their commands. Third, it is the name of the lead character in a 1960s sitcom I liked, *Bewithed*. Finally, the genie (or jinni) is a magic spirit who grants people's wishes in *The Arabian Nights* saga."

Everyone nodded at the lab chief's explanation, and the product name was so decided. For the next few months, Baek Gyu-tae, his research team, and the persons in charge of design, marketing, and procurement devoted themselves to the GiGA Genie development project, which progressed at great speed.

Before naming our product GiGA Genie, the specs for our speaker were hotly debated. We agreed that no matter how nice the AI engine was in the speaker, it still would not be well received by consumers if the sound quality was poor. Good speakers are expensive.

The Procurement Team approached top-end speaker manufacturer with the strategy of purchasing high-quality speakers in large quantities to lower unit cost. Things went well with Harman Kardon, a prestigious audio product maker, and the contract was signed under the condition of purchasing up front the quantity for the upcoming years. The ink on the contract was hardly dry when newspapers reported that Samsung had acquired Harman Kardon for $9 billion. We heaved a collective sigh of relief since we had already closed the deal.

"Thank goodness we cooperated from the early stage and the Procurement Team moved quickly. Heaven must have been happy to see Lab Chief Baek and all the other employees work together. Heaven helps those who help themselves, right?"

The Procurement Team director who participated in the first meeting for the project mentioned the importance of early collaboration. It didn't sound like flattery. The challenging spirit and passion of the AI-related researchers at the KT R&D Center, as well as the early participation of the marketing people accelerated the project pace and enhanced its completeness. Thanks to this, we came out with an IPTV-based AI speaker that differed from Alexa (Amazon) or Home (Google). From the earliest stage of its production, GiGA Genie was touted as the most creative device in KT's long history.

Going straight to No. 1 results from collective passion

In January 2017, there was a press conference for GiGA Genie at KT Square. Amazon's Alexa and SKT's Nugu were already on the market. However, KT employees felt extraordinarily confident because their strategy was to captivate consumers with an "AI speaker that displays things on screen."

"An ordinary AI speaker only listens and speaks. GiGA Genie doesn't stop there; it also shows the images of what the user wants."

GiGA Genie took full advantage of the fact that KT was the top player in IPTV. When you say, "Genie, show me the way to Samseong-dong," the IPTV displays a map to Samseong-dong. This feature not only made

Lab Chief Baek Gyu-tae giving a presentation at the press conference

GiGA Genie function as both an AI speaker and an IPTV-based AI, which domestic media touted as greatly enhancing user convenience and comfort.

The initial praise for GiGA Genie was profuse, and the market penetration was exceptional. A device that was completed in only nine months attracted one million users within a year and a half, and two million in two years. As of 2020, GiGA Genie was installed in 2.7 million households. Looking into the market share of AI speakers in Korea, KT is still ranked first place with a commanding 39% share.

With GiGA Genie's AI engine, KT immediately became the lead player in the domestic AI industry. In July 2017, the KT R&D Center opened the AI Tech Center.

In November, GiGA Genie LTE was released to let users enjoy the

The author signing his name on the exclusive AI server during the opening ceremony of the AI Tech Center in July 2017.

AI service outdoors; and in February 2018, an AI service for children went on the market. Afterward, KT released GiGA Genie INSIDE, which allows users to plug the device into home appliances such as the refrigerator, massage chair, or air-conditioner as well as into automobiles and smart home terminals to access GiGA Genie's call-phrases and services.

GiGA Genie's service availability expanded from households to apartment complexes, hotels, and even automobiles. For example, the Novotel Ambassador in Seoul started using GiGA Genie services, allowing guests to speak to the device in the room to get items delivered. Users can reserve facilities in the apartment community by speaking to the AI speaker or searching for information, such as management expenses (GiGA Genie My Apartment Service). The "connected car" technology established a two-way link between the home and automobile, enabling home-to-car and car-to-home services from the summer of 2018.

In October 2019, with the success of GiGA Genie, KT was able to declare its transformation into an AI company. Management announced an investment of about $300 million and cultivation of 1,000 AI professionals as a top priority.

Like the operating system for a smartphone, GiGA Genie will play the role of a platform that enables AI services in new areas.

The Korea Economic Daily selected Lab Chief Baek as the winner of the 28th Dasan Technology Award in December 2019. He was acknowledged for his contribution to the development of the AI speaker GiGA Genie and AI ecosystem as well as to the development of the realistic media technology based on 5G mobile communications that was used at the PyeongChang 2018 Winter Olympics. I also want to proudly note here that the "athlete's viewpoint video solution" and "360-degree video technology" presented at the PyeongChang Winter Olympics were also products of Baek Gyu-tae's passion and hard work.

Various GiGA Genie products

Faith that our passion is our potential

I marveled more than once or twice at the genuineness of Lab Chief Baek while we made GiGA Genie together.

"This is the most rewarding moment that I've ever had working at KT. I'm doing what I want to the utmost."

"I think I made a good choice by not becoming a professor. It feels good to do the things I want."

"I thought it might be difficult to make it in time, but it occurred to me that this might be my last chance to see AI technology surge with deep learning."

These are what Baek Gyu-tae said as a man approaching his 60s. Someone said that I lit him up, but I thought his pure passion found its way through. It might take time, but passion will always be your pathfinder.

Having left my job, I am half worried, half excited when reading articles about the AI speaker and AI engine these days. KT's AI technology is being recognized globally. The people I met from Google at the 2019 WEF showed avid interest in GiGA Genie. They perceived KT as an AI company, and proposed a partnership between Google and KT for voice recognition technology. Eric Schmidt invited me to a breakfast meeting that he organized, probably motivated by his great interest in KT's GiGA Genie.

However, the global market share for AI speakers in 2020 was, in descending order, Amazon (23%), Google (19%), Baidu (14%), Alibaba (13%), Xiaomi (11%), and Apple (5%). Unknown companies take up the remaining 14%. KT is protecting its position in the domestic market, but the market condition could change at any time. The world economy is being reorganized around the US and China, and it is a fact that their AI technologies are far ahead.

What we can count on now is the passion of our next generation. The deep learning of AI engines, including GiGA Genie, has reached maturity. It has been more than three years since the introduction of its service; thus, big data has been accumulated and the technology has advanced. The next generation has the duty to create better technologies and devices.

It's been more than thirty years since I was delighted at developing the world's first 256M DRAM. The company appreciated our success, and I was even invited to a breakfast at the Office of the President of the Republic of Korea (or Blue House).

I went to the Blue House breakfast with other employees involved in the 256M DRAM project. After breakfast, I shook hands with the President. As I leaned, my fountain pen slipped out of my suit pocket and fell on the floor. The President was faster than me. He stopped the approach of the entourage, and picked up the pen to put it in my pocket himself.

"Do not ever lose to Japan again."

I could still vividly hear the President's voice as he said those words while putting the fountain pen back in my pocket. At the time, it was our assignment to beat Japan with products. The words of the President were a request for us not to satisfy ourselves with one victory and to continue to do our best in the battle against Japan. The passion in my heart to beat Japan in this generation became stronger.

The starting point of every achievement is passion. The bigger your passion, the greater your possibility.

The greater your possibility, the greater your achievement.

Now retired from industry, Baek Gyu-tae also hopes that the next generation will be passionate about achieving the global No. 1 position. If I can, I also want to encourage them, the same way the President picked up my fountain pen for me.

Launching challenges with new technologies

2009

Graphene

The word "graphene" was coined by combining the "graph" in "graphite" with the suffix "ene," referring to molecule with double-carbon bonds. This revolutionary new material is available in film as thin as 0.35mm.

Graphene has chemical and physical properties far superior to substances widely used in industry today. Electrons move at least 150 times faster across graphene than they do over silicon. Graphene is also some 200 times stronger than steel and conducts heat twice as fast as diamond does. Indeed, graphene is already used in a wide range of applications, including rechargeable batteries, solar cells, flexible displays, and parts for the automotive and aerospace industries. Today, vigorous research is being conducted to apply this material to next-generation semiconductors.

2012

Korea Micro Energy Grid (KT-MEG): Korea's Smart Energy System

K-MEG stands for Korea Micro Energy Grid, a system of independent power grids that each make use of small-scale telecommunications infrastructure at the local level. These microgrids both produce and distribute energy to consumers, taking advantage of macro-processes (cloud-based analytics as well as various mobile networks and communication mediums) to achieve self-sufficiency. This microgrid concept serves as the basis for integrated management of the production, storage, consumption, and trading of all energy sources, to include heat, electricity, and natural gas.

KT took over the Korea Micro Energy Grid (K-MEG) project in 2014 and developed KT-MEG, which uses the analytics platform "e-Brain," capable of machine learning, to predict energy output and consumption, thereby optimizing production and trading. For example, the system will analyze customers' consumption patterns and weather conditions to forecast peak demand and then automatically adjust the production and distribution facilities to lower energy costs by 10-20%. Additional savings of up to 40% can be achieved by replacing outdated equipment and other such measures. As such this system can rightly be labeled an "innovative platform."

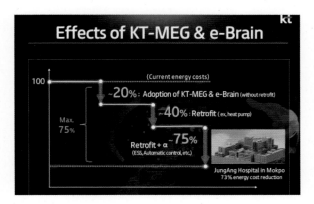

5G

The concept of 5G differs from the earlier advancements leading up to 4G by focusing primarily on raising transmission speed. The 5G network embodies discontinuous evolution, which goes beyond ultra-high speed to achieve ultra-low latency and simultaneous multiple connections, and makes possible the 4th Industrial Revolution. In fact this can be considered a core platform for the 4th Industrial Revolution, connecting with AI, big data, IoT and other network technologies to provide present industries with new opportunities for growth.

The global market research firm HIS predicts that by 2035 the size of the 5G market alone will amount to US$12.3 trillion. The emergence of 5G is expected to add 22 million jobs in the economy as it is applied in autonomous driving, remote medical services, and countless other sectors.

KT presented a trial 5G service at the PyeongChang 2018 Winter Olympic Games, standardized the technology with of demonstration of 5G services during Mobile World Congress (MWC) 2019 in Barcelona, and aims to remain in the lead until 5G is commercialized globally.

Accompany

We Can Go **Further** Together

01

Keep your teachers
in your hearts

| **Hermann Simon** |

When I was young, I thought everyone became an adult when their hair turned gray. I was an energetic young man back in the day. As a student at Busan High School, I ran in the relays at all the athletic meets. At university, I learned to play tennis, won a tennis competition within our department, and participated in the university-level tournament. Whenever I visited Busan, my hometown, I would play tennis on the tennis courts at Pusan National University.

I was full of vigor at that time, yet I always politely deferred to those older than I. Even if they were not as good at tennis as I was, I couldn't act pompous, because to me, they were "adults," while I was not. Adults were those to whom I needed to show respect and from whom I could learn.

Now that I have became older than those adults whom I respected back then, I come to think that there is nothing "free" in this world. Getting to a place where one earns respect is a hundred, nay a thousand times more difficult than respecting someone else. The grayer my hair becomes, the weightier the burden of being an adult becomes.

I have reached the age when I hear news of people whom I respect have passed away. It has been a while since I've asked myself, "What would they have done in this case?" instead of complaining, "This is too much for me." Teachers, whom I cherish dearly in my heart and have left me with heartwarming memories, helped me get through hard times.

Hermann Simon is a world-class business management scholar and a personal friend with whom I've kept a close relationship with for almost 20 years. He once told me that I should keep my teachers in my heart, and I've had many inspirations come from that piece of advice. We first met when I was the director of the Samsung's Memory Business, and we still stay in touch. He is strongly interested in cultivating mid-sized enterprises, and has generously advised me each time I changed my employment position and sought insights on what to do next.

Hidden Champions of the Twenty-First Century: Success Strategies of Unknown World Market Leaders and *Confessions of the Pricing Man* are two of his best-known works, and they are bestsellers in Korea as well. While running a brilliant career as a management consultant, he is also well read in the classics and published collections of aphorisms, available in multiple languages. Hermann is unafraid to learn from anybody, and has devoted much effort to maintaining diverse and close personal networks. I, too, have enjoyed discussing with him the teachers who reside in my heart.

The courage to look back on the path taken

Hermann Simon sent me an e-mail in the early summer of 2020.

He asked me to write a foreword for an English edition of his new autobiography, *Many Worlds, One Life: A Remarkable Journey from Farmhouse to the Global Stage*. Closing his letter, he said, "Feel free to refuse if you don't have enough time or it if it's inconvenient for you. It won't affect our friendship, so don't worry." That was just like him, who was considerate and polite, to say so.

Many Worlds, One Life was his first autobiography. Hermann was born in a small village in northern Germany in 1947, and today he is among the world's leading authorities on management strategy and marketing, particularly in the area of pricing. At the same time, he is considered among the very best German-born business management scholars.

A glance at his career will show that these superlative descriptions are no exaggeration. He taught at business schools in the UK and Germany before working as a visiting professor at leading universities in the US (Harvard, Stanford, and MIT), Japan, and France. Then in 1985, he founded Simon-Kucher & Partners, which has grown into a leading strategy and marketing consultancy, with branches in 26 countries around the world.

However, he did not write *Many Worlds, One Life* to list his achievements. It's not like the typical autobiography one usually envisions. He looks back on his life in great detail, and lays out in everyday narrative, rather than through accounts of heroic exploits, how his world had been formed. For example, he didn't say he was smart or studied hard enough to enter the advanced high school (Gymnasium) as a son of a farmer, but simply said he took the exam without preparing sufficiently and feeling no pressure.

He realized that he was good in academics right before graduating college, so he then decided to pursue a career in academia. Hermann has an amazing network of scholars whom he has met and exchanged ideas with.

What impressed me most in his life was his childhood. He describes the time of his youth as the "Middle Ages," when he grew up in a rural valley community that spoke a German dialect, as opposed to "the present," where he is playing an important role on a global stage. The valley is his own metaphor for the great gap that exists between the two worlds. To illustrate the extent of the cultural and physical gaps he perceives, he talks about vivid memories from his childhood. He presents a vast range of facts such as when and where his parents were born, their marriage, the births and deaths of cousins around him, and the local area at that time. Through these recollections, he tried to capture the essence of the times back then.

Power Pricing, another masterpiece of his, was the reason we first met on September 3, 2001, when I was in charge of Samsung's Memory Business Division. I can say we've interacted frequently during the ensuing two decades. We often exchanged messages and met in person even after I became a chair professor at Sungkyunkwan University, led the Office of Strategic R&D Planning, and served as the KT chairman. While I was at the Office of Strategic R&D Planning, I asked him to be a keynote speaker of the Global R&D Forum, and he gladly accepted. We had several meals together at that time, too.

Even though we knew each other for so long, the childhood story recalled in his autobiography was unfamiliar to me, making the book all the more fascinating to read. Germany was a defeated nation after World War II, and it suffered tremendous war damage. I carefully read how he managed to come from his birthplace, in a small village after Germany had lost the War, to where he is today, and I couldn't help marveling at his courage to look back on the path from where he came.

People our age often long for the good old days and at the same time

The author and Professor Simon having a discussion at the Global R&D Forum in 2011.

regret how dimming memories have raced past in a blur. Most of us, however, continue to live without doing anything about it. Few people have the reserve or the courage to redirect the light illuminating the present back on the past in order to recall and retrace it vividly. Our early days are by and large interspersed with immature mistakes. Considerable regret is also felt about paths not taken. However Hermann decided to deal with these feelings. In the process, he was rewarded by remembering people he had met in the past and forgotten about, particularly the teachers buried deep in his heart who had led him to new opportunities and changed his life.

"When I failed to solve the division problem, my teacher lost patience... I reacted like anybody would... I was scolded and gave up on the lesson."

He decided to get tutoring from a teacher to help him get into Gymnasium, but before long he ended up arguing with the teacher over a math problem and stopped seeing him. Fortunately, they were able to repair their relationship after he entered Gymnasium.

Numerous people who influenced his life were featured in his autobiography. They include his parents; relatives; teachers at Gymnasium; and professors he met in universities, including Philip Kotler, the "Father of Marketing." He also recalled anecdotes that occurred while he interacted with Korean leaders, including myself, as well as with management gurus and religious figures he met around the world. He wrote about each encounter separately, describing what took place without exaggeration or aggrandizement.

He expressed his feelings and the influences they had on him with a very straightforward tone. His story was like German bread—hard and dry, but sufficiently flavorful to satisfy my hunger for humanity.

My first memories-*janggu* rhythms and *maehwa* paintings

In our letters, Hermann Simon and I would sometimes share stories about our grandfathers. My grandfather lived in Korea during the tough Japanese colonial period, and his grandfather suffered difficulties while fighting in the World War. We shared something in common: we lost our grandfathers at the age of four to five, yet we still cherished their memories throughout the years.

After I wrote the endorsements for Hermann's autobiography, I also tried to cross the bridge that connects my time "back then" with where I am now.

I was born in Busan and grew up during the Korean War. I moved to Seoul to attend college, and I've continued to live in the capital. Besides the few years I spent studying in the US, my time "back then" was spent in Busan, while my present is in Seoul. My grandfather was the first person to welcome me to the "bridge that connects my past and present."

My grandfather was Hwang Yeong-du (pen name: Maesan), a prominent painter during the days of the Daehan Empire (1897-1910). By the 1890s, his name was well known in his hometown, and his life as a court painter was even featured in a serial column published by the *Kyongnam Sinmun*, a local newspaper serving South Gyeongsang Province.

People called him a child prodigy, as he started painting at the tender age of ten. In the 1890s, my grandfather participated in a painting contest in front of the King and was invited to a royal banquet. He entered his works in art exhibitions in the Korean capital (then called Gyeongseong) and Tokyo, and even studied modern sciences. However, the Korean people lost their national sovereignty in 1910, and he was unable to realize all his ambitions. Therefore, he left the capital and moved to Jinju around the age of 40. He got married, had a child (my father), spent his later years interacting with the local gentry, and never put his paintbrush down.

My first memory about my grandfather starts with him living in Jinju. My parents sought refuge in Busan during the Korean War, and that was when my mother gave birth to me. My grandfather was unable to leave the old family home (the clan seat). In turn, my father succeeded as the eldest grandson of the head family, and so when he fled to Busan as a war refugee, he carried every one of the ritual items necessary to perform the regular ancestral rites, even during wartime.

The performance of ancestral rites was a common site in our home. Memorial sacrifices to ancestors were held about once a month, including the national holidays, and each time my grandfather visited our home to preside over the proceedings. He would then spend the night with us.

"Gyu, come here. I'll show you how to play the *janggu* (hourglass drum)."

My grandfather adored me, his eldest grandson. After everyone had partaken of the sacrificial offerings at the conclusion of the memorial ceremony, my mother and father removed the sacrificial table. I finally was face to face with my grandfather. He sat me down

The author's grandfather, [Maesan] Hwang Yeong-du

in the *ondol* room (the one with the underfloor-heating) and taught me the *janggu* rhythm by slapping his palms on the floor surface. I still remember the irregular rhythm that I learned from my grandfather, which I demonstrated in a school play after I went into first grade.

Unfortunately, my grandfather passed away even before he could see me enter elementary school. He was already old when I was born and died at the age of 77, when I was five years old. I still vividly remember the time we went to Jinju for his funeral, which took place around Chuseok (the Harvest Moon Festival). My mother, who was preoccupied by everything going on, harshly scolded me when I fell into a ditch. I felt sad, feeling the absence of my grandfather, who always sided with his eldest grandson.

Someone may ask, "You only spent a few years with him in your early childhood. How could that influence your life for 70 years?" But my memories of being with my grandfather have permeated my entire life.

316

My father gave the keepsakes left behind by Grandfather to me, and asked me to keep them well. When my father went on a business trip or traveled to another region, I would open the cloth-wrapped bundles of my grandfather's things, and it would make me so happy. In them I found a rolled up painting of *maehwa* (梅花 plum blossoms), and that piece of Grandfather's artwork especially touched my heart for some reason. The energy it conveyed matched the memories I had of my grandfather, stirring the special feelings of a young boy. Just like that, my time as a young student passed without any trouble as I untied and retied the cloth wrapper over and over again.

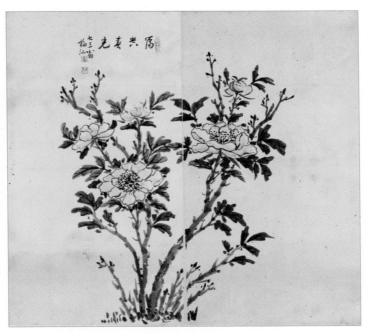

An ink painting of peonies by Maesan Hwang Yeong- du (1953)

I forgot about it for a while when I was in college and studying abroad, but since I returned to Korea, I decided to keep Grandfather's keepsakes at my house and brought them all to Seoul. I opened his paintings from time to time, appreciating the *maehwa*. I may have used being busy as an excuse, but deep in my heart, I made up my mind that someday I would show his paintings to the public.

It was in 2018, sixty-one years after my grandfather passed away, when I sent his paintings to the Gana Art Center in Pyeongchang-dong, Seoul. His old artworks were restored and mounted on new hanging scrolls. Lee Tae-ho, the director of *Institute of Seoul Landscape*, heard about the exhibition, went to Jinju for four days and five nights to ask around about my grandfather's life, uncovered some unknown records, and then organized them in writing. Many oral accounts about interactions with anti-Japanese resistance fighters had been handed down to the present; they supported the documented

The *One Branch of Plum Blossoms* in the author's living room (1956)

evidence and could be published in the exhibition catalog.

Also included in the brochure were congratulatory cards that independent activists of the Enlightenment Party, including Oh Se-chang, Mun Bin, Seo Byeong-du, and Lee Yeong-min, sent to Grandfather when his ink plum blossom painting won an award at an exhibition.

It is said that Grandfather would send his paintings to those who visited him upon hearing he was going to depart for Manchuria to support the Independence Movement. He asked them to use the art whenever needed during difficult times.

I have one of my grandfather's works in my living room, an ink painting called *One Branch of Plum Blossoms* (一枝梅 *Iljimae*), which fills me with courage and comfort. It was produced by Grandfather at the age of 76, one year before he passed.

It is a folding screen approximately three meters wide filled with the image of an old plum tree. Whenever I encountered crises or challenged during my days as a manager, I would gaze at Grandfather's painting and feel the spirit that lingers there, leading me to take a new turn in my thinking about life.

Reading about a teacher in Hermann Simon's heart while in a Korean home

Early in the 2010s, when I was busy as the National CTO at the Office of Strategic R&D Planning, I went with Hermann Simon to visit an old *hanok* (traditional Korean-style home) that belonged to some acquaintances of mine.

Hermann liked to listen to classical music and proudly referred to himself as a Wagnerian. Our conversation began when I boasted I had been to Bayreuth to watch Wagner's Der Ring des Nibelungen (Ring Cycle). Hermann said he went every summer to the Bayreuth Festival, which is in the northern part of the German state of Bayern. He repeatedly used the term "Wagnerian," which denotes an avid fan of the famous German composer.

Loving Wagner to the extent that he could fluently recite Wagner's 10 operas line by line, he told us several stories about the Bayreuth Festival. The old *hanok* and the talk about Wagner curiously blended well to create a fond memory. Hermann loved the atmosphere of the *hanok* very much.

He loved Korea to the extent he called himself "pro-Korean." He had memories of Korean healthcare workers and miners who had immigrated to Germany in droves during the 1970s. He also studied with Korean students when he was in college. He visited Korea often, thanks to the Korean corporations that requested the consulting services of his company. He loved the dynamism of modern Korea, and the orientalism of traditional Korea.

I believe his affection for Korea had a positive influence on our relationship. He was sure to send a copy of his latest book whenever it was published, and he mentioned our relationship during interviews with various media.

He also invited me to his house in Bonn saying, "I look forward to having you stop by one time when you happen to be in Germany." Therefore, while I was on a trip to Germany to visit certain "hidden champions," I took time from my schedule to visit his place. It took two and a half hours on the highway from Frankfurt, but meeting him was always a delight.

Professor Simon sent the author this photo of his study. Behind him is the Korean version of his autobiography.

Located on the Rhine River, his house looked like a country home in Korea-a white one-story structure with a large, well-kept garden. I went there with my R&D companions, and Simon also invited his acquaintances, a few business school professors. Dinner was served in an outdoor pavilion overlooking the Rhine.

Hermann's wife was very friendly. She prepared a great number of dishes, served them, and even shared wonderful stories to us.

She is a career woman who operates her own business and is engaged in social activities. While we were visiting, she took care of her husband first and was very hospitable to guests. In contrast, Hermann looked far different than the stereotypical Western husband, who shows his sentimental side so openly. Rather, he was even worse than Busan men, notorious for their abrupt manner. I joked, "You married a great woman for being a German." We all burst into laughter.

His study was the most impressive part of his house. The room was packed with items from great teachers of humanity. Seeing the collection of books in this traditional European-style study made me realize that his inexhaustible wellspring of insights was here.

As a matter of fact, he published *Geistreiches fur Manager (Wit and Wisdom for Managers)* in 2000. Also translated in Korean, the book features a great number of teachers from both the East and West. It contains aphorisms regarding corporate visions and futures, business strategies and competition, economics, politics, and, of course, the media and the author's own business. While I was reading this book, where encapsulated knowledge was compiled in phrases and sentences, I asked myself, "How could he have written such a book?" I realized the answer when I saw his study and thought that writing

Hinaus in die Welt der Staatsmänner und Manager: Hermann Simon als gefragter Wirtschaftsexperte mit Friedensnobelpreisträger Michail Gorbatschow (l.), mit Ex-Präsident Bill Clinton (M.) oder mit dem National Chief Technology Officer von Korea, Dr. Chang Gyu Hwang (r.)

mentprofessor aus Illinois einmal formuliert. „Marketing ist leicht gesagt und schwer getan", dürfte Hermann Simon augenzwinkernd seinen Sinnspruch für Manager hinzufügen und damit indirekt begründen, warum Vordenker wie Kotler und er selbst rund um den Erdball so ungemein gefragt sind.

Bekanntlich gilt der Prophet im eigenen Lande nichts, doch das stimmt für den Management-Fachmann nicht. Das Ran-

dass man es nicht als separate betriebliche Funktion sehen könne. „Das eigentliche Ziel des Marketings ist es, das Verkaufen überflüssig zu machen. Das Ziel des Marketings ist es den Kunden und seine Bedürfnisse derart gut zu verstehen, dass das daraus entwickelte Produkt genau passt und sich daher von selbst verkauft." Solche wie in Stein gemeißelte Drucker-Sätze als Schlüssel zum Erfolg zeigen sein Bemühen um Klarheit und Überblick. Heute Simons Markenzeichen

An interview with Professor Hermann Simon in *absatzwirtschaft*, a prestigious German magazine specialized in marketing and sales.

that kind of work may have been a pastime for him. Spending much time in a space filled with writings by important figures could have ignited a passion in him that led him to compile the influential words of the teachers he had met before.

A cover of *absatzwirtschaft*

In 2012, he emailed me a clipping from the prestigious German marketing magazine *absatzwirtschaft*. Photos of Mikhail Sergeyevich Gorbachev, Bill Clinton, and myself were on the page.

Hermann Simon selected me as one of the three figures who impressed him in an interview that celebrated his 65th birthday, and included my photo. I felt the depth of our long friendship and his warm heart after seeing my photo in a foreign magazine.

Teaching is not words, but life

"Who are the teachers close to your heart?"

As the introduction of this book suggests, I have numerous teachers whom I've kept close to my heart. I recall an endless number of faces, those of my grandfather; Admiral Yi Sun-sin; William B. Shockley, developer of the semiconductor; Andrew Grove, the eternal head of Intel; Professor Navon of UMass; Professor Dutton of Stanford University; and countless more.

One day I was talking about my dear teachers with an acquaintance. However, I had to stop and be silent when asked if I had some special story that I had heard from them.

I had a vague longing for my grandfather, but I was only five when he passed away. I wonder if there could be any special conversation between a grandfather in his 70s and his little grandson. William Shockley and Andrew Grove were my heroes, and my heart raced when I was in front of them. They helped me to grow and gave me encouragement for the future, yet they were not the type to leave me with important words of wisdom.

In the end, I could not think of any life-changing, definitive phrase that others could easily quote. Nonetheless, I still consider them teachers who had a great influence on my life. I unquestionably gained courage and felt comfort from them whenever I faced difficulties. Then I realized: "Ah! It's not words that changed my life."

My grandfather's paintings were more than just simple words. Professors David Nevon and Robert Dutton, two of my dearest teachers, showed me models of behavior through their life experience. While I studied for my doctorate and at the laboratory, I didn't feel lonely, but instead felt secure, thanks to them.

Indeed, all the teachers close to my heart showed their philosophy and lessons through how they lived their lives. That's why I can never forget them. Every time things got tough, I would wonder to myself, "What would they do if they were in my place?" and then the answer to my dilemma would come easily.

Management is like walking together on a pilgrimage

Hermann Simon is one of my friends who affirmed to me that teaching is not done through words, but through life.

There is a seven-hour time difference between Germany and Korea. It takes 11 hours to travel between the two countries, even on a direct flight. However, he sends e-mails and calls me on the phone whenever he has time. During his visits to Korea, he would always stop by my office and talk about the gifts I gave him, such as a Samsung MP3 player and KT's GiGA Genie, telling me that they reminded him of me all the time. He also freely shares insights that he has learned from business situations, where he has spent most of his life. His propensity to share life stories must also be behind the strong and close-knit network that he enjoys. In this sense, I can say that he is my role model and a teacher whom I keep close to my heart.

To add a bit more praise, his attitude as a professor and a CEO of a global consulting company reminds me of an Eastern pilgrim.

"Let every person and matter serve as your teachers, and always be ready to listen and learn."

This phrase I found in a newspaper, in a piece written by a poet about the teachers close to his heart. When I first read this sentence, I was reminded of Hermann Simon. Only those who are willing to listen can listen, and only those who are willing to learn can accept new things. Hermann has emphasized this in many of his books, and practices it himself.

I particularly agreed with his assertion because of the experiences I had in my early days. During the time I studied as a foreign student in an unfamiliar land, I was astonished to meet brilliant people, far more gifted than I was. At first, I considered them to be competing rivals, and I struggled alone. It didn't take long before I changed my attitude.

"There will always be someone smarter than me in this world. I shouldn't try to beat them, but instead discover a new path."

Indeed, once I changed my mind, our opinions, which had always been at odds, we would connect on a new thesis-antithesis-synthesis approach. As soon as I acknowledged they were not wrong, our research results improved.

I applied this lesson in the workplace when I sat in the manager's position. I particularly emphasized for executives to "meet others outside the office and not just stay inside." I cautioned most against being locked inside your own space. No answers are found by staying shut inside your walls and only reviewing the reports written by juniors. It is better to delegate tasks to subordinates, and communicate with others outside. I have always told everyone why we should be trusting of others and communicate, and I have constantly stated what must be done. The emphasis on learning and listening is what makes managers similar to pilgrims.

For the past 30 years, I have striven to never lose the "attitude to listen and learn" while walking in the same direction together within the organization. The paths lined with flowers were always short, and those through thorns were long, but was able to finish the journeys set out for me, thanks to the many teachers who led me by the hand.

I am still traveling a path, even after my retirement. From now on, I shall continue to walk down the pilgrims' path as I did before, informing young people life's direction.

02 Tearing down barriers leads to innovation

| Eric Schmidt |

The role models for managers are not confined to individual people or leading companies. I believe organizational cultures also represent a domain that needs to be benchmarked.

Organizational cultures have historical aspects to them. They differ depending upon who their leaders have been, what kinds of work they are engaged in, and what visions they have realized. Importantly, once the roots have been embedded, the culture is difficult to change.

I called Prof. Dutton "Bob" when I worked at the Stanford laboratory. Professional titles like "professor" or "doctor" were dispensed with, as were forms of address such as "mister." I could say, "Bob, it is wrong" without hesitation, and without using formalities. That was their organizational culture. For an outsider from East Asia like me, I was shocked at first.

I experienced similar situations with respect to informality at Intel and HP. I believe their organizations were driven forward in one direction through discussion and cooperation rather than by relying on seniority.

I consider the "open culture" to be the reason the US could become an advanced country, despite having problems with racism, income inequality and so on. Another contributing factor has been individuals' dedication to self-criticism and self-correction.

I was a lucky person. Whenever I faced difficulties, I was able to meet someone who reminded me of my initial goal. Over the past thirty years, I served in different positions in different organizations, and went through hard and difficult times. I could envision the path I wanted to take, which seemed so close yet so far.

The headquarters of Google (Googleplex) in California was a unique space I saw at a time I was agonizing over my organization and leadership. Whenever I met Eric Schmidt, then-CEO of Google, I observed him focusing on my question, "What kind of leader creates the dream job?" I found him speaking the same language as myself, since he had been a CTO before becoming the CEO.

No working! Go play!

I first visited Googleplex in the early 2000s. It was not like how it is today, but its scale could be described as "campus size."

Like the typical Silicon Valley start-up, Google started out inside a garage. Sergey Brin and Larry Page, the co-founders of Google, were both Ph. D students at Stanford University. They rented a friend's room that was connected to the entrance of a garage.

Fueled by venture capital investments, their business grew fast, and the cofounders planned and constructed the Google headquarters based on their resolve to allow employees to focus solely on their jobs. The facility was opened in August 1998.

Three or four years later, I was invited by Larry Page, the first CEO, to visit Googleplex. Larry handed over the CEO position to Eric Schmidt in 2001 and focused on product management and engineering. Sergey Brin, the other co-founder, took charge of engineering and business contracts, while Eric Schmidt, the second CEO, managed the vice presidents and the operations groups.

The purpose of my visit there was to consult with them on DRAM sales and the construction of a data center. Initially, Google opted to equip their data center with a large quantity of low-cost PCs instead of investing in the expensive IBM servers. That decision cut the data center construction cost by a third. However, Google soon occupied two-thirds of the global Internet search market, outstripping the data center's operational capacity.

In 2003, Google earmarked $200 million for new equipment purchases, and thereafter, the annual budget was raised to $3 billion. Under these circumstances, Larry Page ordered massive quantities of DRAMs from Samsung Electronics.

When the meeting was about to end, Eric Schmidt came into the room. At the time, he was widely recognized in the industry. Prior to coming to Google, he had served as the CEO of Novell before becoming the concurrent CTO and CEO of Sun Microsystems. He was admired for his leadership in strategic planning, management, and technology development.

Of course, his business acumen was based on his accomplishments as a scientist and engineer. He earned a PhD in Computer Science at UC Berkeley, was recognized for inventing Java code, and was an expert in

Unix. Needless to say, he was the smart, creative figure whom the Google cofounders were desperate to attract.

Eric and I shared opinions on ways to work together as organizational leaders going forward. To my surprise, he did not present himself as being obstinate or headstrong. Rather, he seemed to be gentle and accommodating to the extent that he reminded me of the two professors from my alma maters. His personality must have been an important factor that made two young Google entrepreneurs decide to hire him in his mid-40s as the CEO, and he has had a tremendous impact on the company's products and services.

As I looked around Googleplex, I felt that the personal touch Eric Schmidt conveys is much akin to the open atmosphere of Googleplex. The employees were working freely in an open space without partitions. I noticed that some brought their dogs to work, while others were with their children in the lobby.

"No Working!"

Encountering the slogan hung up at Google gave me a shock similar to the one I felt when I had first come to the US in the mid-1980s. On several occasions, Eric explained Google's generous benefits for employees in the following way:

"Our goal is to eliminate everything that makes our employees uncomfortable. In addition to the regular fringe benefit package, we provide the services that any hardworking engineer would want such as a high quality dining facility, gym, laundry room, massage room, barber shop, car wash, dry cleaners, and commuter bus. Investment in any method that motivates people to be fully engaged in their work cannot be seen as a waste of money."

Google's organizational culture didn't just stop there. The company encouraged their people to play rather than just work. Google has employees spend one of every five workdays, that is, 20% of their total working hours, in pursuit of a project they are passionate about. The company is proud of repeated technological innovation breakthroughs that have been made thanks to their employees doing something they wanted to do instead of the regular work.

After my first impressive meeting at the company and with Eric Schmidt, I began to pay attention to the influence of Google's organizational culture on its business achievements.

Reflecting on the older generation's dereliction of duties

My second visit to Google was in early August 2010. I was on my way to Seattle to participate in the Korean-American Scientists and Engineers Association (KSEA) meeting.

In those days, I was working as the National CTO and looking for future revenue sources to fuel the Korean economy. My schedule was extremely tight and included visits to Hewlett-Packard, SRI International at Stanford University, and the Lawrence Berkeley National Laboratory at UC Berkeley. Nonetheless, I had a reason to meet Eric Schmidt.

That year, the G20 Leaders' Summit was scheduled to be held in Seoul. Currently, the G20 Summit and the B20 (Business 20) are separated, but at the time, B20 was one of the sessions during the G20 Summit.

The G20 Leaders' Summit was being organized by the Ministry of Knowledge Economy, which had asked Eric Schmidt to be a keynote speaker. He had replied that he couldn't due to a conflicting schedule. I had decided to stop over in Silicon Valley to ask him once more in the capacity of the National CTO. Of course, I sent Eric a letter ahead of time. He made time for our meeting despite his busy schedule.

When we met, he appeared more accommodating than I expected. I said I was looking forward to working together in sophisticated technological fields like search engines and memory, as Korea served as a testbed for global IT industries.

After sharing a friendly chat, I said, "I actually came here to ask you again to be a keynote speaker at the G20 Summit." Eric said he would adjust his schedule to accommodate it.

The Googleplex that I revisited this time was far bigger and much more energetic than it had been seven to eight years prior. That was

The author visiting Google to meet Eric Schmidt and ask the favor to be a keynote speaker at the G20 Leaders' Summit.

apparently because the company's size had grown more than eleven times during the period. Sales revenue was below $3.2 billion in 2004, but by 2011, the figure had reached $37.9 billion. Eric Schmidt and the two co-founders emphasized that such growth had been possible because of four factors within their organizational culture: (1) a corporate culture that respects creativity, (2) unrestricted use of 20% of total working hours, (3) a working environment where employees can concentrate on their jobs, and (4) an internal policy that values communication. He said that without these four essential factors, Google would have not been able to make such strides as a technology leader.

After returning to Korea, I thought deeply for a few days about that business trip. Then I sent a local daily newspaper an opened piece entitled "No Working! Go Play!" In it I included the impressions that Google had left on me.

Typically, companies start up a new business in one of three ways: (1) through mergers or acquisitions, (2) through the decision of the company owner or CEO, or (3) through the ideas of the employees. Traditionally, Korean companies have relied on the first and second ways. They rarely adopted new ideas of their employees. We need more leaders who will rack their brains to find the way for Korea in the next ten to twenty years. We were desperately in need for leaders who can sacrifice quick achievements for a much solid future. The members of the older generation who were obsessed with short-term outcomes and thwarted the younger generation's risk-taking approach were seriously failing to perform their duties. However, Google is using openness as a means to link employee ideas with great results.

We in Korea must also change. Our emphasis on the merit-based system has reached its limit. As soon as possible, we have to get away from the environment in which results are the only thing considered important.

I didn't feel that comfortable after sending in the article. As part of the older generation in his early 50s, I had a painful time for self-reflection.

The No. 1 Workshop: begin by dispensing with ranks and positions

I said I was lucky earlier in this book. There are several reasons for that, but getting opportunities has been the most important one. After spending some time to self-reflect, I could again serve as the head of an organization with plenty of potential. I resolved to create a new organizational culture that is unprecedented, but is essentially required for KT.

Many were calling out for improvements in KT's organizational culture. The company had already invested in several reform campaigns, including Six Sigma and the creative management espoused by Professor Gary Hamel. However, those died without showing much result, which left skepticism within the organization, and people asking, "Can we ever improve?"

I saw a desperate need for change starting from the bottom up and from the branches in the field. I also realized that we had to generate meaningful results through communication between the Head Office and the rest of the organization in the trenches. To this end, we needed our own original method, without complicated frameworks or outside consultations.

Our first priority was to expose the problems quickly. Improvement was not easy to accomplish because the people at both the Head Office and the branch offices tended to cover up or ignore the chronic problems that existed. Aggressive efforts were needed from the people in charge and the specialists to look squarely at the problems and offer solutions on the spot.

First, I was concerned about how to build an organizational culture where employees would not be reluctant to take risks. This led to other questions: "What happens when they are subjected to disadvantages after taking risks and then failing?" and "What if they weren't restricted by their work descriptions or by the organizational structure?" I created the No. 1 Workshop as a way to answer these concerns of mine.

The No. 1 Workshop was designed to have specialists and related department employees engage in intense discussions over one night and two days. In the process, I thought it was important to let them talk freely and horizontally, without regard for individual rank or position. I also stressed that no one would be held responsible for his or her proposals,

KT's employees in discussion during an event that lasts one night and two days.

and no one would suffer any disadvantages even if the idea did not work in the end.

Much effort was made at the company level to prepare for these workshop sessions. First, the members in each organizational unit were asked to point out the chronic problems they had. Then, the Corporate Culture Office finalized the issues that most urgently needed to be addressed from the company-wide perspective. Working-level personnel related to each task were invited from the more than 40 affiliates in the KT Group. Last, executives were dispatched to each session as sponsors who played the role of "trusting in and listening to the participants." They were also responsible for deciding whether ideas from the discussion would be put into action, and if so, they were to ensure the implementation was completed prior to the deadline.

The results were immediately apparent. The first day of each workshop session was officially scheduled to end at 6 p.m., but the discussions would often continue until the following dawn. Free expression of opinions guaranteed anonymity, and active implementation of adopted ideas made employees steadily more enthusiastic about the effort.

The No. 1 Workshop was a venue for solving all kinds of issues- from addressing workplace complaints by employees to approaches for improving work efficiency and ways to raise customer satisfaction.

The suggestions raised at these workshops were also applied to new product development and launch. For instance, the No. 1 Workshop was the catalyst for developing an LTE for corporate use, a B2B product, in 2016. An employee who was involved in B2B sales said, "I got this idea when I saw that people at our clients carried around two smartphones, one for business use and the other for personal use."

This observation prompted research into finding a solution where one smartphone could be used for dual purposes: business and personal. That single comment by the employee resulted in the corporate-exclusive LTE service, through which one can access their company's intranet and be guaranteed with security on one's personal smartphone. Multiple related departments worked together on the project, and as a result, the service attracted more than fifty corporate clients within five months of the launch. KT was able to establish itself as the leader in this new market segment.

Another issue put up for discussion at the workshop was the difficulty in securing the space for installing the mobile base stations needed at newly-built apartment complexes. Spirited debates raged among employees working in the trenches, employees from the Head Office, and B2B specialists during the No. 1 Workshop sessions. The participants finally agreed on the idea of portable base stations that could be carried like a suitcase. The idea was commercialized and garnered successful results.

About 84,000 employees participated in No. 1 Workshop sessions by the end of 2020, and more than 5,300 issues were dealt with. These discussions showed demonstrable results in terms of increased sales revenue and reduced expenditures. As more employees became involved in the problem-solving process, their job satisfaction, work engagement levels, and sense of responsibility were all elevated.

Communication, cooperation, and empowerment: three actions that make work enjoyable

What does a happy workplace look like?

The answer I found, as someone who has worked for a long time: a workplace where people work by themselves. Larry Page of Google held a similar opinion.

"Autonomy has been the driving force behind our greatest successes and some impressive failures. In fact, this was the basic principle when Google starting out and was what got Google going."

He gave this answer in his book. "Working on my own" is indeed an essential principle for those with creativity and expertise.

Meanwhile, conglomeritis is a unique term found in the Korean language. It refers to the fact that the bigger a company gets and the older it grows, the more severe its bureaucratic nature becomes. Barriers are erected between subordinates and superiors in the organization, while flexibility and vitality deteriorate. We would explain it as a joke, Conglomeritis is difficult to cure completely. It's a dreadful disease, in which complications (a Korean word that also suggests corporate mergers) arise without symptoms."

In fact, there are many managers who are concerned over the conglomeritis phenomena. They say egotism in their organization makes communication difficult and cooperation rare. It gives them headaches when they think about the organizational system. They also say no one wants to take on difficult tasks, and even the members of task forces organized for solving such problems hide behind collective accountability and lack the sense of personal responsibility.

I asked myself, "What does it mean to have autonomy?" After pondering this question for a long time, I came up with communication, cooperation, and empowerment as the answer. These three actions are what I emphasized hundreds of times to KT executives and staff.

Whenever I sensed a crisis coming on, I labored to make a mature organizational culture based on these three actions.

First, I stressed to the employees at all levels that empowerment should be readily given. Empowerment is not simply superiors delegating decision-making authority to their subordinates. By delegating certain tasks, employees can grow by seeing a deeper and wider vision from the perspective of those above them. At the same time, the superiors who empower their subordinates to do tasks on their own are then freed up to work on devising larger strategies, which allow them to communicate and cooperate with other organizational units.

When more communication occurs, trust naturally increases. Even employees at the bottom of the organization can enjoy their work when a virtuous cycle of communication and cooperation is established on the basis of empowerment.

The author answering questions at a special lecture for new KT employees.

Tasks ordered by someone else are usually just simple labor. They are not interesting, and they are the cause for dissatisfaction to grow. Empowerment enables employees to perform their own work autonomously and responsibly. Low-level employees can be happy when they do their work voluntarily.

"Who are the happiest people in the world? I think they are the ones whose work and interests agree. Of course, it is not easy to enjoy work at the office the way you would a hobby. But what if your idea addresses client complaints? What if you create new markets with your own hands? And what if you are turning your company into the top player globally? The work you do will have greater value, while you will find that changing the company for the better is both rewarding and fun."

That is what I told new KT employees during a special lecture.

The leader's job is to inspire a vision in the hearts of organizational members, and get the ball rolling through communication, management, and bold empowerment.

I considered my annual special lecture for new employees to be one of the most important things I did. It took place on the last day of the month-long basic training program for around 500 new recruits each year. I spoke to them as one who has lived much longer. I shared my experiences and lessons learned while going to school, joining the workforce, and rising to top management. My talk would last about an hour, after which the audience had around 20 minutes to ask questions. I also used that time to encourage them to work voluntarily and with autonomy.

Managers do not have to constantly check on the process of projects or correct mistakes in an organization where empowerment is an established practice. When employees make a mistake or see an error, they will at some moment realize the mistake or error on their own, and they grow at their own pace. I hoped that the new employees would come to understood KT's corporate culture and blossom within it.

Innovation should necessarily move from "the edge to the center"

Shortly after I became the CEO of KT, I shared the company's directions with executives by introducing paintings by Pablo Picasso and Marcel Duchamp.

"This is *The Dream* by Picasso. It shows a three-dimensional structure on a two-dimensional surface. Can you see both the front of the face and the profile?

Professor Shane Greenstein introducing KT.

The author giving a special lecture at Harvard University's Memorial Hall in 2016.

This is the innovation that breaks off from the traditional concept of space.

Next is *Nude Descending a Staircase No. 2* by Marcel Duchamp. Can you see a human figure descending the stairs? This is the innovation of the sense of time that shows the past, the present, and the future at the same time."

I told them that we should look for the potential and possibilities inside of us, the same way the two artists enabled us to see the invisible.

We should unshackle ourselves from the existing paradigm. We should break the limits we set for ourselves to see what we couldn't see before. I emphasized taking the road of innovation by tearing down the walls inside of us.

In 2016, a few years later, I received a deeply moving evaluation before

The author having a conversation with Google CEO Eric Schmidt at a CEO conference for AI companies in January 2018.

I gave a special lecture at the Memorial Hall in Harvard University.

As he explained KT's GiGAtopia and 5G strategy under the theme, "The Power of Future Network," to students, Professor Shane Greenstein introduced KT as a "company that accomplished a rare innovation that goes from the edge to the center, when most companies achieved an innovation that goes from the center to the edge."

Stepping down from the podium after addressing the GiGAtopia strategy to Harvard students, I was very proud and grateful of KT's employees for realizing innovation.

In spring 2020, I resigned from the front line of management. Looking back on the achievements was truly rewarding. A hope filled my heart that future-oriented innovation would continue to happen even though I would not be there.

I am willing to hear something like, "The tradition you told us about is now just an old stereotype for us."

"All you need is the insight that your industry is transforming at a rapid pace, the guts to take a risk and be part of that transformation, and the willingness and ability to attract the best smart creatives and lead them to make it happen."

Eric Schmidt already said what I want to tell young leaders in his book *How Google Works*.

I had a lively discussion on AI and energy with Eric Schmidt at the WEF in January 2018.

I agreed with his ideas on what a leader should do, knowing that he's always paying sharp attention to the future and leading a giant organization.

There are many creative and curious people in our society. I hope they will not be fettered by tradition and fixed ideas. In addition, I want to see an innovative culture become deeply rooted in our society.

03

"Sincerity"
shows you the way

| **Management that**
Opens Hearts |

I suffered with a bad cold for the first 40 days after I began reporting to work at KT as the CEO nominee. At the time, I couldn't figure out why I was in such miserable shape.

When I was in charge of Samsung Semiconductor, even though I used to sleep away from home about one-third of the year, I rarely took ill. I could fall asleep absolutely exhausted at night, but my eyes would always pop open early the next morning. One may attribute it to youth, but back then, I was more than eager to get to work every day.

When I applied for the position at KT, I had uncommon expectations. At KT, a B2C corporation, I was firmly resolved to carry out the challenge of re-creating the successful experience of taking a late mover and growing it into a top player, as I had done in the B2B sector. Everyone thought it would be difficult, and I agreed. But I was confident that once I had taken that first difficult step, the only thing left would be to start running.

However, even one month into my new job at KT, I could not shake off my cold. In hindsight, instead of just being physically fatigued, I think I was also heavy-hearted.

As they had been saying in the media, the situation at KT was not very good. My uneasy mind was sending bad signals to my body. I sat up nights, agonizing and trying to pull myself together. How can I rebuild an organization that has collapsed?

When the levee is about to break, let it break

On March 7, 2014, I received a report about leaked customer data at KT. It was 40 days after my inauguration ceremony. Numerous accidents and mishaps had happened one after another, as if someone had opened Pandora 's box. But then the leak of 12 million customers' data occurred, and I felt like my back was against the wall.

I called for a meeting with the board of directors to seek countermeasures. Their opinions were divided. Half of them said we should monitor the investigation and handle things as they had under the former CEO, and have the working-level executives or head of the responsible division make an apology. The remainder said the CEO should step up and take responsibility immediately.

Each side had its own reasoning. The side that wanted to just keep an eye on the situation was worried about the aftermath. If the CEO came forward and apologized too early, it would amount to an admission of complete culpability, which could lead to an uncontrollable situation, like when a dam bursts.

Those in favor of immediate action were concerned that sitting back and waiting things out would only make matters worse. And indeed, following a customer data leak that had occurred two years earlier, an apology that was offered two weeks later only made the situation worse, both inside and outside the organization.

Because the issue was so critical, opinions were sharply divided throughout the meeting. The final decision fell to me, however. I went back to the basics and thought about it. I could not make a decision that diverged from my obligations as the top administrator.

"If the levee is about to break, it's best to let it break. Let's hold a press conference as soon as possible."

I stood in front of reporters just two hours after the meeting. It was right after I had revised the statement prepared by a staff member, covering it with ink blots. I corrected each sentence over and over again.

"Despite promising to reinforce our security system after the large-scale customer data leak in 2012, we nevertheless have experienced a similar accident, and there is no room for excuses, regardless of the reasons. For KT, which calls itself an IT company, to be involved in such a major leakage of customer data, not once, but twice, can only be seen as an utter disgrace."

I bowed my head in apology and promised to innovate our security system by devoting every resource available, including outside experts. As the new administrator, I was determined to completely rectify past mistakes, reveal the cause of the accident, and reprimand those responsible in order to turn things around and make KT No. 1.

People often say the mind goes blank when they are faced with a serious situation. However, my mind that day was far from being blank. I didn't have enough time to grasp all of the problems in the organization. As I stepped down from the podium, I was resolute and said to myself, "Okay, let's knock down the levee, root out the problems, and start over."

Let's rewrite the future

Forty-three days after taking office as CEO, I sent out an email to all KT employees with the title, "Even one more mistake and we will have no future." It was an expression of my determination to change everything as if our lives depended on it.

"There is no room for retreat. Even one more mistake can mean we will have no future. Now is the time for resolute determination and innovation. Let me be clear: words without responsibility, planning with no execution, willful negligence, and letting things go unanswered are practices that will not be tolerated."

"Insensitivity to crisis" is a major symptom of organizations on the verge of collapse. In fact, as it turns out, major accidents are not usually the reason why many companies fail. They disappear in anonymity because they respond to small accidents with the attitude that "Everything will work out," and "I'm sure somebody will take care of it," or "People will forget about it soon."

In the email, I appealed to KT employees to take the path of innovation while maintaining an attitude of crisis awareness.

My first directive was to establish a dedicated organization in charge of information security. KT became the first company in the domestic telecommunications industry to separate the position of chief information officer (CIO) from the chief information security officer (CISO) and create a new team dedicated to information security. I was personally involved in recruiting new personnel to reinforce information protection, and I steadily increased the expenditure for information protection technology. In 2020, KT's expenditure for information protection was $328.5

million, for an increase of 180% compared to the $179.5 million spent in 2013. In addition, the number of IT personnel was increased from 524 people in 2014 to 743 in 2020.

The change and innovation were not limited to information protection. At the time, KT employees did not feel as though they were part of a group, as the walls between the head office and our subsidiaries were too high. No development or innovation could exist where there was no interaction and little communication.

Thus, I employed the phrase Single KT with the intention to unite the organization. Improvement of our structural constitution was a top priority. First, I disposed of, liquidated, or merged non-competitive and capital-impaired subsidiaries that were constantly in the red. Next, I provided support for telecommunications, the main business of the company. To enhance related competencies, I then established new subsidiaries and incorporated other existing ones into the group. KT's identity as a telecommunications company became clear through this cultivation policy, which in turn added momentum along with greater ability to execute and develop core business strategies.

As early as possible, I intended to complete the realignment of the business system so that KT could continue putting customers first.

As I worked to streamline a bulked-up organization, I also sent an email to employees promising that I would open doors of opportunity, through strict evaluation and fair compensation, to those who were ready to take on new challenges.

My email contained messages of encouragement such as, "We can't survive on the old habits of just getting by," "Let's be resolute and do things right," and "Let's create amazing value and impress customers using the hard work of our senior colleagues as a foundation."

In May 2014, two months after the customer data leak incident, I took the stage at KT Square. It was an opportunity to declare a new beginning for KT, both inside and outside the organization.

That day, I also declared our "Global No. 1" vision and announced the "Realization of GiGAtopia" strategy to turn the vision into reality. The strategy was devised to create a new growth engine for KT by putting full energy into GiGAtopia, an ICT convergence ecosystem that connects people and things through the GiGA Internet infrastructure and solutions.

I persuaded employees who were afraid of change that the GiGA Internet, which was ten times faster than the existing one, would restore the status KT enjoyed in the era of the landline telephone. My efforts to convince them eventually took effect and the results from new change and innovation came faster than expected.

In May 2014, the author declared KT's "Global No. 1" vision and explained his related strategy.

In October 2014, KT commercialized the GiGA Internet nationwide, marking a quantum leap in internet speeds which had been at a standstill for about a decade since 2006. As we went from wired communications into the GiGA era, KT's sales increased. In less than two years after launch, the number of subscribers surpassed two million and sales increased to $506.7 million. Later, I would hear comments from employees such as, "Seeing you bow before the public changed my way of thinking," and "You renewed my faith and made me want to get back to work," or "At first I wasn't sure the plan would work and thought about complaining, but it really worked." Thanks to the employees who were instrumental in bringing about the necessary change, we were able to write a new future for KT.

As KT overcame huge missteps and rejoined the "one trillion club" (companies that achieve 1 trillion won [$838 million] in operating profits), it also upgraded its global competitiveness with the development of a future growth engine and technological advancement. Meanwhile, in July 2014, KT became an official sponsor of the PyeongChang 2018 Winter Olympics and in March 2015 declared the 5G era for the first time in the world. In February 2018, KT successfully provided the world's first pilot service of 5G at the Winter Olympics in Pyeongchang.

The 25th floor of the KT Gwanghwamun Building: "a restaurant of communication"

When I was president of Samsung Electronics, an article titled "Mr. President, did you have lunch?" was printed in a newspaper and became the talk of the town. My name was mentioned in this article, according to which, a new employee of Samsung System LSI had sent a text message to President Hwang Chang-gyu asking if he had eaten lunch and the president had replied, "Yes."

As it turned out, the employee had simply manipulated the messaging app as joke for his friends, but I was not the least bit upset about it. Rather, I had to laugh at the part that described the reaction of his friends, the other employees who didn't find the story strange. In fact I was grateful for his giving them the impression of me as a president with whom employees could exchange greetings. So during a subsequent occasion, I said, "Actually, if had gotten a message like that I would've replied, 'Did you enjoy your lunch, too?'"

In truth, I enjoyed having meals with other employees as it provided an opportunity for friendly conversation free of any constraints. At Samsung Electronics I worked to make that kind of atmosphere part of our organizational culture. Communication in the field was practically a trademark of mine.

I therefore decided to "share rice" with other employees at KT as well. For Koreans, rice has special significance as a food, and "sharing rice together" is an expression that carries warmth and familiarity. I felt that when I ate with employees, wherever we happened to be, it made any remnants of distrust and miscommunication vanish. I wanted to re-create that at KT.

Right after I took office in January 2014, during my first year with the company, I started "lunch dates" with employees in the office cafeteria at Seocho-dong, and from 2015, in the 25th floor lounge at the KT Gwanghwamun Building. We limited our menu selections to basic Korean dishes priced at around 10,000 won (about $9.00 in 2014) to keep it affordable for everyone, including me. Because I kept these lunch dates

The author having a discussion with KT employees over lunch.

up until I retired, I could visit any department and there would always be one or two familiar faces that I recognized. I once calculated how many lunch dates I attended, and it added up to more than 420 in over six years. They say I had meals with a total of 5,500 employees.

At first, some employees found it awkward to have lunch with the CEO. However, the atmosphere lightened as the twice-a-week lunch dates continued, and after a few months it became a funny topic around the water cooler that employees were naturally starting conversations with the line, "I was having lunch with the CEO, and…" For me as well, the 25th floor of the KT Gwanghwamun Building was a "restaurant of communication." The food was delicious, but the conversation and atmosphere were even better.

For any employee, having the opportunity to visit the CEO's office and talk with him/her freely can be an invaluable and meaningful experience.

During one of our lunch dates, I asked the employees what their majors were and found out that one person had majored in flute performance. I asked the employee if he could do a congratulatory performance at the KT employee awards ceremony scheduled for the end of the year. Actually, it was arranged as an accompanied performance with the KT Chamber Orchestra.

When it comes to communication, I have always felt that the analog method is the best approach. The great thing about starting the lunch dates was that our executives and team leaders started having lunch with employees in other departments when they heard about what I was doing. As they benchmarked my activities more, our communication became smoother, and the organization became more flexible.

Sending sincerity in an email

If the lunch dates represented a traditional, analog method of communication, then email was a digital means for me communicate with all of the employees at once.

When the going gets tough, an organization needs to move in the same direction in unison. It has to move cohesively and with strength. To do so, every member of the group must share a common goal, and be focused on that goal. As a leader, my mission was to share a vision and lead the organization. Email was a good way to relay sincerity. I started sending emails to all employees after the data leak incident, and continued sending them whenever there was an important issue. I put a lot of time and effort into composing heart-to-heart emails for 60,000 employees.

"Dear KT Executives and Staff Members:

Hello everyone, this is Hwang Chang-gyu, and I am writing today as member of the KT family.

While it is a great personal honor to be the new CEO of KT, one of Korea's leading companies, I also feel the weight of tremendous responsibility on my shoulders.

The No. 1 KT management meeting, which is held every week and attended by key members of management to discuss important issues, was held last week at the Gangbuk Network Headquarters. The topic of the meeting was innovative cost reduction. I have stressed before that innovation should be about finding structural and sustainable cost reduction methods and not about reducing costs simply by cutting corners. In this meeting we discussed the intermediate outcome.

Reports from the Network, Customer, Marketing, and IT Planning Divisions have revealed a surprising level of innovation in areas and ways that demonstrate a complete break from the past.

Above all, I am delighted that cost-reduction methods were found by working to enhance quality and efficiency through structural improvements rather than the previous way of pinching pennies. For example, a method for collecting and evaluating data in real time was developed, enabling us to prioritize areas with low-quality service for improvement through efficient investment and by reducing the cost of leasing wireless base stations. I also saw a great idea for reducing expenditure for electrical power by changing the structure of cooling panels on repeaters.

Cost reduction through innovation is not simply about spending less. It is an investment concept whereby we can afford to invest this year if we reduce costs next year and the year after that. The results will fundamentally improve our work methods and lead our enhanced competitiveness.

As we closed this most recent No. 1 KT management meeting, I could feel the change taking place at the very core of our organization. This innovation was brought about thanks to keen-eyed employees in the field and through the active support of all KT staff members.

Cost reduction can be enjoyable, and I promise there will be rewards to come. I truly expect we will all have something to be joyful about in the near future. Thank you and have a great holiday."

I continued sending emails like this one, usually under the title "Sharing the CEO's Thoughts." About six months after I became CEO, there was one email I sent that contained my opinions, directions for the company, and the details, background, and development of business strategies. I got a reply back that said, "President Hwang, it's too long to read." I guess I should have expected a response like that because the email was sent in three parts over two weeks and totaled 21 pages on A4-size paper. However, I expected that they would at least feel my sincerity. Below are some other examples of feedback I received from the employees.

- It's not the first time I received an email from a CEO, but it was the first one containing details about business divisions and directions. It wasn't like the typical email from a CEO, and it was worth reading.
- Your email made me rethink the meaning of an open organization. I realized that my job connects me throughout the company with every other employee. It also made me re-evaluate my own work.
- Your detailed explanation using examples helped me understand the meaning of vision. I can also see how we accomplished what we have.

I was the first CEO to send emails like this, and the first to send them regularly. I also was the one who felt the effect of this communication more than anyone else.

There's a Korean saying that goes, "Even a whale will dance if you compliment it." Well, I don't mind saying that sometimes the replies from the employees made me feel like dancing. I could also feel the gap gradually narrowing between management and employees and even between employees as well. And that made me work even harder.

In August 2018, as I had promised in an earlier email, "something to be joyful about" actually happened. A daily newspaper ran an article about the joyful occasion with the title "KT CEO Hwang Chang-gyu Buys Pizza for All Employees to Celebrate 1 Million GiGA Genie Subscribers." The employees and I were all surprised that we reached the goal of one million GiGA Genie subscribers just a year and a half after its launch.

"Dear KT Executives and Staff Members,

This is the power of KT.

By building on successes such as we have just experienced, we will create an even more robust future for KT. It is true that we are currently facing difficult conditions surrounding the telecommunications industry and there is a sense of crisis and anxiety about finding the next breakthrough that will open up future business. Despite this, I want you to always remember that we are unbeatable and No. 1 in the industry when it comes to capability and organizational culture."

I sent this email message to all KT employees and celebrated with them over pizza. It was a deeply moving occasion showing that wholehearted effort leads to good results.

The story behind the map of must-visit restaurants

In November 2018, there was an unexpected accident at the KT branch in Ahyeon-dong. A fire broke out in a conduit for communication cables, and it led to a disruption of service in the local area. The inconvenience it caused for citizens was indescribable.

After visiting the accident site, I decided to provide damage relief for our customers. I was extremely busy with efforts to help small local businesses and prevent recurrence. In addition, I sped up our efforts to combine advanced technology with strengthened safety with the goal of achieving zero–defect operation. At the same time I was also working on the telecommunication network improvement plan.

Every day was filled with intense effort. Amidst all of this, I got a call from the executive I had put in charge of preparing a relief plan for the affected small businesses in Ahyeon-dong.

"What do you think about shutting down the KT company cafeterias?"

The idea was to send KT employees out to have lunch at local restaurants in the affected areas. By doing so, we could feel firsthand the difficulties our customers were facing. It would also enable us to express our sincere apologies to small business owners, many of whom are also our customers. "That's a great idea," I answered.

At the time, KT had about 5,000 employees at its headquarters in Gwanghwamun. Most of them had no experience in face-to-face customer service. No matter how much I emphasized the value of being customer-oriented, it is not easy to feel the value of this unless they actually meet the customers in person. Moreover, the fire at the Ahyeon-dong branch caused great damage to numerous customers, including local business owners. It would be a win-win situation for our employees to meet customers and get a better understanding of their responsibilities and the importance of their tasks. It would also help the small business owners by increasing their profits.

The "lunch with customers" started immediately. The cafeterias were closed not only at the headquarters in Gwanghwamun, but also at nearby branches. KT employees headed to restaurants in Ahyeon-dong for lunch. I also visited the local restaurants almost every day. The employees participated in the lunch-with-customers campaign for two months, and I continued going for three months. The restaurant owners at first thought it was a one-off event and eventually opened their hearts as we visited them continually.

In time, by having lunch with customers, we became aware of stories we had never heard, and that broadened our outlook. An employee who discovered many restaurants serving delicious dishes at low prices commented that, "The more I frequented the local restaurants, the more I came to consider the owners as part of my extended family." An owner of a restaurant in Chungjeong-ro said, "It was really hard after the fire, but I'm grateful to KT employees who visited us often. I hope they will continue to come." We were able to overcome the accident this way. I was thankful to both the business owners who welcomed KT employees, and the KT employees who met our customers joyfully.

In February the following year, KT's PR team published the "100 Must-visit Restaurants in Ahyeon-dong." Even after the "lunch-with-customers" campaign, which had been conducted on a corporate level, the employees continued to visit the restaurants in Ahyeon-dong on their own, and the accumulated number of visits came to more than 20,000.

The map of must-visit restaurants in Ahyeon-dong.

There was a "list of must-visit restaurants" shared among employees. One of the PR team members heard about this list, and came up with the idea of making and distributing a map. As a result, they actually made a map that included all those restaurants. It was distributed to all KT employees and was quite popular.

KT cafeterias also provide delicious meals that are as good as the food served at any good restaurant. They prepare healthy meals using fresh ingredients without MSG. Eating at the cafeteria saves time since it is in the building, and more than half of all KT employees eat there. Nevertheless, our employees had lunch with our customers without a single complaint. Witnessing the employees endure the inconvenience of the frigid winter outdoors during the accident, I felt that KT's organizational culture was truly becoming more customer-oriented.

In September 2019, I made a surprise visit to the Communications-based Infrastructure Innovation Presentation held at the Daedeok

The author and KT employees examining a fire-extinguishing robot at the Outside Plant (OSP) Innovation Center in Daejeon.

Innopolis in Daejeon. It was an unplanned visit, and I apologized about the fire at the Ahyeon-dong branch again in front of reporters and promised to prevent any recurrence.

"I would like to sincerely apologize again. After the regrettable accident, KT came to realize the value of wired networks, which is its foundation. We are now striving for R&D infrastructure and innovation by using our full competencies and technologies."

That day, KT introduced the development of a management system called "Outside Plant" (OSP), which protects the massive network infrastructure. The system gave KT the ability to use 5G- and AI- based robots to detect potentially harmful conditions in cable conduits and is capable of extinguishing fires before they can spread. The system is highly reliable for preventing recurrence.

Since the fire incident at the Ahyeon-dong branch, KT employees continued to eat lunch outside voluntarily for months, even after the cafeteria re-opened. Meanwhile, it took about ten months to finish development of the system for preventing recurrence.

Their will and effort to prevent the same mistakes from happening again remain strong to this day. For this I send my gratitude to the many KT employees who visited the site and prepared for the future together.

Sharing hearts through shared music

Six years can be either short or long. I had my farewell ceremony at KT in March 2020 and I felt sad about leaving. For this reason, I asked the new CEO for two things.

First was the GEPP. I hoped that platforms or systems that prevent the spread of infectious disease would be developed continuously since this is an important issue both domestically and globally. Second, I asked the new CEO to keep up interest in the KT Chamber Orchestra. I hoped the employees would be given the time and space to enjoy music. The new CEO nodded in agreement.

In May 2014, right after I announced GiGAtopia as the new KT CEO, I visited the KT Chamber Hall in Mok-dong with other executives. Listening to the KT Chamber Orchestra's performance brought back many memories related to music from my youth.

I was a boy who loved music. Domestic and global circumstances were gloomy back then, and I didn't have many opportunities to listen to music. Once I heard a piece of music I liked, I rarely forgot it. I loved listening to classical music on the radio, and I would save my allowance to collect LPs.

The author and KT Chamber Orchestra (at left, musical director Professor Kim Yong-bae, at right, conductor Professor Lee Taek-ju).

When I was in high school, I performed Händel's Hallelujah as a choir member.

One of the luxuries I enjoyed after becoming a college student was watching the performance of a national orchestra while sitting up high in the National Theater of Korea.

I remember one occasion when the French Cultural Center invited the Lyon National Orchestra to perform at the National Theater of Korea. As is normal at invitational events at a cultural center, the first two pieces performed were the national anthems of France and Korea. That day, I listened to Korea's national anthem in 3/4 time for the first time in my life, and it was jaw-dropping. I was filled with amazement and overwhelming emotion. The foreign conductor arranged the Korean anthem using the basic rhythmic pattern of the waltz, delivering a moving yet cheerful performance.

The strong feelings conveyed through music mesmerized me. I couldn't help but love this marvelous art that instantly transforms feelings and enriches emotions.

On the same day, the Lyon National Orchestra also played Modest Mussorgsky's Pictures at an Exhibition arranged by Ravel.

Music is both relaxation and consolation for me. It is also a source of inspiration that gives me a lot of ideas. On holidays, I started and ended my days with music. Music also was a good background when I was reading books and thinking about new ideas.

Starting over as a manager, I had this strong desire to enjoy music with employees after listening to a performance by an orchestra sponsored by the company. Immediately, I started to invite employees to concerts. Not just executives. Call center agents and on-site workers, new employees, and candidates for promotions, whom I seldom meet in person—I invited them all, as long as I had an excuse.

At first, it was not easy to fill the 400 seats at the KT Chamber Hall. Some must have been reluctant to come all the way just to listen to music on the weekend. But as the number of employees who went to the concert increased, it instantly went viral. As KT employees, including myself, filled the seats each time, members of the KT Chamber Orchestra were touched by this and said that they were even more motivated, and that the atmosphere was even more energetic. Going to the Saturday concert once or twice a month, then having dinner with employees at a Chinese restaurant was one of the most enjoyable moments that I had over the last six years.

Beginning a few years ago, a regular concert was held twice a year at the hall of the Seoul Arts Center (SAC) with 2,300 seats, as more employees started to enjoy the concerts. During concert days, employees would sit by the SAC World Music Fountain or on the marble floor to enjoy picnics

The author with the family of a KT employee at a special concert by the KT Chamber Orchestra at the Seoul Arts Center.

arranged by the company. It was like going on a family outing.

I greeted the families of the employees as I went around the venue. For me, sharing music was like sharing one's heart.

The ability to listen to music is a human sense that one develops early in life and loses only very late in life. We don't have to be taught about music to enjoy it, and it soothes our emotions. I hoped employees also felt the same relaxation and consolation that I felt through music. I also hoped that they would experience the indescribable emotions that only music can arouse.

My wishes came true during my time with KT and the KT Chamber Orchestra. KT became a mature and harmonious organization thanks to the members of the orchestra, including the conductor and employees who each did their own part. I am extremely proud to have turned the "Single KT" slogan into reality during my six years with the company.

Innovation
and
Contribution

Chapter
5

Participate in Things that **Benefit the World**

01

Design technologies for humankind and society

| The World's First 5G |

There are invisible dividing lines in our society. Even creativity is like that. People tend to think of creativity as the exclusive domain of writers or artists. When you tell students of natural sciences and engineering they should have creativity, it is hard to get them to agree. They don't look at their life at work as something that requires creativity.

What about social contributions? It is easy to just donate or support the disadvantaged. People seldom think about technology, which can transform and advance the lives of all people. Those who contribute to humankind and society by designing technology are rarely in the spotlight.

What I have experienced as an engineer and a manager were results achieved by going beyond stereotypes.

First, for an engineer the future is more like something that needs to be imagined and created, rather than predicted and prepared for. Thus, creativity and imagination are essential. As I researched semiconductors, I constantly imagined how the technological advancements would change our lives. Hwang's Law, which led the mobile era, was formulated based on imagining and realizing the future that was coming. I could step up the momentum of change by making a habit of studying and developing not only the technologies we needed at the moment, but also those that would be needed in the next 10 to 20 years. My declaration from two decades ago that mobile would be at the center of the IT industry is now our reality. In the future, the conditions of communications will have evolved even further.

Engineers also feel pleased and rewarded when designing technology that improves people's lives. They are no different from others who do their best in their jobs, thinking they are contributing to humankind and society.

Over the last several centuries, technology has been the greatest driver of human prosperity. These days 5G is serving in that role. Fifth-generation telecommunications, or 5G, clearly differentiates itself from the earlier generations, which focus solely on speed. The latency in 5G is extremely low, requiring only one-tenth the time 4G needs to transfer massive data streams. As a result, data transmission volumes are growing exponentially, and 5G is being applied as infrastructure that advances diverse industries.

The world has a number of prominent telecommunication service providers and related companies, but KT in Korea was the first to roll out a working model of 5G technology. It is no exaggeration to say that all of humanity benefits from technological advancements in the telecommunications industry, given its distinctive characteristics.

Unfortunately, technology is not readily visible. Users generally do not realize what is actually going on even when the communication environment is convenient and in abundance. However, what is deemed impossible becomes possible thanks to the dedication of many people behind the scenes. Here, I would like to set the record straight on the activities of engineers who have benefitted the world through the commercialization of 5G and B2B businesses.

"If we don't reach an agreement, I will jump off."

Korea hosted the Winter Olympics in Pyeongchang in February 2018, and the Games were a great celebration for KT as well. Why? After painstaking preparation, this was the venue where KT unveiled the world's first working 5G technology. I traveled to the Olympic venues at least five or six times as the clock ticked down to the start of the Games. I checked the progress of the preparation work, and reassured the employees working at the site.

In January 2018, a month ahead of the Opening Ceremony, I took the high-speed train (KTX) to Pyeongchang to take part in a special occasion to encourage the employees who were getting the relay and 5G pilot networks ready. The 5G network between Pyeongchang and Gangneung had been fully installed, and the people in charge of operating the telecommunication service network and broadcasting relay network were busy putting the final touches in place before the pilot service launch.

The Head Office arranged heated vests as a surprise gift for the workers. The average winter temperature in the Pyeongchang area is around -10°C, while the wind chill is nearly -20°C. We hoped that we could help keep the workers in good shape by providing them with a thousand heated vests. I

In January 2018, the author hands out heated vests to on-site workers conducting the final checks prior to the PyeongChang 2018 Winter Olympics

visited the Alpensia Ski Jumping Center for the ceremonial presentation.

The Pyeongchang 5G Center for showcasing KT's 5G technology was located at the Alpensia Ski Jumping Center. The site had been visited without fail by tens of thousands of KT employees who had been to Pyeongchang since December 2015, when KT signed the agreement to supply its telecommunications service for the Games. The KT people were there to install the network, test the technology, and operate the system once it was up.

As the time for the Olympics approached, KT stationed over a thousand personnel between Gangneung and Pyeongchang to maintain, repair, and operate the telecommunication service network during the Games. I made sure to be in the commemorative photo in front of the Ski Jumping Center, expressing my best wishes for a highly successful Games and flawless debut of commercial 5G services. A few days later, I ran into KT Vice President Lee Yong-gyoo.

Vice President Lee was the head of the 5G Platform Development Headquarters back then and was in charge of the B2B business using 5G. He also had an inextricable connection with the PyeongChang Winter Olympics, for he was the very one had who led the Special Interest Group (SIG), in which global telecommunication service providers participated until recently. The Group created the Pyeongchang 5G-SIG specifications.

Vice President Lee said, "I had an unforgettable experience on the ski jump tower" and proceeded to relate a heroic story, warning that I might be in tears after hearing it.

It happened back in March 2016. Vice President Lee had gone to Pyeongchang with dozens of executives and staff members from five companies—Nokia, Samsung Electronics, Ericsson, Intel, and Qualcomm. The SIG was a consultative body organized to establish the 5G standards and specifications to be used at the PyeongChang Winter Olympics. The members were top engineers and CTOs from each participating company. Vice President Lee Yong-gyoo led the online meetings with the individuals in charge at the five companies for several months in order to reach an agreement on the 5G Pyeongchang standards and specifications, based on the 5G network management standardization plan proposed by the KT Institute of Convergence Technology.

Setting protocols for mobile telecommunications normally takes several years through a joint research effort called the 3rd Generation Partnership Project, which involves multiple telecommunications standard development organizations. Thousands of engineers from hundreds of global businesses work for four to five years to map out the system specifications applicable worldwide.

Some may expect results would be guaranteed to some extent when Ericsson and Nokia, the world's top two telecommunications network equipment vendors; Qualcomm and Intel, the leading CPU makers; and Samsung Electronics, the top handset manufacturer, all join the consultative group. However, that was all hype. Certain steps unknown to most regular users must be completed before they can take advantage of a new telecommunications service. These include setting the protocols, producing the chipsets, building the network infrastructure, and manufacturing the handheld devices.

However, deciding on the protocols for telecommunications services involves the interests of various players. Intellectual property rights are always an extremely sensitive issue for companies, and each interested party has a stake in the outcome. The makers of the network equipment, CPUs, and devices all propose their own technologies, offering the technical data to support their claims of superiority and insisting that their products be selected as the standard. Difficulties naturally arise during such proceedings, while Vice President Lee Yong-gyoo was required to complete that procedure among five companies within just five to six months.

To proceed smoothly, Lee organized videoconferences from 10 p.m. to 1 a.m. on weekdays, adjusting by necessity to the work schedules of the global corporations in the US and European time zones. Once a month, representatives gathered in Seoul to confirm the conclusions of the meetings, and regular meetings were held on various topics. Of course, the meetings were conducted in English. Lee Yong-gyoo, a native

Vice President Lee Yong-gyoo giving a presentation during a discussion on 5G standards.

Korean speaker, unwaveringly led the meetings as the chair, resolving divided opinions.

The fifth regular meeting took place in Pyeongchang in March 2016. The number of participants surged, and there were various events, including a tour of the stadiums at the PyeongChang Olympics venue. It was a decisive day for Vice President Lee.

After the meeting, the SIG representatives went to the top of the ski jump tower. It wasn't accessible to the general public, but Lee received permission from headquarters to go up. The SIG members were all amused and excited to see the sports arena; only Vice President Lee headed to the ski jump tower with resolute determination.

At last, dozens of SIG representatives were gathered at the top of the tower, which was dozens of meters above ground. The engineers

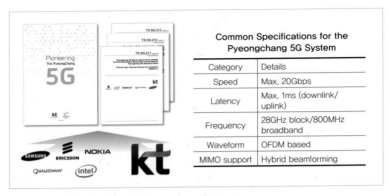

Common Specifications for the Pyeongchang 5G System	
Category	Details
Speed	Max. 20Gbps
Latency	Max. 1ms (downlink/uplink)
Frequency	28GHz block/800MHz broadband
Waveform	OFDM based
MIMO support	Hybrid beamforming

Common Specifications for the Pyeongchang 5G System

were busy taking pictures of the stunning scenery before them. At that moment, Lee called everyone to gather, with the ski jump tower looming over the abyss behind him. He wanted to say just one thing:

"Let's reach an agreement, or else I will jump off."

Although four months had passed, yet many issues remained unresolved with respect to the Pyeongchang 5G-SIG specifications. Generally, telecommunications service standards should be set at least a year and a half before the technology is put into use, because it takes time to produce the necessary chipsets, network equipment, and devices. Moreover, various technologies that are to be used during the Games must be approved by the International Olympic Committee and athletes of each sport, and that means time is needed to get this done. Although two years remained until the PyeongChang Winter Olympics, it was not enough. Vice President Lee was desperate and had to play his last card. He risked his life to ensure a successful debut of 5G at the PyeongChang 2018 Winter Olympics.

I personally signed the standards document, attached my letter of gratitude, and handed it to Vice President Lee. Only when the PyeongChang

2018 Winter Olympics were about to start did I realize why his eyes were sparkling so much that day.

5G at the PyeongChang 2018 Winter Olympics brings glory to Korea

As it is widely known, KT's 5G service debuted successfully at the PyeongChang 2018 Winter Olympics. Representatives from many global companies in the telecommunications industry were amazed by what was accomplished in just three years. They said it was unbelievable.

The story began at the 2015 Mobile World Congress (MWC Barcelona), held in Barcelona, Spain in March 2015. In my keynote speech titled "5G and Beyond, Accelerating the Future," I was the world's first to announce the kind of future that would be created by 5G, and I received an ovation from more than 2,000 people in the audience. Their applause indicated what they anticipated and how amazed they were at the new world that 5G would unfold.

On that occasion I argued that 5G would be the ultimate network, solving issues related to transmission speed, system capacity, and interconnections in the era of hyperconnectivity, where all people and all things are linked. I went on to suggest that it would grow businesses and transform lives at a level beyond what earlier technologies ever could. I also proposed that global companies should work together to accelerate the coming of the 5G era. My speech was concluded with a public announcement that we would provide the world's first 5G pilot service during the PyeongChang 2018 Winter Olympics.

The author with IOC President Thomas Bach at the Official Partner Signing Ceremony for the PyeongChang 2018 Winter Olympics.

Naturally the audience was stunned to hear this. The mainstream tele-communications technology at the time was based on 4G, which even in an IT-leading country like Korea had just been commercialized in the second half of 2011. As of 2015, the latest telecommunications standard had been in widespread service for only three to four years. The consensus was that the time was far too early to discuss 5G, considering that historically it has taken around ten years for a new cycle in telecommunications evolution to begin.

Global corporations that participated in GSMA's MWC thought so, too, as 4G-related technologies were still under development. The GSMA roadmap anticipated that 5G would only be realized after 2020. Needless to say, their reaction to my predictions was natural.

The world was in for another surprise when I declared, "We will provide the 5G pilot service for the first time in the world at the PyeongChang 2018 Winter Olympics." Most of the people in the audience were skeptical when a Korean telecommunications company unfamiliar to them declared that it would present the 5G service at a global event in less than three years.

"We should prepare aggressively to realize the kind of future that 5G can make possible. Let's go riding off into the sunset together. And let's create the future together."

I wrapped up my 20-minute keynote speech with these two simple remarks and stepped down from the podium. Then I visited a series of exhibition stands for global companies, and embarked on a daring journey.

MWC Barcelona is the world's largest mobile event, with more than 2,400 corporate exhibitors from over 200 countries, and up to 110,000 individual participants. More than 200 of the companies at the show are Korean. Normally, the global companies rent exhibition spaces that are roughly equivalent to an entire hall at the Convention and Exhibition Center (COEX) in Seoul. The leading IT companies dispatch anywhere between dozens to hundreds of representatives to promote their technology during the four-day trade show.

I went to the Qualcomm, Ericsson, Nokia, Intel, and Samsung stands to greet the CTO or CEO and stressed that we should immediately begin the technological development to commercialize 5G. Fortunately, their stance and attitude had changed 180 degrees; perhaps because they were impressed by my keynote speech. The Ericsson vice chairman responded positively, saying his company would step up R&D efforts to make products

The author trying out 5G technology when visiting the Ericsson headquarters in Sweden in May 2015.

compatible with 5G. I immediately replied that I would visit Ericsson within a few months. Nokia, a major competitor of Ericsson, might have heard Ericsson's proactive response, also gave me a favorable answer.

Exactly two months later, I flew to Europe with other executives. First, I visited Ericsson in Sweden, where an R&D officer showed us a prototype that works with 5G technology. I sensed they had exerted great effort in a short time to apply the 5G technologies they had been developing for years. Meanwhile, Nokia, based in Finland, also indicated they were ready to forge ahead with 5G technology development and said they would like to join the consortium if KT leads it.

The companies slated to take part in the SIG were thus decided, and Vice President Lee Yong-gyoo personally contacted the relevant people at each company to accelerate the process. The most helpful ally was

Samsung Electronics, the Korean global player. Therefore, the handheld devices used commercially at the PyeongChang 2018 Winter Olympics were made by Samsung. After overcoming some setbacks, KT and Samsung Electronics succeeded in making the "5G first call" (first ever data transmission) in October 2016. This was a brilliant feat achieved not only by the two companies, but also by Korea. While the first-ever 3G call was accomplished in Japan and the first-ever 4G call happened in Finland, the 5G first call was conducted in Korea, which is meaningful beyond words.

I commemorated this moment by sending a text message along with pizzas delivered to KT employees and outside partners.

The 5G era is coming soon. Leading the 5G technology standards means leading the industry and the new era. Each country is struggling to be in front, but Korea was the one to start it first, and is already in the lead.

Indeed, KT's technological prowess was enhanced significantly during the three years spent preparing for the PyeongChang 2018 Winter Olympics. More than 100 contributions related to 5G technology were published in technology-related journals, both domestic and international, and over 60 related technology patents were registered and acquired. The doors to 5G service at the PyeongChang 2018 Winter Olympics were opened by the immense efforts made to demonstrate the technology, persuade other companies, negotiate their needs, and lead the patents and standardization.

We received compliments left and right. NHK, a public broadcaster in Japan, aired a documentary that showed Japanese officials visiting the 5G Exhibition Hall in Pyeongchang. They were investigating the status of Korean 5G technology as a reference while they prepared for the Tokyo 2020 Olympics. China Business News reported that "cutting-edge technology shone brightly at the PyeongChang 2018 Winter Olympics."

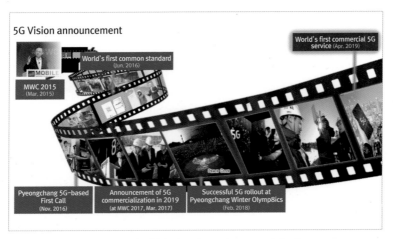

Three-year process between the 5G declaration and commercialization

The French daily newspaper *Le Figaro* covered KT's 5G Exhibition Hall in Pyeongchang, reporting that 5G would "be the launcher of a new industrial revolution" and demonstrated to viewers how fast and dynamic sports action appeared via 5G. Britain's *Financial Times* remarked that seeing 5G work was like putting people on the moon in an article titled "Superfast 5G promises to be a game-changer for humanity." Deutsche Presse-Agentur (DPA), a German news agency, reported that The PyeongChang 2018 Winter Olympics was a venue for discovering technologies several years ahead into the future, and that Korea had proved its capacity in IT and telecommunications to the world.

In this book, I'd like to convey my gratitude once more to all the executives and staff members of KT's Network Division, Institute of Convergence Technology, Marketing Division, IT Division, and other units; the employees who worked so hard on-site to operate the network in -20°C weather; and everyone who toiled for 1,000 days to get the 5G

A dove of peace created with 5G technology at the opening ceremony for the PyeongChang 2018 Winter Olympics.

technology ready for the PyeongChang 2018 Winter Olympics.

Designing technologies for new opportunities

KT management finalized plans to commercialize 5G in the spring of 2019, a year after the PyeongChang Winter Olympics. Vice President Lee Yong-gyoo also took charge of developing new business by expanding 5G to the B2B sphere within the scheduled time. He is still dedicated to the mission of identifying industries that improve society through the 5G Innovation Platform.

In February 2019, one month ahead of KT's 5G commercial launch, I was back in Spain to deliver a keynote address at MWC Barcelona 2019.

The theme of my keynote speech was coprosperity for humankind and contributions to social advancement with the 5G Innovation Platform, a goal similar to the mission of KT's 5G Platform Development Headquarters.

In my keynote speech, I reminded the audience that KT's 5G mobile service had been demonstrated at the PyeongChang 2018 Winter Olympics, a feat I had promised at the same venue four years earlier. I also made sure to express my gratitude to the global partners who participated in the process. Next, I presented the world's first 5G phone designed according to KT specifications and declared that we would commercialize 5G mobile service for the first time in the world. I added my prediction: "5G will bring about surprising social and industrial changes, not only realizing true, real-time mobile communication, but also saving lives and shifting the paradigm of the manufacturing industry."

I have emphasized from the very beginning that 5G innovation would be outstanding in the B2B domain. I was confident that unprecedented kinds of value would be created when 5G is combined with innovative technologies like AI, blockchains, big data, and IoT.

I added, "5G will make possible what used to be only in our imaginations, and it should ultimately become a technology for people, a technology that contributes to human advancement. 5G's hyperconnectivity will distribute the benefits of the Fourth Industrial Revolution to all industries and individuals fairly and economically."

I thought of creating a future for the nation through the convergence of IT and existing major industries when I was the National CTO. That idea was turning into reality.

For instance, the 5G Platform Development Headquarters implemented the Smart Factory Solution with Hyundai Heavy Industries from

May 2018. That November, six months later, we confirmed whether any changes had occurred after converging KT's 5G, big data, and AI technologies with HHI's robotics development and naval technologies. In those fields where the 5G was applied, productivity rose 30%, product defect rates fell 43%, and costs were lowered 16%. The convergence created new businesses by controlling the gantry cranes from the ground, operating driverless forklifts, and managing the ships at sea around the world from the control tower at Busan Port.

Healthcare is one of the most vigorous projects run at the 5G Platform Development Headquarters. KT has stepped up its introduction of new 5G-based healthcare services, establishing 5G networks at the Samsung Medical Center, Asan Medical Center and other major hospitals in Korea to provide remote medical training and improve work

The author listening to CEO Han Young-seok of Hyundai Heavy Industries while he is explaining the progress of the Smart Factory Solution.

efficiency at isolation wards. KT has also constructed 5G networks in 31 neighborhoods on Jeju Island to allow for multi-access edge computing (MEC) infrastructure, an innovative technology that provides users with higher speed and ultra-low latency.

The role of technology is to eliminate hurdles thought impossible to overcome

At the end of the 20th century, opinions on technological developments were mainly divided into two camps: utopia and dystopia. Still today, some insist that developing new technology contributes to human advancement, as it has done so for centuries, while others voice gloom and doom, concerned that technology put to bad use will lead to the destruction of the environment and loss of human dignity.

I believe the role of technology is simple: to eliminate hurdles. The technology of flash memory alone has altered the world. Just twenty to thirty years ago, photography was a domain controlled by professionals. However, the invention and distribution of the digital camera equipped with flash memory made it possible for anyone to take quality photos wherever and whenever they want. The same goes for broadcasting. Nowadays, one-person media is very common. As digital filming and editing became available, the domain that used to be exclusive for experts collapsed.

In the same vein, telecommunication will be just like a public utility in the future and will help us to eliminate accidents, resolve environmental issues, and address problems associated with an aging society. For instance, if you incorporate 5G and cloud computing in robots, they can be operated remotely. Put the controls and the organization in the cloud, and robots' built-in functions can be reduced. The robots can be made to move about freely and perform tasks wherever you want them to. If you deploy these robots at dangerous industrial sites, work accidents can be decreased tremendously.

When automobiles are combined with 5G, exhaust emissions are cut dramatically, helping to mitigate climate change. Connect 5G to smart cities and smart farms, and the problem of a dwindling labor force as society ages is addressed; and when healthcare services are combined with 5G, remote and accurate medical care becomes possible, elevating the quality of life.

Of course, we still have a long way to go. However, we have companies like KT, which started out of the gate a long time ago.

In 2014, I declared GiGAtopia, replacing the *u* in *utopia* with GiGA. Thomas More coined the term "utopia" as a combination of *u* the Greek prefix that means "non-existent," and *topia*, which means "place." Dreaming of a world without wealth or poverty, he dismissed utopia as a figment of the imagination.

However, when I declared GiGAtopia, I set forth the ambition to realize an ideal future with the aid of intelligent networks. Actually, ICT serves as the driving force for new growth, and KT has been leading economic development through energy, security, B2B, media, AI speakers and other businesses. 5G has only recently been commercialized but will bring numerous changes to people's lives as well as to economic areas. The global market research company HIS estimates the 5G service market alone will amount to $12.3 trillion by 2025, while associated markets such as content and app development will generate $3.5 trillion in production, and 22 million new jobs will be created.

The recent COVID-19 pandemic has been accelerating the pace at which 5G is changing our lives. The limitations posed by the *untact* ("contact-free") lifestyle are now being eliminated as we move forward into the era of *ontact* ("online contact").▪

For example, we used to think of virtual classrooms and videoconferencing as being futuristic, but now such activities have become a regular part of our lives. Large volumes of video data can be exchanged easily today, and no one feels inconvenience while studying or working online.

The pandemic has prevented broadcasters from holding large-scale offline events, so they have created TV programs that connect dozens or even hundreds of viewers online. Such performances are unimaginable under the Long-Term Evolution (LTE) standard. Seeing hundreds of faces appear on a single screen is a great spectacle, indeed.

Thus 5G, which can absorb enormous traffic volumes, has become a ubiquitous technology, like air, in our daily lives.

Every technology is made at the hands of human beings. The people who dedicate themselves to contributing to humanity and society with genuine and good intentions will continue to bring about technologies that eliminate various hurdles, as well as provide economic benefits. I am looking forward to the accomplishments of next-generation engineers.

▪ The neologisms *untact* and *ontact* have become common terms in Korean society. *Untact* combines the prefix *un* with the word *contact* to describe contactless consumption patterns such as purchasing from self-service kiosks, shopping online and settling payment with a mobile device instead of paying in person. Robot baristas, AI chat bots and virtual make-up studios are further evidence of the contactless trend that accompanies an aging population and shrinking labor force. *Ontact* takes the term *untact* a step further, to embrace interaction in virtual space, particularly during a pandemic. Examples include online classrooms, increased use of Zoom calls, and interactive concerts online.

Below is an article I published in *Maeil Business News Korea* on July 23, 2012, when I was serving as the National CTO. To prepare for the PyeongChang 2018 Winter Olympics, I studied which themes and technologies had been successfully applied in previous Olympic Games, and then I organized my findings. I suggested that the PyeongChang 2018 Winter Olympic should be differentiated with smart technologies, such as 5G.

(Summary) I checked whether any of the recent Olympics had had a similar theme or concept. What I found was "culture and tourism" in the Athens 2004 Summer Olympics, "reenactment of the old glory of Italy" in the Turin 2006 Winter Olympics, "the rise of China" in the Beijing 2008 Summer Olympics, "green and eco-friendly" in the Vancouver 2010 Winter Olympics, "global capital" in the London 2012 Summer Olympics, "the rise of Russia" in the Sochi 2014 Winter Olympics... It seems like cutting-edge technology could be a theme to make the PyeongChang 2018 Winter Olympics stand out.

The question is "How?" How could we incorporate our science and technology in the Olympics?

This was one of the questions that preoccupied my mind after Pyeongchang was selected as the host last July (in 2012). First, the message needs to have a Korean flavor. The technology should convey our unique story so that anyone who experiences the 5G service will instantly think of Korea.

Second, the technology must speak for all people. The technology shouldn't cause stress to the participants in the Olympics. Instead, it should provide the best convenience and efficiency.

Third, this must be sustainable technology that can be used after the Olympics are over. For instance, we can imagine a "virtual stadium," which could be anywhere, to include locations like Africa or the Middle East, which are usually not associated with the Winter Olympics.

If we apply our unrivalled 3D TV technology, 5G communications (that followed 4G, and first commercialized by Korea), and hologram technology at stadiums on the other side of the planet, viewers will feel as if they are seated in the stands. They can enjoy a variety of winter sports that might feel novel to them, and they can fully experience the excellence of technologies "made in Korea."

매일경제

2012년 07월 23일 월요일 A38면 분석과전망

스마토피아 평창

매경시평

황창규
지식경제부 R&D전략기획단장

"
2018 평창 테마는 '첨단기술'
아프리카 가상경기장 만들고
단지 곳곳 에너지그리드로
기술·산업 금메달 도전
"

'PyeongChang…'. 자크 로게 IOC위원장이 짧고 담담한 한마디는 수십 가지의 의미를 담았다. 뛰는 가슴이 좀 진정되자 불쑥 이런 생각이 들었다. "2018년이면 다양한 미래 먹거리 연구개발(R&D)사업이 상용화된다. 평창이 선진국 입지 구축의 모멘텀이 될 수는 없을까?"

화려한 전시성(展示性) 기술로 올림픽을 분식(粉飾)하자는 게 아니다. 럼, 화려하더라도 선수, 임원, 기자, 관광객 그리고 수십 억 세계인들이 평창을 통해 우리 기술의 우수성을 몸소 체험한다면?

최근 올림픽 중 이런 콘셉트와 유사한 테마가 있었는지 확인해 봤다. 2004년 아테네 '문화 와 관광', 2008년 토리노 '이탈리아 옛 영광의 재현', 2008년 베이징 '중국의 부상', 2010년 벤쿠버 '친환경 그린', 올해 런던 '국제수도', 2014년 소치 '러시아의 부상'…. 첨단기술이라는 테마는 차별화가 가능해 보였다.

문제는 'How'다. "우리 과학기술을 어떻게 올림픽에 담을까?" 평창이 결정된 지난 7월 이후 내 머릿속을 가장 많이 지배했던 질문이 된다.

우선은 대한민국의 냄새가 나야한다. 기술에 우리 고유의 스토리를 담아 이를 체험한 누구라도 코리아를 떠올려야 한다. 둘째, 기술이 인간을 자연스럽게 감싸야 한다. 올림픽 참가자들이 기술 때문에 스트레스를 받아서는 안 되며 무의식 중 최상의 편의와 효율을 만끽해야 한다. 셋째, 올림픽이 끝나도 활용 가능한 '지속형 기술'이어야 한다.

예컨대 '가상 경기장(Virtual Stadium)'을 생각해 볼 수 있다. 장소는 아프리카, 중동 등 동계올림픽과는 그다지 인연이 없는 나라다. 우리가 독보적 위치에 있는 3D TV의 차세대 기술, 역시 우리가 최초상용화한 4세대 이동통신을 이용 54대 이동통신, 그리고 홀로그 램 기술 등을 지구 저편 경기장에 적용하면 실제로 관중석에 있는 듯한 느낌들을 즐길 수 있을 것이다. 그들에게는 아직 신기 한 겨울 스포츠의 박진감도 즐기고, '메이드 인 코리아' 기술의 우수성도 뼛속 깊이 체험할 수 있으리라.

또한, 국가 R&D사업 중 '한국형 에너지 그리드(K-MEG, Korea Micro Energy Grid)'가 있다. 전기의 효율을 추구하는 스마트 그리드보다 한 차원 높은 기술로 전기는 물론 가스, 공기, 물 등 모든 에너지를 융합한 최초의 차세대 에너지종합공급시스템이다. 이를 단지 내 곳곳에 적용한다면 올림픽 종료 후에도 실증단지로 얼마든지 활용할 수 있다.

올림픽에 '메이드 인 코리아' 기술을 적용할 영역은 무궁무진하다. 단, 검증이 완벽하게 끝나야 한다. 올림픽 무대가 테스트 필드는 아니기 때문이다.

여기지 못한 걸림돌들이 분명히 있을 것이며 남은 6년이 길지는 않다. 하지만 비전·의지·열정이 있다면 못할 것도 없다.

'코리아 브랜드'는 이제 '부지런히 선진국을 쫓는 나라'에서 '강하면서도 세련된 나라'의 이미지를 지향한다. 수출 세계 7위, 9대 무역대국, 일곱 번째 20-50(소득 2만불, 인구 5000만명) 클럽 가입국 등의 타이틀은 '강함'을 상징하는 정량적 지표다. 올림픽과 같은 글로벌 이벤트의 전략적 활용은 '좀 더 세련된 코리아'를 만든다.

'스마토피아 코리아', 즉 IT를 기반으로 다양한 산업이 융합되면서 모든 기술이 인간 중심으로 재배열될 미래 스마토피아시대는 대한민국이 선도할 것이며, 이것이 '디지털 코리아'를 잇는 차세대 비전이 되어야 한다는 강한 신념이 나에게는 있다.

비전의 국면적 합의, 그리고 열정만 있다면 '스마토피아 평창'은 '스마토피아 코리아'의 필요충분조건이 될 것으로 확신한다. 정부·산업계·연구계의 중지를 모아 구체화하고 현실적인 성장이 로드맵을 차근차근 그려 나가자. 그런면에서는 종목별 금메달에, 평창에서는 기술과 산업의 금메달에 도전하자.

02

Dream of IT that conveys
hope and respect for life

| GiGAtopia |

Sustainability is an important goal and task for both people and companies. Everyone who is alive dreams of tomorrow; likewise, businesses without exception are run by making promises of something better tomorrow. Global society is also promoting international cooperation on sustainability to mitigate the effects of disease or environmental degradation.

A prime example of this effort is the UN's establishment of sustainable development goals to address economic, environmental, and social problems around the world over the 15-year period between 2016 and 2030. These SDGs are a collection of 17 medium- and long-term development plans.

KT has been endeavoring to achieve the SDGs technologically through the 5G intelligent network and platform service. Even since I started working for KT, I also strongly expressed my determination to support KT to make it a company that contributes to our society.

Employees who are familiar with the concept of "a company that serves the people" were supportive of my resolve. We strove to unearth models that contribute to society through technology and service, going beyond simple volunteer community service programs. We have implemented numerous projects, including GiGA Story, which involves the installation of ICT infrastructure on remote islands or uninhabited areas in Korea and abroad. We have also built an ICT rescue center in Annapurna and established a smart farm in Sharjah. Employees worked with dedication throughout every process.

There's a saying that every beginning has an end. However, over the past six years, the employees' commitment was not aimed at an endpoint. Every day was another beginning.

Solve the community's problems by doing what you're best at

One day in 2014, a member of KT's Sustainable Management Committee (SMC) brought me a handwritten note that read:

"Dear IT Supporters,

I'm OO. The smartphone activity we experienced on Children's Day was so fun. I rarely use a smart device because I live on an island. How nice it would be if we could study with a smart device every day.

iPad Teacher! Can you come again?

Korea is commonly acknowledged as an ICT powerhouse, but disparities exist among regions, classes, and generations. According to 2016 statistics,

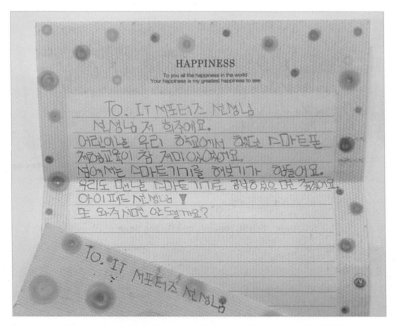

The handwritten note by an Imja Elementary School student that inspired GiGA Story.

the information have-nots in Korean society access digital information at only 58.6% the rate that the social mainstream does. At first glance, this discrepancy might seem to be merely whether one knows how to use a smartphone. However, ICT illiteracy poses enormous disadvantages. The disparity must have grown these days as people do everything on mobile devices, including networking, exchanging information, shopping, and learning.

To reach Imja Island (Imjado), you have to board a ferry at the rural hamlet of Jido-eup, in Sinan County, South Jeolla Province. More than half of the island residents are over 65 years old, and Imja Elementary School has fewer than 20 students. The SMC recommended a project for

Imja Island, and I could only agree.

The GiGA Story projects began with Imja Island. KT's IT Supporters program is confined to offering IT classes. On the other hand, GiGA Story focuses on improving local residents' quality of life by installing the network infrastructure and offering new services. The children in the project area are able to learn remotely using IoT, and the local residents can use a smartphone to check on the status of their crops in real time.

The second GiGA Story project took place in Daeseong-dong, a Paju city district that is located on the demilitarized zone (DMZ) between North and South Korea. Daeseong-dong has an elementary school with only around 30 students. The telecommunications network was so poor that the school principal could not make phone calls from his office. The principal contacted us after the head of a school in a neighboring village told him

A photo taken together with the author after establishing a 5G network in Daeseong-dong, a community on the DMZ.

that his children were enjoying their classes thanks to the IT Supporters. The project started out with the goal of providing children with access to the ICT environment. It was then expanded to bring ICT to the local farms, resulting in both remote-controlled smart farms and remote classes.

The 5G Village in Daeseong-dong on the DMZ reported in *The New York Times* (December 2, 2019)

The story about Daeseong-dong drew attention from the foreign media, and *The New York Times* even reported it the front page of its International section. For foreign press correspondents, the DMZ looms as an unfamiliar and deadly place in a distant land. North Korea is just across a river. The local residents have faced grave danger when inter-Korean relations sour, but they have been unwilling to leave their ancestral homes. The foreign media reported that KT's 5G network has been a gift that offers a new world to people who have endured anxiety and discomfort for so long.

It typically takes a year for the GiGA Story infrastructure to be fully installed in remote locations such as an island. Six of these projects have been completed just recently, including Imja Island, Daeseong-dong, and Baengnyeong Island. The SMC often asks itself, "What do we do best? What are the things that only we can do?"

Making kimchi for impoverished households or delivering charcoal briquettes to heat their homes in winter are typical corporate social responsibility projects performed by Korean companies. However, they do not represent the things that only KT can do well. We went out looking for things we could do for society that involve information technology. We went through some trial and error, but ultimately we focused on activities that supported local communities.

Let technology fill gaps in medical care

Doctor Lee Guk-jong, a trauma surgeon at Ajou University Hospital sent me a special gift in December 2017, a copy of *The Song of the Sword*.

The card that came with the award-winning novel by Kim Hoon bore a greeting in densely written script. It was the penmanship of a person who has been handwriting his own messages for a long time.

Dr. Lee has been widely covered in the media. For example, he operated on *Samho Jewelry* Captain Seok Hae-gyun in Oman in 2011. Captain Seok had been shot when his chemical tanker was hijacked, and he was rescued by Korean Navy commandos six days later. Dr. Lee also saved the life of a North Korean soldier who had been shot multiple times while fleeing south across the DMZ in 2017.

Such high-profile accomplishments notwithstanding, the SMC was more interested in what the good doctor had divulged through various channels about the difficulty he faced in operating a Level I trauma center. I suggested that the SMC let employees look closely at what Dr. Lee needed, considering that we had already visited such places as Baengnyeong Island and Imja Island to provide help to people in need.

At the end of 2017, KT signed an MOU with the Ajou University Medical Center. The regional trauma center calculated the amount of financial support they urgently needed, and KT decided to provide it for three years. It was based on the principles of the SMC, which determined to continue cooperation, instead of supporting a one-off event.

I asked the director of the 5G Platform Development Headquarters to accompany us before I left for the Ajou University Medical Center on the day of the MOU signing. I thought it would be a good idea to check the IT equipment used in the hospital to see if there were other things we could offer technologically. After the ceremony, Dr. Lee personally showed us around the facility. The South Gyeonggi Trauma Center had opened inside Ajou University Hospital as the nation's ninth regional

Professor Lee Guk-jong showing the author around the Southern Gyeonggi Trauma Center

trauma center in June 2016. We quietly followed him.

The other KT executives and I looked around the regional trauma center, intensive care unit, wards, and rooftop helipad. We also listened to Dr. Lee detail the inadequacies of the trauma center and to his proposal that we apply information technology in the medical field.

"We have 'doctor helicopters' (reserved for emergency medical service) but no 2-way radios. It's been seven years since I first asked for them. It doesn't matter how high up the organization I go. They all say we can have helicopters, but none of the other things we've requested. They haven't even approved the radios we've been asking about. This is the seventh year we've asked for them, don't even mention the $20 million budget we requested. No progress."

He talked about how the EMS helicopter was not equipped with radio communication, which forced medical staff to communicate with the medical team through the KakaoTalk mobile messaging app. He said

Gyeonggi-do Fire Services EMS helicopter

only the pilot and crew were allowed to communicate by radio while aboard firefighting helicopters. The law prevented medical personnel from using the two-way radio on the EMS helicopter.

I immediately checked whether KT Powertel (now IDIS Powertel) could provide LTE radios. It was possible to communicate with up to 8,000 persons simultaneously and even do a videoconference over Radger, a dedicated LTE terminal. I thought it would be useful for doctor helicopters, so I told him that we would provide 70 radio sets and cover the associated costs for the next three years.

However, that was not everything the regional trauma center needed. Numerous other tasks remained to be done. For example, emergency medical supplies needed replacement, while ICT medical solutions had to be developed and employed.

The "golden hour" refers to the doctor's window of opportunity for treating victims of serious trauma with the greatest odds of saving the patient's life or preventing irreversible damage. Thus the travel time from Ajou University Hospital to any accident site within its jurisdiction should always be within an hour.

The doctor helicopters normally follow major roads as they navigate their way to the accident scene.

Telecommunications signals normally relay best when the base stations are installed at locations that are higher in elevation than the users are. Therefore, KT rearranged the base station grid, to include the installation of new antennas along the Gyeongbu (Seoul-Busan), Yeongdong (Seoul-East Coast), and Seohaean (West Coast) Expressways. The radio signals need to be directed in a straight line toward the people receiving them, so the antennas are always installed pointing downward. However, antennae in that position will not transmit radio signals to helicopters flying in the air above. The engineering team developed an antenna that points skyward and used it on the base stations positioned along major expressways. This technology was introduced in my keynote speech at the 2019 MWC, and the audience praised the idea.

A new intercom was also created that enable people inside the helicopter cabin to communicate. This system is linked with the two-way radio for enhanced utility. When transferring urgent care patients, the helicopter crew needs to communicate closely with both the medical team at the hospital and the medical staff aboard. However, the loud noise of the helicopter hinders conversation, so the engineering team equipped the new intercom with two channels.

Actually, KT does not manufacture machinery directly, but our staff toiled to accommodate Dr. Lee's needs. They developed the network and information technologies themselves, while asking a KT affiliate to produce a vest for use when providing emergency medical care. They stood by the principle that those who work in the medical field should save lives through the art of medicine, and those in technology fields should save lives through the art of technology. The letter from Dr. Lee was a token of his gratitude for everyone who shared their time and contribution to help others.

ICT rescue center established on Annapurna, at an altitude of 3,700 meters

KT's SMC has continued to search for places where its information technology expertise can be applied to save lives. The relationship with the professional climber Um Hong-gil began with a global GiGA Story project and resulted in the opening of the Nepal Annapurna ICT Rescue Center in October 2019.

At first, we planned for another domestic GiGA Story like the ones on Imja Island or in Daeseong-dong. However, when our SMC personnel traveled to Nepal, they discovered something more important and planned for a project there.

The Annapurna region is composed of one 8,000-meter peak, thirteen 7,000-meter peaks and sixteen 6,000-meter peaks. This is known as one of top three trekking courses in Nepal. Unfortunately, fatal climbing accidents there totaled 172 between 2010 and 2017, and the national safety response remained lacking. Notably, telecommunication signals throughout the region were weak, it was hard to contact a rescue center even when a climber was in distress, which added to the danger.

The SMC decided to establish the Nepal Annapurna ICT Rescue Center (apart from the GiGA Story projects) after talking with Climbing

Rescue exercise using drones at the Nepal Annapurna ICT Rescue Center, established at an altitude of 3,700 meters

Team Captain Um Hong-gil and local residents. They concluded that rapid rescues in dangerous situations would be possible if the climbers and rescue workers could communicate via long-range radio repeaters. The project was quickly executed to construct the Nepal Annapurna ICT Rescue Center at a point in the Machapuchare region 3,700 meters above sea level. The building that houses the Nepal Annapurna ICT Rescue Center was donated by the owners of a lodge who help mountaineers and is managed by sherpas.

However, establishing a rescue center outfitted with medical equipment in a foreign country was not easy. First, we had to obtain permission from the Nepali government to set it up and various other approvals related to the management and deployment of operating staff. Fortunately, the Gandaki provincial government supported us. The Um Hong Gil Human

Foundation was also involved in the establishment of a civilian ICT rescue team supported by KT. The Foundation helped us with the project maintenance and oversight. We asked the Nepal Mountaineering Association to operate the rescue center and organize a rescue team.

The SMC improved the external appearance of the rescue center, and also provided ICT solutions, maintenance, and training to the rescue team. This turned out to be a huge project involving much hard work. The ICT solution included beacons with position tracking systems, two scout drones, one rescue drone, 40 wireless radios and intercoms, a radio control system, and long-range wireless repeaters. The Center also needed portable medical equipment.

In addition, the SMC staff helped to get the equipment up to the Nepal Annapurna ICT Rescue Center. Vehicles can go up to around 1,700 meters above sea level in four to five hours. However, the last 2,000 meters up must be traversed on foot, and that takes about two days to reach the rescue center.

The Nepal Annapurna ICT Rescue Center opened six months after the project began. The long-range radio repeaters at the rescue center enable climbers and the rescue team to communicate. This capability made possible location tracking, rescue supply transport by drone, and rapid response using the rescue equipment.

In January 2020, I was told the SMC needed to go on an urgent business trip to Annapurna. The day before, news broke about four Korean climbers who had gone missing in Annapurna. Upon hearing the news, the SMC decided to dispatch its personnel. Two SMC staff members and one drone expert flew to the Nepal Annapurna ICT Rescue Center.

However, bad weather hit on the day they arrived, preventing them from going near the scene of the accident. The next day they headed out with Team Captain Um Hong-gil, carrying the equipment for locating the missing climbers. They got ready to do the search, but the conditions didn't improve. The search for the climbers was called off after seven days. Nepali natives said it was regrettable that the missing climbers hadn't stopped by the Annapurna ICT Rescue Center before the accident, so that they could have taken advantage of the tracking devices available there.

The SMC members were deeply saddened and after they returned to Korea they had difficulty in accepting the words of gratitude from the bereaved families. Having to give up the search was not the fault of the search party or equipment. However the training for the rescue team was subsequently reinforced, and ways were sought to improve the equipment in preparation for the next accident. They all wished to save at least one life with their hard work.

A smart farm in the desert and a customized high-tech facility for persons with disabilities

Thanks to the activities of the SMC, I had a chance to meet a princess from the Middle East.

Sheikha Jameela is from Sharjah, one of the United Arab Emirates. She was invited to the inauguration ceremony for Pyeongchang Forum 2018, held on February 8, 2018. Sharjah is a small emirate, four times the size of Seoul with a population of 1.4 million, and is famous for its history and arts.

Sheikha Jameela remains unmarried and has been dedicating herself to operating the Sharjah City for Humanitarian Services (SCHS), the largest support agency for persons with disabilities (PWD) in the Middle East. About 2,000 PWDs benefit from the education and rehabilitation programs at the SCHS.

I greeted the princess when she came to watch the PyeongChang 2018 Winter Olympics. She was dressed in simple clothing and gave the impression of a kind and loving person. Her modest and calm movements while seated appeared to be like someone of her mother's generation..

However, when our conversation began, she asked some very unexpected questions. She seemed to be aware of my career, which started with semiconductor development, and now as the head of KT. She bombarded me with questions about the directions of future technology. I shared my usual thoughts about prospective opportunities in the fields of IT and biotech. Sheikha Jameela told me about the times when she visited Google and Microsoft to ask for their support in teaching information technologies to PWDs. I could see that she is gentle-hearted but has a go-getter attitude, which has enabled her to carry out various projects.

As our conversation continued, she brought up one occasion when she visited a smart farm operated by KT in Namyangju. She said she looked around the facility for hours longer than the scheduled time, and asked if we could build a similar smart farm in Sharjah. She remarked that an ICT-based smart farm would be a perfect place for PWDs to work, and proposed its establishment repeatedly. After our hour-long conversation, the princess gave me a bust as a present sculpted by a student with a disability.

When the PyeongChang 2018 Winter Olympics were over, I discussed the smart farm that Sheikha Jameela had mentioned with KT's persons in charge. The UAE has vast deserts and imports most of its vegetables from Iran. Fruits are at least available because they are easy to store for long periods, but vegetables are not easy to find because they spoil quickly. Moreover, whenever Iran and the US are on bad terms, the vegetable supply dries up, causing prices to soar and making things difficult for everyone. Thus, vegetables become even harder to buy for PWDs, who represent a vulnerable social group.

I then could understand why Sheikha Jameela had asked me so earnestly. Our conversation naturally turned toward a discussion on finding a solution. However, we came to a dead end.

Typically, smart farms are established in greenhouses in regions with a cold climate. This approach reduces the cost of heating and allows farmers to grow vegetables without having to depend on outside weather conditions. However, Sharjah is a hot region, so lowering temperature would be a critical task for a smart farm there. Regular air conditioning

A smart farm to be used by persons with disabilities is dedicated in Khor Fakkan, Sharjah, an emirate of the UAE.

would be very costly and not easy to afford. Moreover, a large amount of water is required to grow crops. Where could we get water in the middle of the desert?

It seemed that it would be difficult to find a technical solution. Our first meeting ended with an agreement to find a solution first. A second meeting, which I thought would never happen, followed soon after. A suggestion was made: lower the air temperature with a recirculating farming and cooling system. This approach would minimize water and electricity consumption without having to resort to air conditioning.

Then, our SMC personnel headed to Sharjah. It took a day to fly from the Incheon Airport through Dubai to Sharjah. We executed the pilot project with a strong resolve that we could build a smart farm in that region.

On April 6, 2018, two months after Sheikha Jameela had visited Pyeongchang, we held our final meeting, and the project details were finalized by October. We were to construct two structures, each with 600 m^2 in floor space, that would be equipped with ICT facilities to provide the optimal environment for cultivating crops. It only took a month and a half to complete the smart farm.

To reciprocate the princess' visit to Pyeongchang, we went to Khor Fakkan, Sharjah, where the smart farm was established. Our three-day schedule included only one night at a hotel while two days were spent either on the airplane or on the road. The great local interest in the smart farm prompted the Deputy Ruler of Sharjah to attend the ribbon-cutting ceremony. They were especially interested in the augmented reality (AR) glasses and ICT sensors. The AR glasses enable the wearer to receive training and instructions remotely, while the ICT sensors collect data on conditions outside and inside the greenhouse and allow the systems to be remotely controlled.

Those technologies allow the farmers to reduce manual labor and facilitate farm operation, which will grow basil, mint, and other herbs as well as certain vegetables such as lettuce. Plans call for the herbs to be processed and sold as tea, soap, or spices. Sheikha Jameela thanked us and said growing crops at the smart farm would create some jobs and help with the rehabilitation of PWDs. Even for me, growing vegetables in the desert was a marvelous and surprising achievement.

How technology offers warmth

I was invited to attend Dreamforce 2019, which was held at the Yerba Buena Center for the Arts (YBCA) in San Francisco in November 2019. Dreamforce is organized by Salesforce Dot Com and is the world's largest B2B software event, drawing some 170,000 individual participants. I went to the stage with two other panelists to discuss the topic "Is 5G the Future?" Ellen McGirt, Fortune magazine's senior editor, was the host.

I explained that demand for digital transformation makes companies increase their demand for software that is based on 5G, which provides high speed, seamless connectivity, and massive density. This is sparking tremendous changes in large companies and SMEs.

I introduced Hyundai Heavy Industries, KT's client, as a major example and talked about its system for reinforced security and real-time monitoring of manufacturing processes, which are done in a facility with

Discussions on 5G were the highlight of Dreamforce 2019 (from right to left: Ellen McGirt, Fortune magazine's senior editor; Casper Klynge, Denmark's tech ambassador; Mats Granryd, GSM Association's Director General; and the author)

the floor space equivalent of 70 soccer stadiums. Casper Klynge, one of Denmark's tech ambassadors, and Mats Granryd, GSM Association's Director General, expressed their concern, warning that technology was not always neutral and that it should be used for human benefit.

When only ten minutes were left in the session, I addressed the audience: "Actually, I negotiated with the host before the session. For the last question, I wanted her to ask me, 'What will 5G do for countries, and for the whole world, that go beyond convenience and comfort?' But the host didn't ask me this question. So, I will just pretend that she did and give an answer."

The host was slightly surprised, and the audience burst out laughing. I quickly delivered the message that I wanted to get through. It was the story about six GiGA Story projects in Korea, GiGA Island in Annapurna, and the smart farm in Sharjah. I finished my talk with the story about the project we did in Daeseong-dong along the DMZ, where we built 5G infrastructure to enhance the quality of life for all residents. These were real-life stories, not a science fiction movie, underscoring the point that technology can offer warmth to humans.

Already more than one year has passed since that discussion. With the acceleration of the Fourth Industrial Revolution, an evolved intelligent network combined with 5G network, IoT, big data, and AI is making its appearance. Now, no one doubts that technology will be the way to solve environmental and health problems, as well as other issues humans face.

And now, we have to ponder how to fairly distribute the economic growth and prosperity gained through the ICT revolution. Technology is neutral in itself, but its temperature will rise when we act thoughtfully for those who are disadvantaged. And its warmth will give a firm answer to the sustainability of humanity.

03

We will save the world soon

| GEPP |

"How can I achieve technological innovation to develop the economy and change society?"

As an engineer and an administrator, this topic has been a lifelong concern of mine, and one that gets my heart beating. When I came to KT, innovative technology was important, but I continually stressed the need to develop people-oriented technology. My ideas also meshed well with KT's deeply rooted spirit as a "company of the people."

KT's roots date back to the late Joseon Period (1392-1897). The Hanseong Telegram Service was founded in 1885 and later became a regional communications office after the establishment of the Republic of Korea in 1948. In 1981, the state-run Korea Telecom Authority was launched, marking the beginning of the nation's telecommunications industry and leading to the era of "a telephone in every home." The name was changed to Korea Telecom (KT) in 1991 and the company became privatized. However, the KT identity as a "company of the people" did not simply disappear, and the will to perform its social responsibilities as a people's company with a 130-year history remains strong to this day.

"Innovative Technology for People: PEOPLE, TECHNOLOGY"

KT conducts various campaigns as part of its promise to contribute to sustainable development, not only in Korea, but throughout the whole world. Meanwhile, KT's SMC carries out a wide range of projects to bring innovative technologies to people both at home and abroad.

During my six-year tenure as KT's CEO, I traveled with the SMC staff deep into the mountains of Korea and to many corners of the world. Seeing the members of the team giving their heart and soul in unseen places made me at times delighted, at other times touched, and sometimes apologetic. In particular, the process of building the Global Epidemic Prevention Platform (GEPP), introducing it at global conferences, and transplanting it to countries vulnerable to infectious diseases, was akin to creating something out of nothing.

"Isn't there something we can do to prevent the spread of infectious diseases?"

In May 2015, Korea was turned upside down due to the rapid spread of a highly contagious viral infection called Middle East Respiratory Syndrome (MERS), which claimed the lives of 38 people.

Cases of MERS occurred mostly in the Middle East. However, within less than a month after a man in Korea was confirmed as having MERS, the number of infected people went up to more than 100. Citizens were soon in a panic over the news that more than 16,000 people had been put in isolation and 186 were confirmed as infected. But how could this virus have spread so quickly?

Early on, health authorities had recognized the danger of MERS and were taking special containment precautions regarding travelers arriving directly from countries where infections were occurring. However, there was a major weak point in the system. Even though a person had been in a country known to have MERS cases, if the person entered Korea via a third country, they were not placed under any special quarantine.

The first confirmed patient contracted MERS in Saudi Arabia but arrived in Korea via Bahrain. His stopover in Bahrain, which was not one of the countries with MERS cases, prevented the health authorities from detecting his stay in Saudi Arabia. Therefore, he was not classified as a suspected case. Unaware that he was infected, he visited three hospitals while experiencing symptoms before being diagnosed as a confirmed case. Doctors did not suspect MERS because they were not aware he had visited Saudi Arabia.

As a result, the reason MERS spread so quickly was that the patient did not realize he had been exposed to the virus. He had no idea his symptoms were related to MERS because he did not even recognize the possibility of exposure.

"Can't we prevent the spread of infectious diseases if a person who visits a country with confirmed cases is aware that he or she visited that country and goes to the hospital, or if hospitals can verify that kind of information?"

KT came up with the idea of preventing the spread of infectious diseases by isolating those who have been in contact with infected individuals if danger is uncovered by tracking the patient's movements via the mobile data.

Already in 2014, during an outbreak of avian influenza (also called AI or bird flu), KT had used big data to determine that the cause of AI's spread was not migratory birds but vehicles transporting bird food.

This infectious disease was stopped by accurately predicting the locations of farms where AI could occur.

KT passed its MERS-related idea on to the Korea Centers for Disease Control and Prevention (now Korea Disease Control and Prevention Agency) and initiated a project to prevent the transmission of infectious diseases. With government support, Korea's three main telecom service providers jointly created a system to prevent pandemics, and this became the prototype for the GEPP.

Trial application of GEPP service helped end the first MERS outbreak in 2015. By examining the mobile phone data of MERS patient No. 12, it was possible to quarantine those with whom the patient had contact, which helped end the MERS outbreak.

GEPP's capabilities were validated during the second MERS outbreak in 2018. A single confirmed case occurred, but there was no further spread, and the situation was over in 38 days. This result was in contrast with the outbreak of 2015 in which 38 people died and it took 69 days to end.

GEPP, "A Great Idea to Benefit Humanity with Technology"

"But can we really stay safe in a global society?"

This question was posed at a gathering to celebrate the achievements of GEPP after ending the first MERS outbreak. I began to ponder that question at the event, which I attended along with other SMC members.

Around 15 million people visit Korea each year, and more than 30 million Koreans go abroad annually for business, study, travel, and other reasons. In a global age where people travel around the world as easily as going in and out of a room, we cannot guarantee our safety by only protecting our own families. This presented me with new concerns and worries.

"How about developing GEPP further and providing it to the whole world?" I proposed a new vision and mission.

Since we had recognized the necessity of a project to prevent the spread of infectious disease through contact tracing, I now thought we should turn it into a platform for global society at large. And that was the beginning of this new "global project."

KT's SMC, which was in charge of the GEPP project, is a unique organization at KT. At the end of each year, KT accepts department transfer requests from employees. SMC members are selected from among these applicants. So, there are no new employees in the SMC and most members have been with KT for a long time. Their previous jobs vary widely as they come from across the KT organization and have worked in management support, marketing, or research. Most SMC members, however, see social contribution as their calling. They share a remarkable sense of mission and have no qualms about working long hours.

The uniqueness of KT's SMC inspired trust throughout the entire organization. Its members completed whatever task was given to

Executive Director Lee Sun-joo of KT's Sustainable Management Organization (second from left) having a friendly conversation with employees.

them. I decided to assign the work of expanding the GEPP globally to the SMC and had high expectations for their performance. A few months later, however, the ball was back in my court.

In the spring of 2016, SMC Head Lee Sun-joo came to my office. "We have a good opportunity to promote the GEPP. Would you be able to help us with that?" She told me they had been sending GEPP-related information to the UN and trying to establish contact with the organization, one of the largest in the world. Somewhat unexpectedly, Lise Kingo, the CEO of the United Nations Global Compact (UNGC), showed great interest. The UNGC is a UN agency that was established to attract corporate participation in sustainable development as promoted by the UN. The UNGC actively works to find solutions for various global issues.

A few months later, in June 2016, I boarded a flight to New York to participate in the UNGC Leaders' Summit, an annual event at which participants in the UN and UNGC gather to discuss sustainable development. It is the largest event held by the UN. The first UNGC Leaders' Summit was held at UN Headquarters and UN Secretary-General Ban Ki-moon gave the opening keynote speech.

The preparations for my own attendance at the summit were handled almost entirely by the SMC and I was invited as a keynote speaker. The SMC members and I together drafted the keynote speech saying that to achieve the Sustainable Development Goals ("SDGs"), global telecom service providers all over the world must take on the role of solving "the issue of sharing big data to prevent the spread of infectious diseases."

The event took place over two days from June 22nd to the 23rd, and we were to give our presentation first at the general meeting. There was an opening ceremony at the United Nations Secretariat Building the day before the event. A UN general assembly was held to celebrate the

Celebrating the UNGC Leaders' Summit 2016 at the UN General Assembly

The author introduced the GEPP for the first time through his keynote speech at the UNGC Leaders' Summit.

Leaders' Summit. First, I met with the UN Global Compact's CEO Lise Kingo, and the following day I gave my keynote speech.

The Leaders' Summit was held at the New York Marriott Marquis Hotel to an unexpectedly great response. During my 20-minute speech, I informed the audience about the GEPP's importance. Then, while stressing the need for global telecom companies to take on a new role to realize the SDGs, I announced the "Big Data Initiative on Disease Diffusion Mapping" to prevent the spread of infectious diseases.

I continued by proposing that since telecom companies possess big data generated by the world's 7.3 billion mobile phone users—including data on their location and movements—that if they collected and scientifically analyzed these data, they would be able to effectively prevent the spread of infectious diseases. I also suggested that these service operators needed to work with their governments and participate in the GEPP together.

"At KT, we are ready to share our international mobile tracing data, our big data solutions for infectious disease prevention, and the experience we've gained from successful projects."

Lise Kingo, the UN Global Compact CEO, came running up to me as I descended the podium. I am somewhat awkward with Western-style greetings, but we exchanged a light hug.

The response from officials of different governments and international organizations was very enthusiastic. They praised the idea, saying that it was rather extraordinary.

The UN Secretary-General also viewed KT's proposal as a great idea, and at the luncheon with the UNGC CEO later said, "This idea will serve as an example case in which digital technology contributes to all of humanity,".

The SMC members were even more pleased with the responses than anybody else, with one of them saying, "I'm thrilled because not only did the GEPP garner attention from the global community, but we now have the opportunity to achieve something truly meaningful." As for me, I was also eagerly anticipating the next move of KT's SMC.

Global mission to prevent the spread of infectious diseases

In 2017, I became a full-fledged missionary for the global initiative to prevent the spread of infectious diseases.

In February, through another keynote speech at the Mobile World Congress, I pressed for participation from global telecommunications

The author delivering a keynote speech at a B20 event as part of the G20 Summit held in Düsseldorf in April 2017.

companies in the response to infectious disease. In April, I became the first Korean businessperson to be invited as a keynote speaker at the B20 Digital Economy Conference, held in Düsseldorf, Germany, and called for greater international interest in the cause of our infectious disease prevention project using big data. In May, I participated in a panel at the B20 Health Initiative held in Berlin to introduce KT's efforts for digital inclusion. I stressed the importance of having the cooperation of global society to prevent the spread of infectious diseases.

Once every month, KT's SMC and I packed our bags and hit the road, working tirelessly in support of the GEPP. It was a highly rewarding experience for us to see firsthand how global society moved.

The general idea of the GEPP was reflected in a joint declaration at the G20 Summit held in Hamburg, Germany, in 2017. In addition, at the

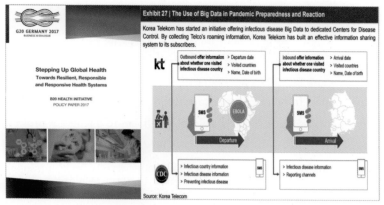

The GEPP, shown in a joint declaration of the G20 Summit held in Hamburg, Germany, in 2017.

concurrently-held B20 Health Initiative, it was recommended in a policy paper that member nations of the G20 should support not only private-public partnership across various sectors in response to infectious disease spread, but also the use of big data in the healthcare industry.

In September, the ITU/UNESCO Broadband Commission (under the UN) officially launched working groups that will utilize ICT to prevent the spread of infectious diseases. This demonstrated clearly that the "Big Data Initiative on Disease Diffusion Mapping" was being executed in full swing after the UN-level discussions.

In October, I was getting ready to attend the World Economic Forum (WEF). Chairman Klaus Schwab had already shown a lot of interest in plans for a global disease prevention project.

He proposed a partnership between the WEF and KT, saying that his organization had already appropriated a budget for solving problems related to infectious disease epidemics. He asked me to explain the GEPP

Chapter 5 Innovation and Contribution : Participate in Things that Benefit the World / **421** once more and invited me to be a panelist at the WEF in 2018.

In 2018 at Davos, Switzerland, I explained the motivation behind the development of the GEPP and its application as a WEF panelist for the session on preparing for infectious diseases in the future. I requested active support from international organizations such as the ITU, WHO, and the WEF, since we needed a global agreement to pursue the project. At the general assembly, WHO Director-General Tedros Adhanom Ghebreyesus had high praise for the ITU report, saying, "It is important that we share information about excellent cases such as these working groups that help to prevent infectious disease."

In Korea, the news media had reported on the GEPP and the meeting with Bill Gates and the story became a hot topic. The Bill & Melinda Gates Foundation was conducting a project that supplies vaccines to prevent epidemics to underdeveloped nations around the world.

As I mentioned earlier, Bill Gates, who also participated in the WEF, invited people from countries that the Gates Foundation was supporting and the officials of IT companies to a breakfast meeting, and that was where I first met him. I introduced myself as the "CEO of KT" and explained to him in detail the usefulness of the GEPP. He showed a lot of interest and said that the idea was "creative and fresh."

KT remained persistent in seeking global cooperation on the GEPP. In September 2018, KT led a working group of the ITU Broadband Commission, under of the auspices of the ITU, and presented a report on epidemic response using ICT at the Broadband Commission general assembly held in New York. Practical discussions were made possible thanks to the participation of not only KT, the chair organization, but also of personnel from related institutions in seven countries, including Kenya

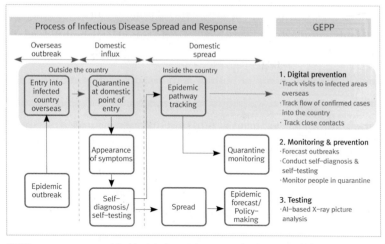

| Process of Infectious Disease Spread and Response | | | GEPP |

Overseas outbreak ← → **Domestic influx** ← → **Domestic spread**

Outside the country | Inside the country

Entry into infected country overseas → Quarantine at domestic point of entry → Epidemic pathway tracking

Appearance of symptoms

Epidemic outbreak

Self-diagnosis/ self-testing → Spread

Quarantine monitoring

Epidemic forecast/ Policy-making

1. Digital prevention
· Track visits to infected areas overseas
· Track flow of confirmed cases into the country
· Track close contacts

2. Monitoring & prevention
· Forecast outbreaks
· Conduct self-diagnosis & self-testing
· Monitor people in quarantine

3. Testing
· AI-based X-ray picture analysis

GEPP processes use mobile big data from telecommunications companies.

and Malaysia; 16 related organizations, including the Novartis Foundation, Intel, and Ericsson; and experts from four organizations, including the World Bank and the Pan American Health Organization (PAHO).

From 2016 to 2020, I maintained an extremely hectic schedule with single-minded devotion to the GEPP project. Looking back on those years I have to ask myself where I got the energy for all of that. Even for the SMC it was a next-to-impossible schedule as they had to constantly adjust the itinerary, pack the necessary documents, and contact various organizations practically nonstop behind the scenes. Fortunately, the SMC's hard work has resulted in achievements that should benefit all of humanity.

In 2019, one after another, KT "exported" the GEPP to Kenya, Ghana, and Laos. Instead of accepting payment, KT signed an MOU with each government, launched the GEPP, and installed the system to demonstrate the effects of the service.

These three countries all have something in common in that they serve as transfer points between African and Asian countries, which makes them particularly vulnerable to epidemics. Kenya, a country in East Africa with a humid environment and an inadequate healthcare system, is a major transportation hub that connects Europe and Africa. Meanwhile, the government of Ghana, a major country in West Africa, puts great effort into healthcare and has relatively high acceptance of ICT. However, it faces a high risk of infectious disease since it shares borders with countries suffering from Ebola infection. In Laos, epidemics occur frequently along the Mekong River, but the country lacks trained personnel for effective healthcare.

KT's Big Data Development Team played an important role in developing a smartphone app. When the app uses the related mobile data to detect that a person has visited a country with an active epidemic, the person is perceived as a target by the KCDA (Korea Disease Control and Prevention Agency), which then sends the person a text alert. The KDCA can then

2016. 6	2017. 4	2017. 9	2018. 1	2020. 1
UNGC	**G20**	**ITU**	**2018 WEF** Davos Forum	**2020 WEF** Davos Forum
Leaders Summit	Multi Stakeholder Conference	Broadband Commission		

History of GEPP-related activities of international organizations.

take care of the individual until the end of the viral incubation period. If that person visits a hospital, her/his travel history can be automatically provided to doctors or pharmacists, which further helps in medical treatment.

KT developed this system in Korea and updated the app so that the system can be customized according to the country using it, which was a difficult task to complete. Yoon Hye-jeong, who led the Big Data Business Support Group, flew herself to Kenya to take the lead in the first demonstration of the GEPP. When she came back to Korea, she was sporting a dark tan.

In February 2020, while we were preparing to distribute the GEPP to neighboring countries, following its introduction to the three afore-mentioned countries, we received good news saying that we had won an award in the UN SDG Mobile Contribution category at the 2020 Global Mobile (GLOMO) Awards.

The GLOMO Awards are a prestigious event in the ICT field and are organized by the GSMA, which selects companies and services that have realized major innovation and achievements throughout the mobile industries in the technology, terminal, and content areas.

According to the reviewing committee, "The GEPP is a well-designed and essential tool for global public healthcare. Its approach and ecosystem cooperation have resulted in the development of a brilliant solution."

Receiving a GLOMO Award was like a warm hug for the employees who devoted so many hours of their time for the GEPP. Unfortunately, however, the celebrations for this wonderful achievement were short-lived. Soon, the spread of COVID-19 consumed the world. And once again, humanity is living in fear due to another pandemic of infectious disease.

"Not through medicine but through technology."
Researching epidemic disease with the Gates Foundation

There is always a glimmer of hope. I received a message that we would be partnering with the Gates Foundation in carrying out a project responding to infectious diseases. The official title of the project is A Next-Generation Surveillance Study for Epidemic Preparedness. More specifically, this project will combine IT and biotechnology to predict the pathways of influenza transmission and search for prevention measures. KT decided to develop an AI-based algorithm for early diagnosis of the influenza virus and a prediction model of the virus' pathways of transmission using telecommunications data. The Gates Foundation and KT agreed to allocate $10 million in funding for a three-year period.

I praised Lee Sun-joo, the Executive Director of KT's SMC, for her hard work and asked her how all this happened. Lee said that the SMC had been knocking on the door of the Gates Foundation ever since I met Bill Gates in 2018. In a timely manner, staff members from the Gates Foundation visited the KDCA, and KT took the opportunity to introduce the GEPP and highlight our epidemic management competencies, and this led to the joint project.

Our society is still in hibernation due to COVID-19. The entire world is working on developing treatments and medications, but there is no guarantee when these will be ready.

These days I often think, "What would it have been like had we quickly established the GEPP and prevented the spread of COVID-19?" If the GEPP had been distributed throughout the world at the end of 2019 when the first case of COVID-19 was detected, it could have saved a lot of lives.

KT signing an MOU with Trevor Mundel, president of Global Health at the Gates Foundation.

Up to now, humankind has overcome countless tribulations through advances in medicine. In the future, however, it is expected that technology will play a bigger role in helping to ease this enormous burden.

The GEPP can locate people who have visited countries with epidemics using big data and mobile tracing, and alert people who have had close contact with those individuals. In this way, the GEPP can prevent the spread of infectious diseases. The final step is global cooperation. I hope that the objectives of the GEPP can be achieved as soon as possible.

"I'm an engineer. And as one, thoughts about how I can help more people or make society and the world better are always on my mind. I've come to the conclusion that the answer is technological innovation." ▪

▪ From the author's UNGC keynote speech in June 2016

Let go of fear and live a brilliant life through encounters and lessons

I was asked how wanted to be remembered as a CEO during the orientation ceremony graduation and special CEO lecture for newly hired KT Group employees in 2019. This was also something I had even asked myself, so I didn't hesitate to answer.

"I want to be remembered as a CEO who established KT's future, KT's driving force, and KT's spirit."

I had always lived with this mindset at all the organizations I was in. I wanted to make a better organization and achieve better performance. Even after resigning, my heart never changed. Only the things I can do and things I ought to do are different. I started to write down my encounters with people I met and the lessons I learned from them in hopes that someone becomes a better person because of me.

As I met different kinds of people, I sometimes heard words that I'll never forgot.

The words that made the deepest impression on me are: Chairman Lee

Kun-hee's "When will your subordinates become winners?;" Steve Job's "Dr. Hwang, until when do you think Hwang's Law will continue?;" and Marc Benioff's "Hey, Mr. 5G." However, as I said before, what raised and developed me were not just a few words that are engraved in my mind. People's thoughtfulness, hospitality and bitter lessons ceaselessly filled me with inspiration and made me race towards my vision.

I strongly believed that technology would change our lives when I announced Hwang's Law and declared the mobile era. Embracing the nomad spirit, I worked together with employees to open new markets and produce new semiconductors. The depth of the technology was bottomless, but the areas of their application were not wide.

When I became the National CTO and focused my competencies on that work, I coped with a wider range of technology and was concerned about issues of a larger scale. I learned the basics by broadening my outlook, meeting world-renowned scholars, and visiting global research centers, but to apply what I learned in real life was another thing. I needed new capacities to draw a technological roadmap at the national level that reflects 5G and the Fourth Industrial Revolution, and then link it to industrial fields.

When I got on the same boat with 60,000 employees as the CEO of KT, I was identified as a management "specialist." I strove to orient the organization's direction by emphasizing communication, cooperation, and empowerment, which I had always done. Planning and implementing projects such as the GEPP to contribute to humankind was a rewarding experience.

I was indebted to the hard work of those who taught me throughout the entire process. The roots of all my accomplishments are the lessons

I have learned. My teachers showed me where to go through their life stories. In particular, Chairman Lee Kun-hee taught me how powerful support, trust and empowerment of authority can be. Steve Jobs taught me the marvelous outcome and uniqueness that comes from fierce passion.

Klaus Schwab, who studied new technologies and the future his whole life, is an old friend of mine who shares his insights about the future. I will never forget Andy Grove, a down-to-earth and friendly CEO who showed me that paranoid meticulousness is necessary when it comes to the management of both organizations and technology. Thanks to him, I was able to direct all the passion I had in my 30s to research.

Carly Fiorina, who was always an attentive listener; Tim Cook, who practiced cooperation and convergence as a leader; and Hermann Simon, who always contacted me first and shared the ideas of gurus in management. Each of them has endlessly taught me lessons and gave me encouragement as my teachers and friends. They were behind my endeavors in the academic, government, and corporate arenas for the past four decades.

As my big journey of writing a book draws to a close, I want to tell my readers to "let go of fear when meeting other people and learning something new." I probably repeated this message earlier several times. But I'd like to say it again.

There are many "special" individuals in the world. Sometimes, we think of them as special, but they may not be much different from us. I have seen so many people who practice over and over again, and I myself have also practiced nonstop. I had to take deep breaths before taking the next step forward. When you let go of fear, you will have better encounters, learn more lessons, and grab unexpected opportunities. The next step will come naturally.

When you are young, you have endless possibilities. It is okay to make mistakes and fail. If you just have the will to keep moving forward without stopping, you will be surprised when you realize all the dots connect.

Every one of us must depend on the wisdom of others. And going through life is something each of us has to do. So, how about following the path of encounters and lessons where you get to meet others and learn from them? I am sure no one will be lonely on that road.

It may have been a coincidence, but I heard of Chairman Lee Kun-hee's passing while I was reminiscing my past during the writing of this book. Numbed by the tragic news, I spent several hours doing nothing.

I wasn't the only one who had to say farewell to a cherished and precious person, yet my heart still ached.

Chairman Lee Kun-hee shone the light in his heart on me. Although my outlook was narrow and I lacked experience because I had worked in academia for a long time, Chairman Lee gave me the chance and fully supported me.

"Mr. Hwang, you have been chasing a really big goal. You became a winner and reached this far. If you don't invest now, when will your subordinates become winners and how are we going to maintain the top position globally?"

His calm voice coming from the phone still reverberates in my ears.

He was not one to show his emotions. However, when we succeeded in developing the world's first 256M DRAM, he prepared an extravagant banquet for us. He didn't hide his delight, personally giving tailor- made watches as souvenirs to the guests.

After we acquired technologies that had once been owned exclusively by companies in Japan and the US, I said to him, "We are now a top player that receives royalties." I recall him nodding many times and saying, "Good job." His eyes were full of unrivaled passion and virtue.

He kept advocating for "Global No. 1" when he was alive, but it was not for his own good. It was his ambition to protect the country's industrial businesses, hoping to open up a better future for Korea by establishing high-value industries.

His endless hunger for talented people was no different from a person who plants an apple tree in preparation for decades ahead.

I responded to journalists as I came out of Samsung Medical Center after attending the funeral by saying,

"My heart aches that we lost a guiding light in our society. We need to do our best to fill in this gap."

Those were the only words I could utter. I couldn't fully express the emptiness and grief I felt. I think there are two things I can do to lessen my debt.

First, to remember. I will remember the hard work and accomplishments of Chairman Lee Kun-hee, so they don't just vanish as time passes.

Second, to help. I will help the next generation by staying next to them and supporting them, so they can do their best in their respective areas of endeavor.

I did my best to ease the heavy weight my heart feels in commemoration of Chairman Lee Kun-hee, who dedicated his life to Korea as a pioneer of crisis management.

May his soul rest in peace.

1985	- Completed PhD at the University of Massachusetts Amherst
	- Worked as a research associate at Stanford University
1988	- Received the offer to be the director of the Semiconductor Planning Department of Samsung Electronics
	- Visited six major semiconductor companies in Japan and Osaka University
Apr. 1989	- Joined Samsung Electronics as the Senior Researcher (Director) of the Semiconductor Device Development Department
1990	- Conducted Technology Exchange Meetings with six major companies in Japan
	- Selected as a technical program committee of the VLSI
1991	- Conducted Technology Exchange Meetings with NEC, Toshiba, and Hitachi
1992	- Led the development of the 256M DRAM
Aug. 1994	- Completed the world's first 256M DRAM
1998	- Became the head of Samsung Semiconductor R&D
	- Organized the Flash Research Society
1999	- Became the vice president of Samsung Semiconductor R&D
Dec. 1999	- Became the CEO and vice president of the Memory Business Division of Samsung Semiconductor
2001	- Became the president of the Memory Business Division of Samsung Semiconductor
Aug. 2001	- Attended the Zakuro meeting (decided to conduct the flash memory business as an independent corporation)
	- Decided to invest in the 12-inch wafer production line
2002	- Declared Hwang's Law at the ISSCC
	- Presented on Professor Clayton M. Christensen's paper (IEEE

Spectrum)

- Attended a meeting of presidents of electronics-related affiliates (to report on the future of flash memory)
- Supplied the NOR flash memory to Nokia (64M, 128M)

2003   - Chairman Lee Kun-hee meets Chairman Jorma Jaakko Ollila at the Nokia headquarters
- Developed the world's first fusion semiconductor OneNAND
- Led the Semiconductor Future Research Team (CTF, etc.)

2004   - Became the president of the Semiconductor Memory Business Division of Samsung Electronics
- Replaced NOR flash with OneNAND for Nokia mobile phones
- Awared Distinguished Alumni Award(University of Massachusetts)

Dec. 2004   - Met Apple's Steve Jobs
- Supplied the flash memory to Apple (iPod nano, iPhone, iMac, etc.)
- Conducted the Samsung Mobile Solutions Forum (Taiwan)

Mar. 2005   - Started the semiconductor case study at Harvard University
- Gave a special lecture at Burden Hall of Harvard University (declared Samsung's lead in the mobile market)
- Awarded the EIA Leadership in Technology & Innovation Award
- Selected as one of the "10 Big Thinkers" by Newsweek
- Supplied the mobile DRAM to Nokia, Apple, etc.

2006   - Received an award at Korea's 4th Award Ceremony for Best in Science and Technology
- Awarded the IEEE Andrew S. Grove Award
- Developed the world's first CTF 32G NAND with 40nm design rule
- Developed the world's first 64GB SSD (installed in MacBook Air)

2007   - Supplied the AP to Apple (iPhone)

Sep. 2007   - Developed the world's first CTF 64G NAND with 30nm design rule

2008   - Became CTO and director of Samsung Advanced Institute of

Technology (SAIT)
- Published a paper on graphene in Nature
- Established the Medici Research Society

2009 - Consulted for Samsung Electronics
- Visited US East Coast (Harvard University, MIT) and West Coast (Stanford, UC Berkeley) to study future technologies

2010 - Became the Head of the Office of Strategic R&D and Planning of the Ministry of Knowledge and Economy (National CTO)
- Presented the National Vision 2020

2011 - Organized the Overseas Advisory Committee for the Office of Strategic R&D Planning (leader: Professor George Whitesides)
- Decided the national future technologies (graphene, electric vehicles, K-MEG, etc.)

2013 - Became chair professor of Sungkyunkwan University

Jan. 2014 - Became the 13th CEO and chairman of KT

2015 - Selected as a GSMA board member of GSMA
- Gave a keynote speech at the MWC (declared 5G)

Jun. 2016 - Announced the GEPP at UNGC Leaders' Summit
- Established the world's first 5G specifications

Sep. 2016 - Announced the development of GiGA Genie AI speaker

Oct. 2016 - Conducted the KT case study at Harvard University (GiGAtopia)
- Gave a special lecture at Harvard's Memorial Hall (5G as the future communications innovation)

Nov. 2016 - Succeeded with 5G-based First Call at the PyeongChang 2018 Winter Olympics

Mar. 2017 - Gave a keynote speech at the MWC (declared 5G commercialization)

Jul. 2017 - GEPP selected as the agenda in the joint statement of G20 Summit

Jan. 2018 - Announced the GEPP at the WEF

Feb. 2018 - Succeeded in demonstrating 5G at the PyeongChang 2018 Winter Olympics

	- Conducted case study related to KT-MEG (energy-related platform)
	at Harvard University
Jan. 2019	- Elected as a member of IBC, the top legislative of the WEF
Feb. 2019	- Gave a keynote speech at the MWC
	(announced 5G commercialization)
Ap. 2019	- Commercialized the world's first 5G
	- Presented 5G at IBC
	- Gave a keynote speech on 5G at Dreamforce 2019
Jan. 2020	- Presented 5G at Congress Center during the WEF

List of Names

Steve Jobs	Apple Founder
Klaus Schwab	World Economic Forum (Davos Forum) Founder
Marc Benioff	Salesforce Founder
Elon Musk	Tesla, SpaceX, and SolarCity Founder
George M. Whitesides	Harvard University Professor
Andy Grove	Intel Founder
Carly Fiorina	Former HP Chairperson
Eric Schmidt	Former Google Chairperson
Hermann Simon	Simon-Kucher & Partners Founder

ENCOUNTERS
WITH GREAT MINDS

A story of the global No. 1 in semiconductors & 5G

First Edition (1st printing): Mar 20, 2022
First Edition (2nd printing): Apr 25, 2022

Author | Hwang Chang-Gyu
Translator | Timothy Atkinson
Publisher | Yun Ho-Gwon

Publishing Company | Sigongsa Inc.
Publishing Registration | May 10, 1989 (No. 3-248)
Address | 7F, 22, Sangwon 1-gil, Seongdong-gu, Seoul, 04779,
          Republic of Korea
TEL | Editing: +82-2-2046-2864, Marketing: +82-2-2046-2800
Fax | Editing & Marketing +82-2-585-1755
Website | www.sigongsa.com

ISBN 979-11-6579-913-7 03320